For Wendy
our dear, caring
& friendly —
& sexy
neighbor !
with loves —
Richard [signature]
3/28/07

And Me too !
[signature]

Before I Forget...Again!

My second memoir covering

1968—2002

By

Michael F. Wynne-Willson

ISBN: 1-4107-8046-5 (e-book)
ISBN: 1-4107-8047-3 (Paperback)
ISBN: 1-4107-8048-1 (Dust Jacket)

This book is printed on acid free paper.

Michael F. Wynne-Willson's first memoir, Before I Forget, is available at www.1stbooks.com

All photographs, unless otherwise noted, were taken by Anne and Michael Wynne-Willson

1stBooks - rev. 11/20/03

DEDICATION

This, my second memoir, is dedicated to my wife Anne
With all my love and gratitude.
The many reasons for this are within!

CONTENTS

"Manners Makyth Man"

(The Motto of my Father's School,
Winchester College, England
Established Over 600 Years Ago!)

FOREWORD

To those who had the intestinal fortitude to plough through the pages of **Before I Forget Book 1**, there is no need to read the rest of this page! It is for those who have not read it to clue them in as to its content.

Book I, like so many of this kind of memoir, started on the day I came on the scene in north London on September 13th, a Saturday, in 1919. From then on until 1967 I tried to relate a few of the less humdrum experiences that happened to me in the intervening years while introducing those who helped make them or forced them upon me.

I wrote about my education at Radley College near Oxford in the U K and at St. George's School in Newport, R I. Next, more or less, came the 'Unpleasantness' known as WW2 and my service in the Royal Air Force Volunteer Reserve for six years. I was *not* in the Battle of Britain and that, in retrospect, was just as well for my future. I was, however, learning to fly with the RAF at that time, and that wasn't dull either! All that does take a few pages for sure, but I had a great time reminiscing and going through my logbooks, so forgive me, please, if I overindulged. It was a fascinating, exciting, terrifying, energetic and at times horrifying experience. It surely must have been one of the greatest wastes of just about everything for all time, so far. Yet, in retrospect, as there has been no world war since, nor are we hailing a dictator, that assessment may be an incorrect one.

While at St. George's in 1936-1937 I met Jackie Chambers. In 1944 we were married in Middleburg, VA while I was on a rest from operational flying in Canada. I returned to England that year and rejoined my squadron. Jackie followed me to live, in the harshest of circumstances, as did all there then until we left in 1948 for Hamilton, Massachusetts, via New York City for a short while. Here, all kinds of things happened during the following 19 years which included the arrivals of Wendy and Mark, our adopted children, sundry jobs ranging from Marmalade Maker to Broadcaster to P R Director of The New England Aquarium just to mention a few! It was all by no means humdrum and, frankly, there was never a dull moment. This memoir ended in 1967, the year Jackie, to whom the book was dedicated, died of cancer.

So do press on regardless if you feel so inclined. I intend to have fun writing this as I did the first, so hope you will enjoy reading it, too!

Michael F. Wynne-Willson
Dedham, Massachusetts, December, 2002

Part One

ONE
1968 - 1970

I never gave it a thought. I never even considered it. That I should become a widower at the age of 46 was unthinkable and the situation would only happen to another, not me. How wrong I was and how everything about that state was hellish, to put it mildly. Life seemed suddenly to end, become useless and uncontrollable. Additionally, I became consumed with near anger at Jackie, my late wife, for leaving me to cope almost without warning. This in itself was a completely destructive and unnecessary way of thinking, but that was the way it was for quite a while. Grief, pain, anger, tears, walks muttering to myself, impatience—you name them—they were all a steady diet of mine and I had to pull myself together for my kids, friends and, most of all, myself. I had to stop wallowing in self-pity and it had to be sooner rather than later. Luckily, I think the outcome was about mid-way between those time frames.

By way of brief background: Jackie was the eldest daughter of Suzanne de LaSalle who had been brought up in Paris, and married Robert Chambers, at the end of World War I. Suzanne's third marriage (when Jackie was 20) was to Bobby Clark of Middleburg, Virginia, one of the Singer Sewing Machine heirs, and 17 years younger than she was. Suzy and Bobby had a son by the name of Tony to whom Jackie was devoted. Most sadly, both Bobby and son Tony met early deaths. It was from Tony, and after her death Suzy, that Jackie realized her inheritance. On Jackie's death, unbeknownst to her, the money passed to our children, Mark and Wendy.

Not long after Jackie's funeral in 1967 at Christ Church, Hamilton, MA. Letters poured in from all over the country and the U K as well as from our dear friends nearby. Wendy and Mark coped in the best way they knew how—which can't have been at all easy for them. Kindnesses, both great and small, occurred daily and what we'd have done without the regular arrival of Ruth Ellen Totten's superb Chinese dinners, goodness only knows! Ruth Ellen, General Patton's daughter, lived near us and had spent much time in the Far East and had brought home a superb chef who created these delicacies for us. Also, it was Ruth Ellen who lost her soldier husband on the very same day that we lost Jackie and, it transpired, that their funerals were both in the morning and on the afternoon of the same day. That was a hard day for Hamilton.

3

It is amazing the happenings that stay vividly in one's mind at crises such as this. I remember specially our close friends Moody Ayer and Connie Taylor arriving to remove all Jackie's clothes, for instance, and wondering why on earth that was necessary. I remember, too, suggesting to Moody that she take Jackie's mink stole, recently given her by her mother, Suzanne, to give to her young daughter, Ruthie, for use later in her life.

Another dear friend suddenly appeared out of the blue from Pennsylvania, Frances Spackman. She stayed with a nearby friend in Manchester-by-the-Sea so she could be close by to help, if needed. I remember sitting down and writing answers to all the letters with tears streaming unashamedly down my face after the kids had gone to bed and with our animals, Minus, Duchess and Perky by my side,. Eventually, I decided I was a king-sized pain to all including me and I should stop feeling such self-pity, p d q! This I did because I decided I was a very, very lucky man. There was a lot of living to be done, especially for my kids.

Somewhat unsurprisingly, the first call I got from overseas was from my sister Betty who, bless her heart, announced that she was on her way over to help me cope. I shall always be incredibly grateful to her for making this considerable effort, for air tickets were most expensive back then and it meant that Harry, her husband, would be left alone. I've had a nasty suspicion that I was too miserable and self-centered then ever to appreciate fully what she did for us all. Her task was far from easy. Trying to organize and help the kids who were brought up a bit differently to those in the U K; trying to cook in a strange kitchen with different utensils and menus; having to buy different food must have been challenging for her. She coped nobly for quite a while and then left, promising to try and find another to follow shortly after. This she did in the person of Marjorie Lord. Again Marjorie, under the most difficult of circumstances, did wonderfully even though the kids gave her quite a hard time.

After Marjorie stayed as long as she could, I heard about a 'house-keeper' person who was available. In due course she, in addition to her small, yappy and over-sexed dog moved in, professing that her forte in the culinary world was lasagna. Between her, the dog and the three of us plus animals, life became a total, utter disaster, complete with a massive conflict in personalities! Her snotty, yapping, dog had the vilest of habits but mercifully spent most of its time in his mistress's room, so wasn't all dumb! I expect you get the picture, but there is really nothing to be said for a housekeeper under such traumatic circumstances.

4

Believe it, or not, I was often more sorry for her than I was for us. There was no possible way that she could win, regardless of her efforts to please. With that dog, it was totally impossible. Life took a magnum leap forward after she quit in a huff one day, and that was that. Lasagna has not been at the top of the menu for any of the family since!

During this time the kids went off to school regularly at Brookwood in Manchester and did all the things that kids do, only more so I felt! I continued doing public relations for the Boston Zoological Society and kept my most favorite invention, The Zoomobile, going in all directions all the time. The N E Aquarium was being built quickly, however, and its Director was beginning to make noises about my promised transfer to that exciting and unique facility. It was in July 1967 that I made the move and was appointed Director of Public Relations. It was not a big move physically! It was down a long passage in the ancient building on Long Wharf, at the foot of State Street in Boston.

Bluntly, I was glad to leave the BZS even though it had been challenging, to say the least. My original conception that after all the zoos—for there were and still are two—were not going to become world-class exhibits due, particularly, to the location of one in Franklin Park and of the other in Stoneham, a northern suburb. Now, 31 years later, little has changed and hopes for better seem every bit as remote as always, as I mentioned in Book I, though I certainly trust I'm proven wrong.

Ed Taft, a member of a respected Boston family, came to be Director of the Aquarium from a career in the Cable & Wireless Co. An energetic and kindly man, he was responsible for the complex work of seeing that the vision and drawings of architect Peter Chermayeff, of the young and successful Cambridge Seven group, worked and grew out of the ground as designed. Like Ed, the trustees were, in the main, from wealthy and fairly prominent families in the Greater Boston area. His secretary, at that time, was Anne Patterson whose parents lived in Chestnut Hill and Marion in the summer.

The Aquarium, because of its newness and uniqueness of plant and structure, was a vibrant place in which to work. It was the greatest shock and loss when Ed, driving alone in his Porsche, was killed instantly in an accident on the Massachusetts Turnpike.

It was a few days after Ed's shattering death that his wife, whom Jackie and I knew a little bit, came and asked me if I would give the reception following his funeral as I'd had recent experience! I must admit

5

to being a bit surprised and not a little un-nerved as I knew few, if any, of his or her families, but felt that I really should do it knowing what a state of shock and misery she must have been in. I think about 70 guests showed up in Hamilton where we were still living, so it was just as well I decided to have the affair catered! Now that I come to think of it, I could have done nothing else! Anyway, I was pleased that it turned out to be an up-beat affair and not a bit gloomy, which is just what Ed would have wanted. I think that must have been my first effort at entertaining on my own, since losing Jackie.

With Ed gone, the NEA trustees led by David Stone, Dusty Howland and Arthur Lyman, started the search for a replacement as Director. Quite soon it became apparent to those of us on the staff that Donald DeHart, then an executive at Gillette, was the front-runner and, before long, was confirmed in that position. This appeared to be a highly popular choice all round.

On joining the NEA, I found out that my position was for P R Director on a part-, not full-time basis! It was decided that they were unwilling to pay me a full-time salary so they'd like me to find another source of income as well! Sadly, I was unlike some who were on the staff who were able to donate their services to non-profit organizations. I was lucky, however, as soon after receiving this rather disturbing news I did find additional PR work with the Harbor National Bank, where Dan Needham of the law firm Sherman, Powers and Needham was president, and whose offices were quite close to the NEA. It is anything but easy to serve two masters but Dan was a most understanding and helpful one and realized that the NEA was going to demand the lion's share of my working day. Consequently, he let me parcel out my own time as I saw fit and right. After Jackie's inheritance (see Book I), you might well ask why was this business of two jobs necessary for me? Let's face it: we had a super house with a 30ft. living room, children in a private school, horses and cars...and here I was working at two jobs to make ends meet!

It was deemed necessary that I journey to New York City and present myself to Holmes Clare, a lawyer, and to be introduced to others at a luncheon atop the Chase Manhattan Bank building. They, apparently, felt it necessary to cross-examine the 'widow of the deceased' as they insisted upon calling me! Why this was desired I never really gathered because all I could do at that juncture was to do as I was told. Since my kids had their inheritance, all of these formidable types seemed now to be on their payroll one way, or another!

Be that as it may. Dressed in my very best suit this country bumpkin was whisked up endless floors and into a magnificent, chandeliered, dining room in which were several snappily dressed men in business suits. Not one to be caught napping, nor to be backward in coming forward under such circumstances, I strode in, put out my hand and introduced myself to one and all. This was not one of my major moves as all were butlers! From that moment on, Clare and all his cohorts had no doubt whatsoever that they had a real country bumpkin on their hands and behaved accordingly! No wonder that things went from bad to ghastly from then on.

It actually took about four years to get the kids' trusts moved out of the hands of Clare and Chase and into the far more capable and friendly hands of the Bank of Boston. This move was brought, eventually, to a successful conclusion by the endless and patient work of a unique, friendly and mildly eccentric legal eagle by the name of Norman von Rosenvinge, also of Boston.

Regardless of all the problems mentioned, including those of having to deal with Clare who, I'm sure, was quite convinced that he should have been the kids' father rather than me, I learnt quickly that dealing with large sums of money belonging to others is no picnic. It is certainly great to have...what a dumb thing to say...but it sure brings a peck of problems along with it. Sadly, these were to involve my then in-laws and, in time, my daughter Wendy for a while. No one, *but no one*, should allow a teenager to inherit a boodle of money. Massachusetts did at the age of eighteen, I found to my chagrin. I'll argue that from experience 'til I am blue in the face or in a pine box! I hasten to add that, in spite of all the hassles, I don't think the kids suffered at all at that time and all seemed to continue fairly normally with their schooling and other interests. Wendy continued to ride successfully and Mark to have fun with his friends and to study hard. He was showing considerable success with his work and showing, thank goodness, that he was not taking after his old man!

Some may remember that, at the very beginning of Book I, I introduced you to Aileen Farrell, the lady who pulled me out of a boiling bathtub when I was very young and who taught at my Dad's school. She was, also, Jackie's headmistress at Foxhollow School. It was in 1966 that she moved her school to Lenox, Massachusetts, and it was there that we hoped to send Wendy after she would graduate from Brookwood. I mention Aileen again here because she became as devoted to my second wife Anne as she had been to Jackie and we saw and kept in touch with her regularly. In fact, in the early 60's, Jackie was elected President of

7

the Foxhollow Alumnae Association and that kept us regularly on the Mass Turnpike to and from Lenox. I had been associated with Aileen and Foxhollow for so many years that I was, almost, voted to be the only alumnus, as opposed to alumna, of that all-girl school!

While reminiscing about Aileen, I should again mention Dolly Sawyer, wife of Dan, who lived next door to us now in Hamilton. They were not only our good friends, and had been since our arrival in Hamilton in '48, but Dan was also our architect for the house they sold us and we enlarged. We discovered a giant coincidence much later when Dolly was talking to Anne and asked her if she was any relation to Cam and Peggy Patterson and when Anne said 'Yes", Dolly said, "I was married to Newell Bent, your mother's older brother, so I am your aunt!" When Peggy, Annie's Mum, heard this she darn' near blew her mind and said, "That is one person I never thought you'd meet!" Dolly was 4 years older than Newell, divorced and mother of two and, I gathered, there'd been a bit of chilliness in Peggy and Dolly's association on that account. Sadly, Newell died while climbing the highest mountain in Chile and was buried half way up. Eventually, Dolly married Dantan, usually known as Dan. As Annie had been adopted by Peggy and her husband Cam, she was both excited and overjoyed to find a real aunt living right next door and they became great friends.

My Favorite Photo Of Dave Taylor
Courtesy Of His Son, Bill
(Globe Photo)

At the Aquarium things were coming along apace and the building was emerging, mushroom-like, out of the ground on Boston's waterfront. I was having a rare old time, doing the PR and grabbing as much good and free publicity as possible from all quarters. Of the greatest help to me in this respect was my much-admired friend of many years, Dave (W. Davis) Taylor, then Publisher of the Boston Globe. Dave seemed and was fascinated by this project and worked tirelessly to assist in its growth through his paper and by raising considerable funds for it. It was John, his cousin you may remember, who helped me so generously when Jackie and I started our marmalade business, Mendip Cottage Ltd. (the Ltd. was for funds and no other reason!) back in 1948. How lucky I was and how tremendously grateful I am and always have been to them both for the loyal, warm and understanding friendship of Dave, who survived John. He was a remarkably kind, caring and humble person from whom I have never, ever, heard an unkind word said about any human, living or dead. If only I, and some others I know, were more like him!

For some time I had wanted to promote a cruise for members of the Aquarium Associates, the volunteer arm of the N E A, to some exotic place in the sun where diving, fish-watching and snorkeling etc: could be found and enjoyed. By chance I found that the Grace Line had two very smart and comfortable passenger-carrying cargo ships called the Santa Rosa and Santa Paula. These sailed, on a regular schedule, between New York and exotic-sounding islands in the Caribbean. I spoke of my idea to one of the Aquarium's trustees, Helen Spaulding, who was then Chair of the Associates. Would she go to New York with me to talk and suggest my idea to the Grace Line's President whose name, I am ashamed to say, escapes me after all these years? I do remember that his title was 'Colonel', though! Helen readily and enthusiastically agreed.

In short order we were in New York and were ushered into the president's office in the Grace Line Building. It was with open-mouthed amazement that, after introductions, we heard him say, "What I propose to do, Mrs. Spaulding, is to send you and Michael as my guests on a cruise on one of our ships, so that you may judge for yourselves what a great experience it will be for those who wish to go from the NEA. When would be a good time for you to go?"

Most sadly, Helen found that she was unable to get away so, naturally, I said that I would be and could! A date was duly approved! It was then that I became more than bold and asked the Colonel if, as Helen couldn't make it, I could bring Mark my son with me as he was more than due a bit of fun and change after the loss of his Mum. Wendy decided that she was too involved with her riding and other extra-curricula activities to get away. Being a most understanding and compassionate man, the Colonel agreed at once and booked a first-class cabin for Mark and me to share on the Santa Rosa. This sailed from New York with calls at Caracas, Aruba, Curacao, Haiti and Jamaica, taking about two weeks for the round trip. The timing of this exciting and most colorful experience could not have been better for both of us. We both felt strange leaving without Jackie and Wendy, but the healing process was beginning for us all and we were learning that life goes on regardless.

Neither Mark, nor I, had ever been to such exotic places before and we returned raving about all that we had seen, enjoyed, learnt and at the friendliness of all on board who cared so well for us. All this happened in December '67 and on return I wrote a glowing report to Don, the Aquarium's General Manager, and Helen about how it should take advantage of the most generous preview given to Mark and me and to plan and promote such an event for the membership at large. Sadly, this promotion was not forthcoming, though why I never found out. Perhaps the timing was off, but I always have felt an acute sense of guilt when thinking of Grace Lines and its most generous president, even though it was not my decision.

Before leaving on that voyage, the kids were beginning to bug me about getting out and about and to stop being reclusive. Frankly, I was in no hurry but, as a great exponent of marriage, I must be honest and say that I thought living alone, was strictly "for the birds" and I often longed for companionship, fun and affection, all those things which go hand in hand with a happy marriage! My real problem was that even though I was lucky enough to have many friends and attractive divorcees nearby, they were all friends and probably knew me far too well to let me try to whip up a 'relationship'! How I dislike that totally over-used word today! (1996) Twenty-five years ago it was still used sparingly and was tolerable. Whom, then, should I ask out on a date, I wondered.

Anne Modelling on Bermuda

As I mentioned, Frances Spackman...Mrs. Batman as the kids called her...was married to Horace and was resident in Pennsylvania. She was a great friend of Jackie's and mine and had been wonderful to the kids and me since I'd been on my own. Even before then we got along famously and enjoyed each other's company, but she was married and lived miles away and they had kids of their own! Anne Patterson, Ed Taft's secretary, was around 20 years younger than I, unmarried, highly decorative and, obviously, most sought after and popular with all ages. So! I plucked up my courage and asked her to come with me to a cocktail party in Hamilton. I was delighted when she agreed but felt it necessary to tell her that I was fairly terrified at bringing her into our orbit there and might well keep her in a closet most of the time!

Let's face it, single men were at a premium then and there was a rumor around that I'd recently become loaded, with money that is! This was really a hollow misconception, if ever there was one! The dreary truth was still not common knowledge at that time. Anne's and my problem was, however, that we both thought the other was loaded! She whizzed around in a fast sports car, lived with four charming girls on Lime Street in Boston and carried on, I thought, a fairly jet-set type of life! She, in turn, saw our house in Hamilton and all that it involved with kids, horses etc: and figured that I'd got it made! It is amazing how wrong we both were, but not to worry! We started having great fun together and it was exciting to get a letter from her while Mark and I were on our Santa Rosa cruise in mid December. When we returned to Logan airport, Anne was there waiting for us on the tarmac and, as we came down the stairs from the plane (no automation back then!), she broke away from the others waiting at the entrance and rushed up to greet us from quite far off! Quite a noticeable move I thought and one of great enthusiasm!

Mark at about this time

Our Home in Hamilton

With all due respect to some of Jackie's and my old friends on the North Shore, I think that many figured that Frances and I might eventually pair off as we'd all been such friends for so long and the four of us had had such great times together over the years. Why, you may ask, as she was married? Well! The match had really been put to the fire in this respect because, some time previously, Frannie had suddenly announced that she and Horrie were getting a divorce! That, bluntly, blew my mind as neither I, nor Jackie, had a clue that anything like that was even contemplated! What was worse was that whenever she and I used to go and stay with them I would, invariably, give Horrie the hardest time, jokingly, about the 'girl at the end of the driveway'! You're right! It was that lady he married after all was said and done! Perhaps naive was my middle name, but I never caught on to all that, nor did Jackie, and we were all great friends. Suffice to say Frannie eventually called me to say that she was going to marry an Army officer and I fervently hope that she is living a most happy life. She deserves to for she was a super, fun loving, highly attractive and caring person.

15

Anne and Her Dad Leaving for Church

Anne didn't really want to be a June bride but for sundry reasons, many of which were Aquarium-related, we went ahead and selected June 8th as our personal D-day of 1968! The Church of the Redeemer, Anne's church in Chestnut Hill, was chosen and was close to her parents' house on Middlesex Road where the reception would be held. My Best Man was Kerr Collingwood who, you may recall from Book One again, was my roommate at St. George's in 1936/37. Anne's oldest friend, not in age but in length of time, Judy Gray was her Maid of Honor. Among my ushers were my old RAF chum, Alec Worthington then living in Canada; Phil Reynolds, husband of Lea, and Jack Brengle, husband of Natalie. Other than Alec, all were good friends from my Hamilton days.

Suffice to say, our wedding day was perfect in every way. Peggy and Cam, Anne's mother and father, put on a tremendous, memorable and festive occasion for us that was well attended by many old and new friends and relatives. Sadly, my family again couldn't make it over from England. My Mum was too old to make the trip and my sister and her school headmaster husband couldn't get away. My great friends from St. George's days, Bea and Vaughan Merrick who was my headmaster there, stood up for my family. This was the second time they'd performed this noble task for me!

One of the many high-spots of our wedding day was our being driven away from Middlesex Road after the reception in a spotless, dark green, antique Bentley sports car, owned and driven by Gil Steward Jr., another kind and generous friend from the North Shore. He drove us to the Ritz in Boston and, on arrival, I asked him to come up and join us for a drink! I guess this surprised him a little! That showed that I was getting a bit more sedate with age, perhaps! I was 47 then, and Anne 27!

Both Wendy and Mark seemed to have a great time at the wedding, too. In addition to so many who came, I was so happy that my old chums Roger Smerage and Joe Govoni, our gas-station owner and S.S. Pierce grocery dealer respectively in Hamilton, plus their wives, were able to come and celebrate with us for they'd been almost 'part of the family' for years.

As you can guess, I'd made every effort to have everything ship-shape starting at the Ritz for our honeymoon and the subsequent days of that exciting holiday. At the Ritz I had ordered what I thought and hoped Anne would like for breakfast on our first full day of married life. However, that and dinner the night before were total disasters! You may remember that June 8th '68 was the day on which Robert

Kennedy's coffin was taken in state by train from New York to Washington, D C and nearly the entire route was covered by TV cameras and with people standing alongside it in mourning. It so happened that most of the country was watching this and no exception was the room-staff at the Ritz! We eventually got our dinner that night at 10.45! It was cold, unsurprisingly. The champagne was as flat as milk. The flowers sent by Jackie Lowe, my good friend who was the P R Director of that hotel then, were D O A! Not to worry! When breakfast did arrive next morning, it bore not the slightest resemblance to what I'd ordered, so I decided there and then not to address my list of grievances to the manager until we returned from our honeymoon. Now was not the time to get my tail in a right-royal spin!

June 8, 1968
Courtesy of Harding Glidden

18

That afternoon, June 9th, '68, Tammy Gardner, who had gotten to know the kids prior to this time as their sitter, and was a most charming and attractive young lady as well, drove them both up from Hamilton for lunch so that we could have a final meal together. Later, Cam and Peggy joined us and went to Logan to catch a final, 'farewell' snort at the Clipper Club, and Pan Am's night flight to London which was to be our first stop on our honeymoon.

As was usual for such an event as a honeymoon, the pre-planning had been considerable and a great deal of fun! We both felt that we certainly should go first to the U K to have Annie meet my family. Additionally, we felt that we'd like to go somewhere warm on the Continent, so chose the Algarve on Portugal's south coast. You may remember my old RAF chum, Peter Mackenzie from our Accrington, Lancashire days. (Book1). Anyway, he and his new wife, Marty, had found an estalagem in Albufuera which they thought would be perfect for us. That we included most enthusiastically in our itinerary.

Peggy and Mark on Our Wedding Day

19

Like many of her age back in the late 60's, Annie had never had the opportunity to travel on an ocean liner and she was crazy to do so! With this in mind, we enlisted the aid of her father who was in the shipping business and he put us in touch with a friend of his who knew 'everyone and everything'! He found out that the Italian Lines 'Raffaello' was sailing from Naples to New York, when we wanted to leave Europe and kindly booked us in second class. What to do?! I couldn't possibly afford first class, but that was the way we were going to have to go, surely, on our honeymoon! It was about then that Annie mentioned a diamond ring that she'd found on a street in Washington D C, in 1961 that had never been claimed. So! She trotted herself down to one of the jewelers on Boylston Street and found out that, on appraisal, it was worth quite a bundle! Enough of a bundle, she was told, that it would enable us to forge off fearlessly and book a first-class passage for our 'moon'!

Where would we go between the Algarve and Naples was the next question? We both had a longing to go to Rome and that looked en route! It was when they heard about this that the Merricks gave us two nights at the beautiful and famous Hassler Hotel, over-looking Rome and the Spanish Steps nearby. What a magnificent gift! There was one other stop that we found we had to make due to the airlines we were using, and that was at Lisbon where we had to stop on the way to Faro near Albufuera for a night and then fly on to Rome. We were all set to go!

Our arrival at Heathrow was on time and, in no time, we were at Colet Court Prep School in Hammersmith, next to St. Paul's Public School with which it was associated. Harry Collis, sometimes known as Henry, was headmaster of that prep: school and my sister's husband. There were most of the members of my immediate family all on hand to greet Annie for the very first time! My Mum, who was still in remarkably good shape tho' hampered by a bad hip which shortened her leg, seemed overjoyed to meet Annie, as were all the others, and it was a great 'home-coming' for me as you can guess.

Soon thereafter, Betty gave a big cocktail party for many old friends of mine and guess whom she included? Readers of Book I may remember my having a spot of bother with evacuees from London while on a RAF weekend at the Lygon Arms Hotel in Broadway. Remember that I was not alone and that one Barbara Waldegrave was with me, when I got shot as a fox when on a weekend pass in the RAF? Anyway, Betty invited her to this party and she came and I'd not set eyes on her since 'after the blast!' She'd hightailed it (no pun intended!) back to the safe bosom of her family in London and I'd been carted off unconscious to the nearby WAAF (Women's Auxiliary Air Force) hospital! Suffice to say,

Annie was intrigued to meet her and we, more or less, took up where we left off 26 years before! I admit to being just a wee bit nervous about how she'd handle our meeting, or what she might say, but she did it just like the lady she always had been! The party was a huge success and, though a bit scary for Annie, she handled it beautifully and charmed everyone, as I knew she would.

The Algarve was all and more than we ever thought it could be. In 1968 it was still relatively unspoiled as a tourist resort and we had no trouble finding beaches under a hot sun without another soul thereon. Just what the doctor ordered! Leaving there by air wasn't dull! We climbed on board a Comet airliner, the first type of jetliner ever put into service, and taxied to the end of the runway for take-off. Half way down and roaring along, the pilot aborted the take-off and came to a screaming halt! Naturally we were fairly convinced that we were about to meet our maker, or somebody. Not a bit of it! We turned and taxied back to what was loosely referred to as 'the terminal'. On stopping there, the door was opened; a man entered and walked down the aisle of the plane and stopped half way down; stretched above what must have been his seat on the inward flight just landed; picked up his umbrella and disembarked without a word to anyone. We started up again, taxied out to the runway and took off! Such were the vagaries of airline travel back in those days!

As bad luck would have it, our reservations had become muddled in Lisbon and we had to spend a night there prior to flying to Rome and landing in Madrid en route. Consequently, as the town was most crowded, we eventually found a fleapit of a hotel after the longest search, at which we both felt for sure we should *not* stay, but did anyway and with dire results. Anne caught a fiendish bug and was laid totally low when we eventually arrived at the Hassler in Rome. Never before, nor since, have I seen her so ill. In fact I promptly called the hotel doctor as I was convinced that she had acute appendicitis. Thank heaven, after a day of misery in bed, she started to improve and, with great guts and determination, came with a guide and me to St. Peter's Cathedral and the Catacombs. I was worried that the latter might do her in for good but, somehow or other, she made it both going down and up!

In short order and on the next day, Annie was raring to get going again and was darting into leather and jewelry shops as if tomorrow would never come! Of course, we loved the Hassler and if anyone is ever in Rome and doesn't know where to stay, try it for sure! It is a most memorable place, but I should remind you that we were *given* our stay there! After a comfy train ride to Naples, we boarded the 'Raffaello' on

June 24th and sailed that evening stopping at Algeciras, hard by Gibraltar, to take on passengers at midnight and then headed west for a non-stop run to New York. Before leaving Italy, however, I think I will placate my dear bride by relating the following. Honesty demands that, on one occasion when about to pay the owner of a horse and buggy that, with romanticism oozing from my every pore, I'd hired for a drive round some of the city, I became more than hassled about the correct change I should give him and flatly refused to listen to Annie who was, with maddening calm, suggesting correctly. There followed a notable silence as we headed for our bedroom and her promise 'never to open her mouth again'!

No wonder I kept her in a closet at first!
On our honeymoon in Albufuera, Portugal

When we arrived by taxi from the Hassler at Rome's big railroad station the next morning, I hailed a porter to cope with our luggage and informed him that we'd like him to take us to the train leaving for Milan at such and such a time. Off we went for quite a while as Annie bided her time and when 'le moment critique' arrived' with time running out, she allowed in long-suffering tones that she was under the impression, surely, that we were bound for the port of Naples, *not* Milan a town from which no ship has ever sailed! This, remember was after she promised 'never to open her mouth again'! As you might guess, I've heard that tale reported, occasionally without excessive exaggeration, by Annie many times and, I guess, deservedly!

Everything on board the Raffaello was just as superb and exciting and different as it should have been for a honeymoon and it was hard to imagine anything more luxurious or delightful. July 1st at 6.30 A M saw us sailing under the Verazzano Narrows Bridge and soon it was time to disembark at the dock in Lower Manhattan. As honeymoons go, it really was the very, very best! Regardless, we were both glad to return home by 7.30 in the evening and to a rousing welcome from Wendy, Mark, and Tammy who had been looking after them both and all the animals! We had been away for three superb weeks.

Our new life was off to a great start! Annie came home from our honeymoon to run the formidable establishment in Hamilton with Wendy and Mark, two dogs, Minus and Duchess, a cat Perky and a horse Piglet! Quite an assignment for a 27-year-old, and that didn't include her husband!

My office was now in the N E Aquarium building and I was able to commute by car from Hamilton to Boston on weekdays, taking about forty minutes each way.

Let's take stock then. Wendy is going to Foxhollow School in Lenox, MA. run by Aileen Farrell whom I'd known almost since I was born. It was she who introduced me to Jackie, my late wife, who was Senior Prefect when that school was in Rhinebeck, N Y. and I was at St. George's. Mark is still at Brookwood School in Manchester, MA. and will be graduating from there in June this year, 1969 that is, with early acceptance to my alma mater in Newport.

With the Aquarium due to open officially on June 20th, 1969 too, it can be imagined that this was more than a hectic time for us in the P R department, seeing to it that as many as possible knew when, where and what would be happening on that epoch-making day for Boston's waterfront. Suffice to say, everything went off with a bang in more ways than one!

Paul Newsome, President of the distinguished Boston PR firm bearing his name and members of his staff, augmented mine on this special day and did a 4-star job. I didn't really deserve a letter Paul wrote to Don DeHart about being 'unflappable' that day, but all who were such a help to me did!

Boston's media really gave us brilliant coverage on the day and for months thereafter. As usual, Jess Cain and John Day of WHDH radio and TV, located in town on Morrissey Blvd, were outstanding, as were, of course, Boston's Globe and Herald Traveler. It wasn't long after the opening that I remember well being interviewed at the top of the Giant Tank by a charming cub reporter from Channel 5, Leslie Stahl by name, now a mainstay on CBS-TV's distinguished '60 Minutes' program.

Life wasn't always a bowl of cherries, though. Not long after the opening, all hell broke loose with pipes in the basement of the Aquarium rupturing, apparently without any warning!

Jim Wood, the Chief Engineer, was nearly driven around the bend with what seemed like ever-recurring crises at that time. I believe that the many miles of piping had to be replaced by PVC piping which had just come on the market, a costly and time-consuming process for sure.

My description of these problems are, perhaps, a little vague but it is what I vividly remember! As the Giant Tank was then unique in the country, and probably the world, there was perpetual panic among those closest to the problem that the 2" thick glass panes surrounding it might either crack, or break. If memory serves me correctly, I think the former did occur but the latter did not. That would have let the fish out of the tank and flow onto and up State Street, not to mention the public who invariably had their faces glued to the glass panels!

TWO
1968—1970, continued...

Dan Needham was the president of The Harbor National Bank, where I worked my second job. Compared to the local giants his bank was small and quite new and, therefore, relatively unknown. How to get attention then was one of my primary tasks, and what I chose to do would have caused considerable mayhem today! Located on Franklin Street, the bank did have a sizeable glass frontage, but what to put into it to attract attention of passers by was the major problem. Most bank-related objects for display were born of boredom, so I decided that whatever I put in there should have constant motion to draw crowds and provide interest and intrigue. Realizing that what I was about to do would probably be my undoing, I figured that it would be great fun to have a go anyway!

My first requirement for this project was a reputable baker who could, and would continue if required, to bake a huge loaf of bread daily with dimensions of about three feet across and a foot high. With this accomplished and at a most reasonable price, I felt certain that the baker that I found felt he should handle this insane P R man gently! My next requirement was for at least a dozen mice, black or white, it mattered not! Finally, another necessity was a bowl for water out of which these mice could drink without drowning, or water logging the huge loaf! How I wish I still had a photo of the bank's most conservative trustees, tellers and secretaries all viewing the arrival of this incredible assortment of display material! When all was unloaded, I cut a third out of the loaf, set up the water trough and let the mouse brigade loose within the 5' x 5' x 1.5' enclosure and disappeared, wondering what on earth would happen, if anything.

Within an hour what I had hoped might happen, did! The mice started furiously to tunnel into the loaf, greatly enjoying the freshly baked dough. Crowds started to gather in rows to gape and none could fail to notice the sizeable, attractive sign I'd placed alongside this craziness, proclaiming the several services and advantages to be had by using the Harbor National Bank! As I had soft lights over the exhibit all night long, I felt it suggestive to have yet another sign, illuminated of course, that read, "The Harbor National Bank, the bank that labors both by day *and* night!" This was, of course, assuming that the mice did just that, too!

25

Suffice to say, there had to be a new loaf provided daily with the used one left on display also. In this way, the tunneling of the mice could be seen and admired by all. So that the mice didn't become too fat and lazy, we found it necessary to introduce a new, hungry group daily and return the rotund ones whence they came to their pet-shop on the North Shore! Unsurprisingly, the bank gained a lot of publicity and, equally surprisingly, I was not fired! If the truth was told, I was a bit nervous about the project at first, but I never did hear from Dan Needham whether his fellow trustees told him he must have been insane to hire such a P R person!

THE ANTARCTIC CIRCLE

In October, Anne was invited, once again, to climb into her mermaid suit that she used before at the Groundbreaking and at the Opening Ceremonies of the N E A. This time it was to dedicate the newly decorated and overhauled Aquarium Subway Station of the Mass Bay Transit Association. This wasn't the most epoch-making event of the century in Bean Town, but it was all in the cause of publicizing the N E A and, if I may say so, with considerable beauty as well! Slight bias is evident!

In early November, Mark gained early acceptance to St. George's that delighted us. We had taken him to look at the prep: schools that he wished to visit, but SG was always the one to which he was set on going.

The Harvard-Yale game was a never-to-be-forgotten event this year and, probably, will never, ever, be duplicated. As most who were there or were in some way involved via radio or TV will never forget, it was a 29 to 29 tie with, Harvard getting six points in the last 42 seconds! Jeannie Putnam, my old RAF chum Alec Worthington, Anne and I were there and were lucky enough to be 'way up at the top of the stands for that epic performance! Mark you, Alec knew next to nothing about American football and I probably, at most, five per cent more, but it was the greatest game ever, which few will be likely to forget!

Early in 1969, as the Aquarium's P R Director, I was invited to a dinner at the Harvard Club to lecture to a group of doctors about it. The dinner was good but, principally, I was more impressed by the amount of liquid that was consumed during that and my talk! At the end of the talk, a doctor came to chat with me and said that he really did think that

I would enjoy knowing about a voyage that The Explorers Club was planning and sponsoring for January 1970. "Why?" I asked, knowing too well the state of the family finances and not having a clue whether, or not, Anne would want to join me. "You're just the kind of person that'd love it," he replied, "and besides, it'd be great publicity for the Aquarium!"

At this juncture I felt it necessary to ask just where this 'exploratory' trip might be going. "Oh!" the friendly physician replied, "To the Antarctic! Won't that be fun and fascinating, too?" As it was getting late and I felt that said friend had dined well and really should be heading home, I didn't have the heart to say "No" on the spot, so asked him to mail me all the necessary information so that I could think about it! He agreed and I promptly forgot the discussion for I'd dined quite well, too!

A few weeks later I received from the Explorer's Club of America a large bundle of information regarding this trip, all about the forthcoming maiden voyage of the Lindblad Explorer to Antarctica. My doctor friend hadn't forgotten, even if I had!

Naturally, I read it from cover to cover and when I got to the price of the trip per person I promptly deposited it in the circular file, forever I thought. A little while later, something nudged my thoughts that prompted me smartly to go and retrieve it. "What a really exciting thing to do," I said to myself, "who on earth has been to Antarctica and why on earth would anyone want to go?" I continued. "Precious few," I answered, "and besides, you only go by once so don't miss this opportunity!" Chatty, wasn't I?

After I'd finished the momentous conversation with myself, I made up my mind that without doubt I certainly had to go; that it'd be a natural to have a staff member from the Aquarium aboard this brand new ship built for 'cruising' in Antarctica with ordinary, but nosey, civilians thereon. Also, I'd take a small bet that I might be able to talk the Boston Globe into sending me! Such over-confidence and conceit had to be seen and heard as I broached the subject with that kind, thoughtful and understanding previous mentor of mine in Mendip Cottage days, Dave Taylor, the Globe's publisher. Much to my surprise and utter delight, Mr. Taylor—as I called him then—warmed to the idea. He felt that if some crazed types had built a ship to take common-or-garden civilians down to that freezing wilderness, then the Globe should know why and have a stringer on board who could write a story and have photos available on his/her return to provide the answers.

Armed with excessive enthusiasm and wanting to strike again while my iron was red-hot I then said, "But Mr. Taylor, I'd like to take your old baby-sitter, now my wife Anne, with me, please!" At this, he knew me well enough to respond, "The Globe will assist you in getting there, Mike, as a contribution to the Aquarium, but you raise the cash so that Anne can go with you and good luck to both of you!" He knew that Anne was a darn good photographer and diarist, so I did just what he told me and raised the necessary funds to get her on the voyage with me! That was a big lump of money in those days, and still is to me.

This amount involved contributions of sponsorship from the Aquarium itself that donated our necessary 35mm color and motion picture film, and a high-powered executive loaned me one of the very latest movie cameras as well. Others sponsors were The Hampshire House and Tom Kershaw, who greatly supported our project and made his popular restaurant available for promotional and publicity parties etc; radio station WHDH in town provided me with broadcast facilities and air time to use on an every other day basis from the ship itself. The Harbor National Bank provided sponsorship of the broadcast time and a clothing store, Streeter & Quarles, now no longer in business, provided us both with superb foul-weather gear and the furriest and warmest boots you can imagine! After this was all accomplished, I asked the N E A for final permission to go and was wildly delighted when this request was granted.

Anne knew and was very close to two brothers Tim (Latimer) and Sam Gray who, in the summer, lived close to Marion where Anne's parents had a house on the water near the 18th green at the Kittansett Golf Club. Sam had married Gerry in Chestnut Hill on June 15th, '68, the week after Annie and I were married. They then moved down to Buenos Aires where Sam worked for The Foxboro Company. Most kindly on hearing of our upcoming adventure, they invited us to stay with them prior to boarding the Lindblad Explorer there. Originally, this was not the planned starting place, but the Explorer, as she was making her way from Scandinavia where she was built, had a fire in the galley and, instead of sailing on her maiden voyage from Ushaia in Argentina, near the tip of South America, had to make port at Buenos Aires for repairs. Due to this delay, the group which was due to sail on the maiden voyage was unable to go and we, the next of about 70 people who were due to be on the second sailing, became the first. Most exciting to be on this Maiden Voyage we all thought!

Our schedule called for us to gather at Idlewild, as JFK was called back then, on January 21st. 1970 and board an Aerolineas Argentinas

28

707 for the endless flight to Rio and then B A! It so happened that this was the day on which the very first Pan-Am commercial 747 was due to fly out for London, so we had the chance to see it taxi out and then return with an engine problem! We, too, were delayed for some reason. Weather, I believe.

On arriving without incident, Sam and Gerry met us at the B A airport and took us to their apartment. For two days they showed us this exciting city and, on January 24th they drove us to board the Lindblad 'Explorer' where we could see the ship that was to be Anne's and my home for the next two and a half weeks. Sam, being a most knowledgeable sailor, was just as shocked as I was to see that the ship had a list of ten degrees and the decks looked as if there'd been a party on them for days! After a strong drink in the bar, our hosts departed feeling, they said on our return, more than concerned about our safety on the 'cruise' we were about to take! I was highly nervous myself, but was not about to let Anne know it, hoping that she had, somehow, not noticed!

Hakon Mielche, circa 1965
Courtesy Of The Danish Union

Following this page, you will see 'THE ANTARCTIC CIRCLE', the highly unofficial ship's paper. The copy for this was taken from my series of broadcasts to Radio Station WHDH in Boston while on board at sea. As we and many of our 98 fellow passengers found that useful information about what we were doing, where we were headed and what to expect was limited, we got the idea of putting it together ourselves. I wrote it. Mary Hemingway, wife of author Ernest who was with us, proofed and distributed it and Hakon Mielche, the famous Danish explorer, writer and cartoonist, TV star and one who was to become our dear and respected friend for many years, illustrated it.

So that you may enjoy the superb cartoons that Hakon drew on the pages of 'The Antarctic Circle', I copy from the original script that, due to its being broadcast originally, contains repetition. You will see the names of others who 'contributed' to this opus one way and another as you progress, and I believe that you will be able to gather who's who in Hakon's delightful drawings that grace each page!

[N.B.—While I make no claim to editorial perfection within this manuscript, I must beg the reader's indulgence of typos and errors of grammar and syntax in the little newsletter pages that follow, as they have been reproduced photographically from the originals and offered no opportunity of editorial hindsight!]

The ANTARCTIC CIRCLE

January 26, 1970

On board the twenty-three hundred ton motor vessel Lindblad Explorer, this is Michael Wynne-Willson for Expedition Antarctica. On a course due south now from Buenos Aires for 48 hours and heading for Fox Bay in the Falkland Islands, our ship is making an average speed of 14.00 knots and already has covered 500 miles of a total of 1100 for this first leg of this maiden voyage. Temperature of the air today at 12.00 noon (10.00 a.m. Boston time) was 62°F; the sea water, 58°F under a cloudless, azure-blue sky; our position 42° 5' South, 57° 40' West. The sea, unbelievably for the Roaring Forties in which we are sailing, is dead calm. In fact, the Norwegian First Mate of the Explorer, who has sailed these waters for 38 years supplying Antarctic whaling fleets, told us he had never encountered such warmth and calm.

After leaving New York by air last Wednesday - three hours late due to the zero degree temperature, the eleven-and-a-half-hour flight gave great indication to this reporter and his wife of the enormity of the South American continent. A brief and hot stop (83°F) at haze-enshrouded Rio de Janeiro broke our flight briefly. Two and a half hours later the vast, muddy, sluggish and brown estuary of the River Plate came into view. The town of eight million spread out for miles on the southern shore, and with excitement and not a little perspiration due to our winter clothing and the 85° heat, we disembarked at Buenos Aires, Argentina at noon on Thursday, January 22. It was great to be met by good friends from New England, now living in Buenos Aires, whose warm hospitality we gratefully accepted during our two-day visit to this busy friendly and proud capital, slightly reminiscent of Paris yet mingled with a suspicion of Rome.

As many well know, steak - in all its succulent forms - is the mainstay of the Argentine diet. Just for your enviable comparison, we enjoyed a three course delectable meal for four people, with huge steaks and a good local red wine, for $10.25, tip included. In other words, steak at 70¢ per lb!

21

31

-2-   1/26/70

Tomorrow at the same time - God willing and
a good signal - will try to paint a verbal
picture of life aboard the Lindblad Explorer
and of those who comprise our crew and passenger
list - and also a brief introduction to Amos,
our wandering albatross who, with his 12-foot
wing-span, glides effortlessly and serenely across
our wake.

From 600 miles North of the Falkland Islands and
5,250 South of Boston, Michael Wynne-Willson says
goodnight to you all at home.

The ANTARCTIC CIRCLE

January 27, 1970

This is Michael Wynne-Willson for Expedition Antarctica on board the Lindblad Explorer. Everything looks colder today and is, as we see that the air temp. at noon was 62 degrees; sea temp., 52. Our position 46° 39'S;59° 33'W - or more simply 350 miles from the Falkland Island Now by-passing Fox Bay, we are due to anchor off West Point Island at 6 a.m. tomorrow for our firs full day of exploration and photography ashore.

The officers and crew of our ship are mostly Norwegian - sails under that flag. The chefs, stewards and stewardesses seem mostly Swiss - a country not overly famous for its sailors - but who cares! Our meals are excellent so far and service both efficient and friendly. As this is a small ship (2300 tons) the Explorer accomodates its 100 passengers comfortably, but not lavishly. Cabins are compact and all overlook the sea; bathrooms make the cabins look spacious, but they lack nothing except bath tubs for those of us who prefer horizontal rather than vertical total immersio Most of our days, so far, have been spent in 4 locations - on deck in the sun - taking photos etc. - in the forward lounge where writing, reading and elbow-bending sociability take place. An attractive nautical pub type bar there seems permanently open and is operated by an effecient and totally unflappable Englishman. Luckily he has these characteristics for he has no help out front - the one and only severe tho' not too important, criticism heard regularly to date. The dining room is spacious and attractive - we sit with whom and where we want, a happy and uniqu arrangement. Further aft, the lecture and movie theater where, twice daily so far, we have been delightfully educated and entertained about what we shall see, when to look for it and how to identify - be it bird, seal, penguins or antarctic research station.

Now a brief review of our passenger list. The majority are from all over the USA. In addition English, Swiss, Italian, Danish, Argentinian, South African and Australian nationals are also

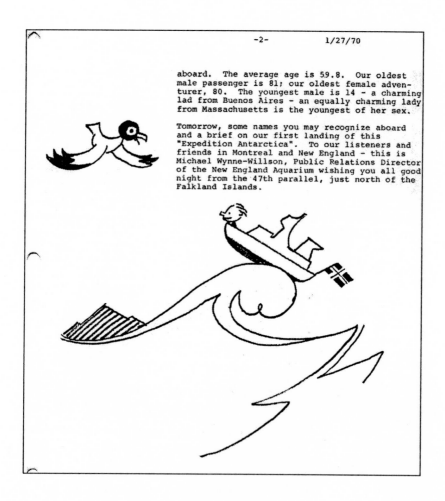

aboard. The average age is 59.8. Our oldest
male passenger is 81; our oldest female adven-
turer, 80. The youngest male is 14 - a charming
lad from Buenos Aires - an equally charming lady
from Massachusetts is the youngest of her sex.

Tomorrow, some names you may recognize aboard
and a brief on our first landing of this
"Expedition Antarctica". To our listeners and
friends in Montreal and New England - this is
Michael Wynne-Willson, Public Relations Director
of the New England Aquarium wishing you all good
night from the 47th parallel, just north of the
Falkland Islands.

The ANTARCTIC CIRCLE

January 28, 1970

This is Michael Wynne-Willson for Expedition
Antarctica aboard the Lindblad Explorer at anchor
in West Point Island Harbor, the Falkland Islands.
As predicted, we made landfall around 6:30 am
and we were on deck to see the jagged and stark
islands, collectively the size of Connecticut,
loom out of the morning mist. We could have guessed
we were close to land, however, for the water, at
that time, literally boiled on the surface with
petrels, albatross, skuas, purpoises and the occasional elephant seal who would vertically raise
his giant head and neck to survey our ship, with
considerable indifference it seemed. "All ashore"
was the cry over the loud speaker system at 9:30
after we lowered anchors in the snuggest harbor
you could imagine. Drawing only 16 feet, our ship
lies 100 yards from a small jetty, and, in no time,
two ships' boats were lowered to shuttle passengers
ashore. All were dressed in the big red parkas
and hoods which are mandatory on leaving the ship
in these and more southern waters - for safety and
quick recognition. We felt a little odd all dressed
so similarly and even more so when we heard we
were off to the rockhopper penguin rookeries - for
they must have looked just the same to us as we did
to them. Guided by the local and most friendly
British islanders from the little settlement of
about 4 cottages. They kindly transported the more
elderly by a land rover over the 20 minute walk
which the majority took in beautiful sunny 65°
weather. Walking up over a high hill, we soon
could hear the noise of the penguins and their 3
month old chicks; notice the slight tho' not too
obnoxious odor and see the huge albatross circling
overhead. Below, some 50 to 70 feet, the sea
pounded the rocks - what a fantastic sight! Standing within two to four feet of them there were
acres of these underwater swimming birds caring
for fluffy chicks. And dotted around, sitting
on their foot-high nests were blue-grey furry
albatross chicks and their enormous sheet-white and
attentive parents. Never has so much camera footage
been used so fast, so long by so many, to misquote
a very famous statesman.

A picnic lunch was served to all who went ashore
much re-loading of precious film and then off in

-2-   2/28/70

brilliant sunshine along the shore to meet relatives of the New England Aquarium's jackass
penguins in the crystal clear water; on the snow
white sand, and unbelievably, way up the surrounding hills guarding their chicks and burrows, a
stones throw from the sheep which provide wool
for the Falkland Isles main export.

Tonight we entertain all the local inhabitants
aboard for dinner. We can't wait for they were
so kind and generous to us. We are the first
people they've seen for months and months.

For Expedition Antarctic, this is Michael Wynne-
Willson joined by his wife Anne on the Lindblad
Explorer. Good night to you all from the calm of
West Point Island Harbor in the Falkland Islands.

ENGLAND YES

ARGENTINE NO

The ANTARCTIC CIRCLE

January 29, 1970

Good evening from the Falkland Islands. At 6 a.m. today the Lindblad Explorer was due to sail for nearby Carcass Island and did, but due to high winds and heavy seas, landing of passengers would have been impossible by small boat, so it was decided to return to West Point Island and to the many friends we made yesterday. Six of the total adult population of nine were the ship's guests for dinner last night and their excitement and wonder was thrilling and almost unbelievable. English accents which, as Jess Cain once said, made mine sound like Rocky Graziano's, abounded at dinner as all on board did their best to entertain our visitors whose major communication with the world and each island is by short wave radio. When we returned for another day on shore it seemed, by the looks of some of our male guests, that the party was a success! Today, for most of our passengers, it was a repeat of penguin rookery visitations, but in different parts of the islands.

For this reporter, the morning was spent with Dr. Gordon Ferguson, the peripetatic doctor whose practice stretches across several of these Falkland Islands, by sea plane and short wave radio. When I met him on the Island yesterday, we both exclaimed instantaneously "I know you" and it took most of last night until lunch at noon today to remember that we met playing cricket in Scotland 31 years ago! The only general practicioner for 4,000 square miles, Gordon Ferguson is employed by the government and has been practicing here for just over a year and finds his a most challenging and rewarding vocation. His patients, the islanders, subscribe $1.40 a year each for their prescriptions, otherwise his services and all drugs are provided free. Living on the island of Fox Bay, he gets home once every ten to twelve days for a night. The rest of the time he stays with his patients, for he knows them all well and is known either as Doc or Uncle Gordie. It was heart-warming to hear him calm, and prescribe to a lady who, over short wave, was

-2-   1/29/70

unable to hide her concern for her ailing daughter
and to assure her that, as soon as the seaplane
could get here to pick him up, he would be over.
This he was afraid would not be until tomorrow,
but a few minutes ago we stood waving to him from
the top deck as he took off once more.

We hope for calmer weather tomorrow to visit anoth
island, but as Capt. Gjesdal said tonight, "We
have to live by the elements and plan day by day".
Thank you for joining us - we hope our signal was
clear. This is Michael Wynne-Willson, Public
Relations Director for The Townhouse, bidding you
goodnight from the Lindblad Explorer, the Falkland
Islands.

SPECIAL EDITION

The ANTARCTIC CIRCLE

Sunday, February 1, 1970

Continuing it's good luck with weather, the Lindblad Explorer is sailing through Drake's Passage in unbelievably calm weather. While still rolling enough for some passengers, we according to Capt. Gjesdal, very lucky.

Breakfast this morning was more sparsely attended than usual due to a. ,The Drake Passage swell and b. ,the results of the Falkland Islands' bash! The islanders entertained us all lavishly and, in an effort to repay the hospitality, the Governor and his wife, plus about 70 residents came aboard last night for cocktails and supper. It was a festive and crowded affair which went on long after the last islander had left the ship. Your correspondent had prudently retired soon after that time, but many rumors are rife as to the floor-show and some unusual exhibitions staged by some passengers. Ian, the lounge bar steward was privy to these events, but true to the tradition of his trade, his mouth is sealed.

Stamps, clothing, trinkets, not to mention delightful penguin neckties were purchased in profusion and the opportunity to photograph our Argentinian Francisco Erizo and our British Keith Shackleton either side of a sign proclaiming "Keep the Falklands British" were eagerly taken.

The delicious lunch at St. Mary's for both islanders and passengers was greatly enjoyed and appreiated and resulted in many being invited to privat homes after tours by landrovers. Additionally, many were invited back to the ship to tour it, but Island Company, Ltd. forbad the entry of many and proved an embarrassment to many a passenger and guest.

An airplane was chartered for photography and aeri views of elephant seals and king penguins. Our Chief Purser reports that he distributed 620 Falkland Island pounds and had about 100 returned so, with use of personal sterling, dollars and travellers checks, it would seem that the Falkland Islanders were, from a mercenary point of view, richer by about 700-800 pounds.

-2- 2/1/70

FLOTSAM & JETSAM

THE ANTARCTIC CIRCLE wishes to congratulate
Capt. Gjesdal for his masterly docking at Port
Stanley. In such a wind it was a proud per-
formance.

There is a demand for ice-picks and toasters.
Any passengers having either, please contact
THE ANTARCTIC CIRCLE offices - cabin nos.
207, 208 and 203. On arrival at the Palmer
penninsular, THE ANTARCTIC CIRCLE is organizing
an expedition to crack ice and bring it on board
for obvious reasons.

The ANTARCTIC CIRCLE

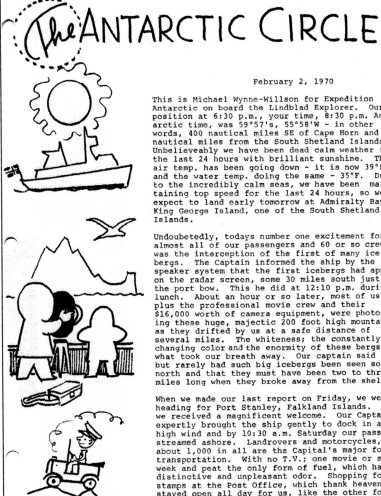

February 2, 1970

This is Michael Wynne-Willson for Expedition Antarctic on board the Lindblad Explorer. Our position at 6:30 p.m., your time, 8:30 p.m. Antarctic time, was 59°57's, 55°58'W - in other words, 400 nautical miles SE of Cape Horn and 130 nautical miles from the South Shetland Islands. Unbelieveably we have been dead calm weather for the last 24 hours with brilliant sunshine. The air temp. has been going down - it is now 39°F and the water temp. doing the same - 35°F. Due to the incredibly calm seas, we have been maintaining top speed for the last 24 hours, so we expect to land early tomorrow at Admiralty Bay, King George Island, one of the South Shetland Islands.

Undoubetedly, todays number one excitement for almost all of our passengers and 60 or so crew was the interception of the first of many icebergs. The Captain informed the ship by the speaker system that the first icebergs had appear on the radar screen, some 30 miles south just off the port bow. This he did at 12:10 p.m. during lunch. About an hour or so later, most of us, plus the professional movie crew and their $16,000 worth of camera equipment, were photograp ing these huge, majectic 200 foot high mountains as they drifted by us at a safe distance of several miles. The whiteness; the constantly changing color and the enormity of these bergs was what took our breath away. Our captain said that but rarely had such big icebergs been seen so far north and that they must have been two to three miles long when they broke away from the shelf.

When we made our last report on Friday, we were heading for Port Stanley, Falkland Islands. Here we received a magnificent welcome. Our Captain expertly brought the ship gently to dock in a high wind and by 10:30 a.m. Saturday our passenge streamed ashore. Landrovers and motorcycles, about 1,000 in all are the Capital's major form o transportation. With no T.V.; one movie or so a week and peat the only form of fuel, which has a distinctive and unpleasant odor. Shopping for stamps at the Post Office, which thank heaven, stayed open all day for us, like the other four

-2-   2/2/70

or five stores, was the first order of business;
shopping for trinkets, delightful penguin ties
followed. We were lavishly entertained for lunch
on shore, then most were invited back to individua
homes or taken on tours of the town. Our host
worked for the British Antarctic Survey and is a
ham radio operator. Imagine our delight when he
raised Jock Kiley in Boston within an hour and
was able to hear all our news.

Yesterday we had a heavy swell which produced its
toll at breakfast. In addition, those who entertained our Falkland Island friends who came aboard
for liquid and solid refreshments at dinner stayed
up late, were also inconspicuous.

All being well, and a good signal, we will have
much exciting news for you tomorrow, our first
day ashore where it is really cold. Michael
Wynne-Willson, Public Relations Director for the
New England Aquarium for Expedition Antarctica,
from the Antarctic, Goodnight.

For THE ANTARCTIC CIRCLE, LTD

Business Manager: Bitten Clausen
News Advisor: Lars Eric Lindblad
Illustrator: Hakon Mielche
Advertising: Topsy Waters
Technical Advisor: Capt. Gjesdal
Secretary: Anne Wynne-Willson
Copywriter: Michael Wynne-Willson
Printer: Suzi Zanatta

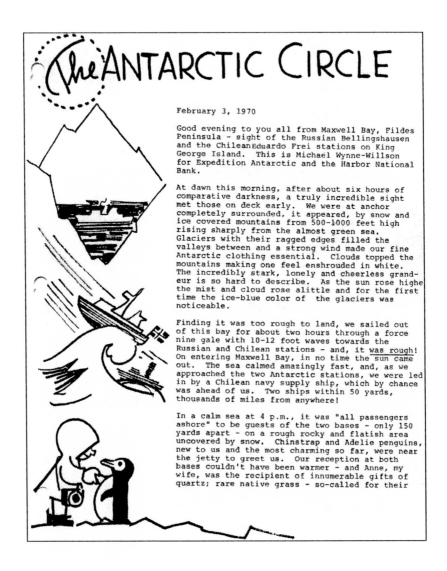

The ANTARCTIC CIRCLE

February 3, 1970

Good evening to you all from Maxwell Bay, Fildes
Peninsula - sight of the Russian Bellingshausen
and the ChileanEduardo Frei stations on King
George Island. This is Michael Wynne-Willson
for Expedition Antarctic and the Harbor National
Bank.

At dawn this morning, after about six hours of
comparative darkness, a truly incredible sight
met those on deck early. We were at anchor
completely surrounded, it appeared, by snow and
ice covered mountains from 500-1000 feet high
rising sharply from the almost green sea.
Glaciers with their ragged edges filled the
valleys between and a strong wind made our fine
Antarctic clothing essential. Clouds topped the
mountains making one feel enshrouded in white.
The incredibly stark, lonely and cheerless grandeur is so hard to describe. As the sun rose highe
the mist and cloud rose alittle and for the first
time the ice-blue color of the glaciers was
noticeable.

Finding it was too rough to land, we sailed out
of this bay for about two hours through a force
nine gale with 10-12 foot waves towards the
Russian and Chilean stations - and, it was rough!
On entering Maxwell Bay, in no time the sun came
out. The sea calmed amazingly fast, and, as we
approached the two Antarctic stations, we were led
in by a Chilean navy supply ship, which by chance
was ahead of us. Two ships within 50 yards,
thousands of miles from anywhere!

In a calm sea at 4 p.m., it was "all passengers
ashore" to be guests of the two bases - only 150
yards apart - on a rough rocky and flatish area
uncovered by snow. Chinstrap and Adelie penguins,
new to us and the most charming so far, were near
the jetty to greet us. Our reception at both
bases couldn't have been warmer - and Anne, my
wife, was the recipient of innumerable gifts of
quartz; rare native grass - so-called for their

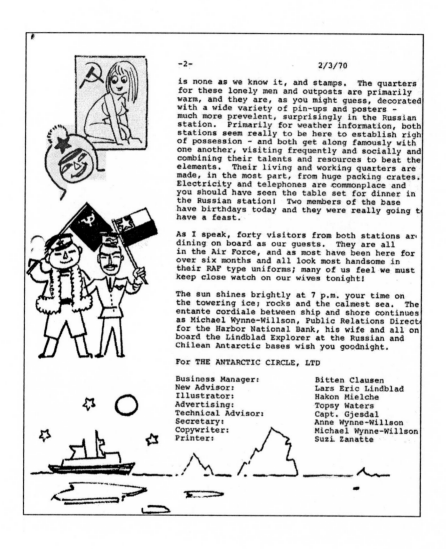

-2-   2/3/70

is none as we know it, and stamps. The quarters
for these lonely men and outposts are primarily
warm, and they are, as you might guess, decorated
with a wide variety of pin-ups and posters -
much more prevelent, surprisingly in the Russian
station. Primarily for weather information, both
stations seem really to be here to establish righ
of possession - and both get along famously with
one another, visiting frequently and socially and
combining their talents and resources to beat the
elements. Their living and working quarters are
made, in the most part, from huge packing crates.
Electricity and telephones are commonplace and
you should have seen the table set for dinner in
the Russian station! Two members of the base
have birthdays today and they were really going t
have a feast.

As I speak, forty visitors from both stations ar
dining on board as our guests. They are all
in the Air Force, and as most have been here for
over six months and all look most handsome in
their RAF type uniforms; many of us feel we must
keep close watch on our wives tonight!

The sun shines brightly at 7 p.m. your time on
the towering ice; rocks and the calmest sea. The
entante cordiale between ship and shore continues
as Michael Wynne-Willson, Public Relations Direct
for the Harbor National Bank, his wife and all on
board the Lindblad Explorer at the Russian and
Chilean Antarctic bases wish you goodnight.

For THE ANTARCTIC CIRCLE, LTD

Business Manager: Bitten Clausen
New Advisor: Lars Eric Lindblad
Illustrator: Hakon Mielche
Advertising: Topsy Waters
Technical Advisor: Capt. Gjesdal
Secretary: Anne Wynne-Willson
Copywriter: Michael Wynne-Willson
Printer: Suzi Zanatte

The ANTARCTIC CIRCLE

February 4, 1970

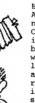

Hello again, Michael Wynne-Willson on Expedition Antarctica from the Lindblad Explorer on the most northern tip of the Antarctic Continent. As the Captain just said to me "that's probably why it is called Hope Bay!" Esperanza base is operated by the Argentinians, and we sailed to it after we had gotten our Russian friends off the ship late last night - not without considerable effort and slight delay we might add. Never has this reporter seen more hand-kissing and cementing of international relations! It is truly great to see all nations working together so amicably and helpfully on and near the seventh continent. By common agreement it seems that this is possible due to the total lack of politicians.

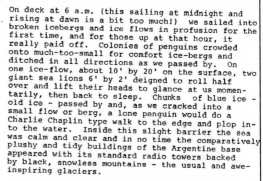

On deck at 6 a.m. (this sailing at midnight and rising at dawn is a bit too much!) we sailed into broken icebergs and ice flows in profusion for the first time, and for those up at that hour, it really paid off. Colonies of penguins crowded onto much-too-small for comfort ice-bergs and ditched in all directions as we passed by. On one ice-flow, about 10' by 20' on the surface, two giant sea lions 6' by 2' deigned to roll half over and lift their heads to glance at us momentarily, then back to sleep. Chunks of blue ice - old ice - passed by and, as we cracked into a small flow or berg, a lone penguin would do a Charlie Chaplin type walk to the edge and plop into the water. Inside this slight barrier the sea was calm and clear and in no time the comparatively plushy and tidy buildings of the Argentine base appeared with its standard radio towers backed by black, snowless mountains - the usual and awe-inspiring glaciers.

Arriving on shore around 9:30 a.m. by outboard propelled rubber boats holding about 15 people, we were taken on personally conducted tours. To date, Esperanza Station is by far the most comfortable and well-equipped which we have seen. Nearby the several buildings - not crates that we've seen before - were two teams of Husky sled dogs, staked out parallel on two long chains, who, like their South American owners, were delighted and pleased to see us, and seemed to say so too.

-2-   2/4/70

On the rocky inclines behind both sides were innumerable Adélie penguin rookeries and, stretch-
ing at least for 100 yards horizontally across a
snowy incline was what is known here as "The Penguin Turnpike". Here the traffic was heavy in
both directions and accidents frequent it seemed
as these mesmerizing birds marched, ran and fell
from rookery to the open sea to feed and reverse
direction to discharge their catch to their fuzz;
 chicks.

One thousand yards up the mountain is an unused
British station built in 1945. Today it is in-
habited by fifteen members of a British motion
picture production company here for several month
preparing a new film called "Forbush and the Penguins". This is surely a great location. One
very rare occurance happened within 200 yards
today. A huge chunk fell off an ice-berg. With
great timing your reporter had, two seconds before. laid down his film camera. Naturally, had
his wife been using the machine it would have
been recorded fully!

Tonight we sail for Deception Island. Please
join me tomorrow night as we head even further
south. This is Michael Wynne-Willson, Public
Relations Advisor for the Townhouse at 84 Feacon
Street reporting from the Lindblad Explorer off
the Antarctic continent. From us to all of /ou,
Goodnight.

PENGUIN
TURNPIKE

STOP

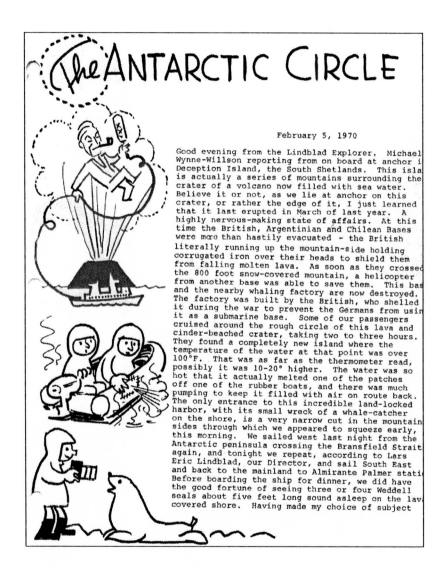

The ANTARCTIC CIRCLE

February 5, 1970

Good evening from the Lindblad Explorer. Michael Wynne-Willson reporting from on board at anchor i Deception Island, the South Shetlands. This isla is actually a series of mountains surrounding the crater of a volcano now filled with sea water. Believe it or not, as we lie at anchor on this crater, or rather the edge of it, I just learned that it last erupted in March of last year. A highly nervous-making state of affairs. At this time the British, Argentinian and Chilean Bases were more than hastily evacuated - the British literally running up the mountain-side holding corrugated iron over their heads to shield them from falling molten lava. As soon as they crossed the 800 foot snow-covered mountain, a helicopter from another base was able to save them. This bas and the nearby whaling factory are now destroyed. The factory was built by the British, who shelled it during the war to prevent the Germans from usin it as a submarine base. Some of our passengers cruised around the rough circle of this lava and cinder-beached crater, taking two to three hours. They found a completely new island where the temperature of the water at that point was over 100°F. That was as far as the thermometer read, possibly it was 10-20° higher. The water was so hot that it actually melted one of the patches off one of the rubber boats, and there was much pumping to keep it filled with air on route back. The only entrance to this incredible land-locked harbor, with its small wreck of a whale-catcher on the shore, is a very narrow cut in the mountain sides through which we appeared to squeeze early, this morning. We sailed west last night from the Antarctic peninsula crossing the Bransfield Strait again, and tonight we repeat, according to Lars Eric Lindblad, our Director, and sail South East and back to the mainland to Almirante Palmer stati Before boarding the ship for dinner, we did have the good fortune of seeing three or four Weddell seals about five feet long sound asleep on the lav covered shore. Having made my choice of subject

2 -   2/5/70

suffice to say my camera was two feet from his or
her nose and molting head. He deigned to raise
himself up and pose, then collapsed, rolled on his
back, burped and went back to sleep. For humans,
they obviously couldn't care less.

Thank you for joining us again - or for the first
time - on this incredible Antarctic Expedition.
This is Michael Wynne-Willson, Public Relations
Director for the New England Aquarium wishing you
all - good night.

The ANTARCTIC CIRCLE

February 6, 1970

Good evening to you all from Michael Wynne-Willson on board the Lindblad Explorer as we leave Almirante Bay after the most perfect day to date, from scenery and animal point of view. In addition, it was all doubly appreciated as it is my wife, Anne's birthday - and it's not every year you have a birthday in the Antarctic - nor under the bluest sky surrounded by 4,000 foot mountains, the surrounding sea covered by small azure blue icebergs and the rumble of avalanches and glacier break-offs from behind and above the entirely scientific Argentinian station at this base. Photographically, it was a perfect day and brought everyone on deck early. This reporter took over 150 photos ranging from scenics to thousands of Gentoo and Chinstrap penguins caring for their furry grey chicks. Fittingly - and I hope you'll forgive a personal point of view - the day started in an epoch-making fashion. We shared our breakfast with our good friends on board, the well known European novelist and illustrator from Denmark, Hakon Mielche, traveling with us on assingment for a Danish weekly magazine, and a most charming compatriot, Mrs. Bitten Clausen. They had arranged a typical Danish breakfast and a gala opening for Anne's birthday with champagne and several delightfully illustrated gifts. Later, Hakon appeared dressed in tails and white gloves and made a striking sight wandering through fields of penguins. This was always something I wanted to do, but it took Hakon really to pull it off.

As our series from the Antarctic close early next week, it would be inappropriate not to give due credit to the man whose ideas sparked this amazing adventure and who has done - with good assistance from many - so much to make it memorable. It is quite incredible that all of us passengers can now, in great comfort and with considerable ease, see and go ashore on this most rugged of lands where we often see - through the marks and crosses overlooking almost every base we visit, that men have recently sacrificed their lives for exploration or science. It is so great to see that Lars Eric Lindblad not only wants people to have the opportunity of seeing this incredibly rugged and beautiful land but obviously cares tremendously about the conserva-

-2-   2/6/70

tion and preservation of beauty. It is he who,
amongst others such as Capt. Mac Donald, Dr. Sewal
Pettingill, distinguished ornithologist from
Cornell, Keith Shackleton, renowned wildlife
artist from England, Dr. George Grice from Woods
Hole Oceanographic Institute and Francisco Erize
from Argentina have done so much to teach us and
guide us in ways of life here in the Antarctic and
how we should conduct ourselves on shore. We are
indeed lucky in our directors.

We wish you a happy weekend and we hope you will
join us on Monday.

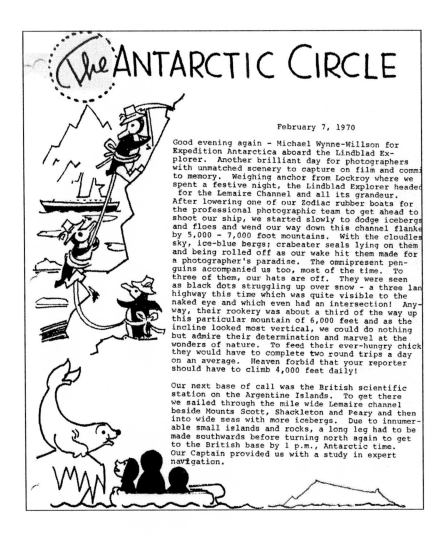

The ANTARCTIC CIRCLE

February 7, 1970

Good evening again - Michael Wynne-Willson for Expedition Antarctica aboard the Lindblad Explorer. Another brilliant day for photographers with unmatched scenery to capture on film and commi to memory. Weighing anchor from Lockroy where we spent a festive night, the Lindblad Explorer headed for the Lemaire Channel and all its grandeur. After lowering one of our Zodiac rubber boats for the professional photographic team to get ahead to shoot our ship, we started slowly to dodge icebergs and floes and wend our way down this channel flanke by 5,000 - 7,000 foot mountains. With the cloudles sky, ice-blue bergs; crabeater seals lying on them and being rolled off as our wake hit them made for a photographer's paradise. The omnipresent penguins accompanied us too, most of the time. To three of them, our hats are off. They were seen as black dots struggling up over snow - a three lan highway this time which was quite visible to the naked eye and which even had an intersection! Anyway, their rookery was about a third of the way up this particular mountain of 6,000 feet and as the incline looked most vertical, we could do nothing but admire their determination and marvel at the wonders of nature. To feed their ever-hungry chick they would have to complete two round trips a day on an average. Heaven forbid that your reporter should have to climb 4,000 feet daily!

Our next base of call was the British scientific station on the Argentine Islands. To get there we sailed through the mile wide Lemaire channel beside Mounts Scott, Shackleton and Peary and then into wide seas with more icebergs. Due to innumerable small islands and rocks, a long leg had to be made southwards before turning north again to get to the British base by 1 p.m., Antarctic time. Our Captain provided us with a study in expert navigation.

- 2 -   2/7/70

This afternoon we visited the base, enjoying a
delightful boat ride of about 20 minutes at
below iceberg level and at seal level. So far,
they have proven shy animals - with the exception
of my rotund friend at Deception Island of whom
I reported previously. The base itself was similar
to most others we have been to - in fact, for a
region supposedly barren of humans, we seem to
see more, more regularly, than one would believe
possible. Is the Antarctic suffering from a
population explosion?

One English scientist stated that he came here
because he was engaged and wanted to think about
the prospects. Possibly he may have time to do
this as he's been here a year and has one more to
go. With mail in and out once annually, it can't
be the hottest courtship, but then, the British
are conservatives, are they not?

People, or no people, it has been a most memorable
day however. Rumors are rife about whether or not
we will see seal rookeries and be able to really
get close to them, and whether or not we will reach
Adelie Island, our most southern destination, due
to pack-ice en route. Time, our Captain and our
Director will tell.

This is Michael Wynne-Willson, Public Relations
Director for the New England Aquarium, where you
can see seals and penguins - and people everyday
of the week - reporting for Expedition Antarctic
and the Harbor National Bank. Goodnight.

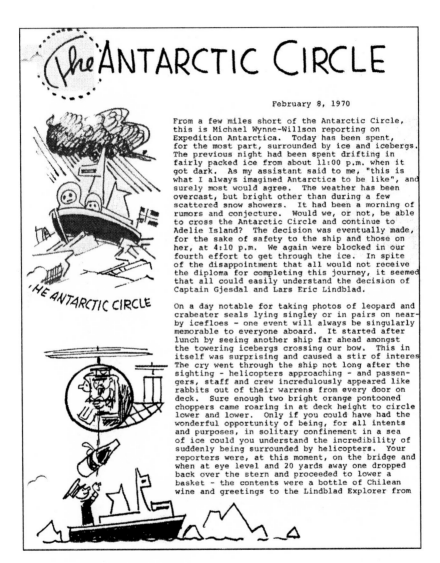

the ANTARCTIC CIRCLE

February 8, 1970

From a few miles short of the Antarctic Circle,
this is Michael Wynne-Willson reporting on
Expedition Antarctica. Today has been spent,
for the most part, surrounded by ice and icebergs.
The previous night had been spent drifting in
fairly packed ice from about 11:00 p.m. when it
got dark. As my assistant said to me, "this is
what I always imagined Antarctica to be like", and
surely most would agree. The weather has been
overcast, but bright other than during a few
scattered snow showers. It had been a morning of
rumors and conjecture. Would we, or not, be able
to cross the Antarctic Circle and continue to
Adelie Island? The decision was eventually made,
for the sake of safety to the ship and those on
her, at 4:10 p.m. We again were blocked in our
fourth effort to get through the ice. In spite
of the disappointment that all would not receive
the diploma for completing this journey, it seemed
that all could easily understand the decision of
Captain Gjesdal and Lars Eric Lindblad.

On a day notable for taking photos of leopard and
crabeater seals lying singley or in pairs on nearby icefloes - one event will always be singularly
memorable to everyone aboard. It started after
lunch by seeing another ship far ahead amongst
the towering icebergs crossing our bow. This in
itself was surprising and caused a stir of interest.
The cry went through the ship not long after the
sighting - helicopters approaching - and passengers, staff and crew incredulously appeared like
rabbits out of their warrens from every door on
deck. Sure enough two bright orange pontooned
choppers came roaring in at deck height to circle
lower and lower. Only if you could have had the
wonderful opportunity of being, for all intents
and purposes, in solitary confinement in a sea
of ice could you understand the incredibility of
suddenly being surrounded by helicopters. Your
reporters were, at this moment, on the bridge and
when at eye level and 20 yards away one dropped
back over the stern and proceeded to lower a
basket - the contents were a bottle of Chilean
wine and greetings to the Lindblad Explorer from

'HE ANTARCTIC CIRCLE

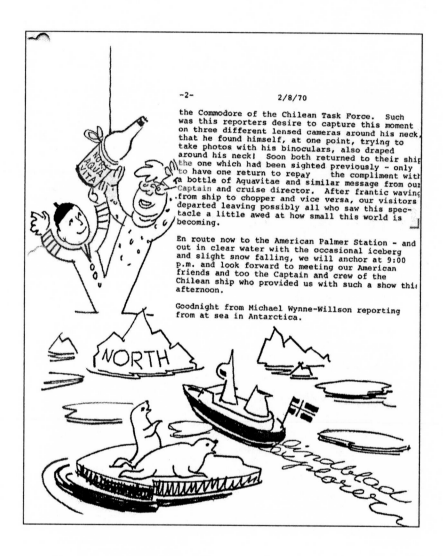

-2-   2/8/70

the Commodore of the Chilean Task Force. Such
was this reporters desire to capture this moment
on three different lensed cameras around his neck,
that he found himself, at one point, trying to
take photos with his binoculars, also draped
around his neck! Soon both returned to their ship
the one which had been sighted previously - only
to have one return to repay   the compliment with
a bottle of Aquavitae and similar message from our
Captain and cruise director. After frantic waving
from ship to chopper and vice versa, our visitors
departed leaving possibly all who saw this spectacle a little awed at how small this world is
becoming.

En route now to the American Palmer Station - and
out in clear water with the occasional iceberg
and slight snow falling, we will anchor at 9:00
p.m. and look forward to meeting our American
friends and too the Captain and crew of the
Chilean ship who provided us with such a show this
afternoon.

Goodnight from Michael Wynne-Willson reporting
from at sea in Antarctica.

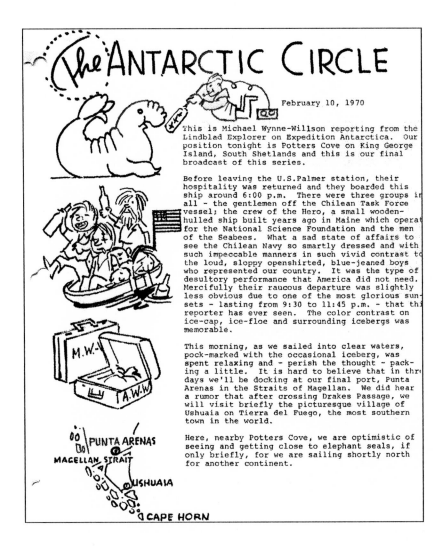

The ANTARCTIC CIRCLE

February 10, 1970

This is Michael Wynne-Willson reporting from the Lindblad Explorer on Expedition Antarctica. Our position tonight is Potters Cove on King George Island, South Shetlands and this is our final broadcast of this series.

Before leaving the U.S. Palmer station, their hospitality was returned and they boarded this ship around 6:00 p.m. There were three groups in all - the gentlemen off the Chilean Task Force vessel; the crew of the Hero, a small wooden-hulled ship built years ago in Maine which operate for the National Science Foundation and the men of the Seabees. What a sad state of affairs to see the Chilean Navy so smartly dressed and with such impeccable manners in such vivid contrast to the loud, sloppy openshirted, blue-jeaned boys who represented our country. It was the type of desultory performance that America did not need. Mercifully their raucous departure was slightly less obvious due to one of the most glorious sun-sets - lasting from 9:30 to 11:45 p.m. - that this reporter has ever seen. The color contrast on ice-cap, ice-floe and surrounding icebergs was memorable.

This morning, as we sailed into clear waters, pock-marked with the occasional iceberg, was spent relaxing and - perish the thought - packing a little. It is hard to believe that in three days we'll be docking at our final port, Punta Arenas in the Straits of Magellan. We did hear a rumor that after crossing Drakes Passage, we will visit briefly the picturesque village of Ushuaia on Tierra del Fuego, the most southern town in the world.

Here, nearby Potters Cove, we are optimistic of seeing and getting close to elephant seals, if only briefly, for we are sailing shortly north for another continent.

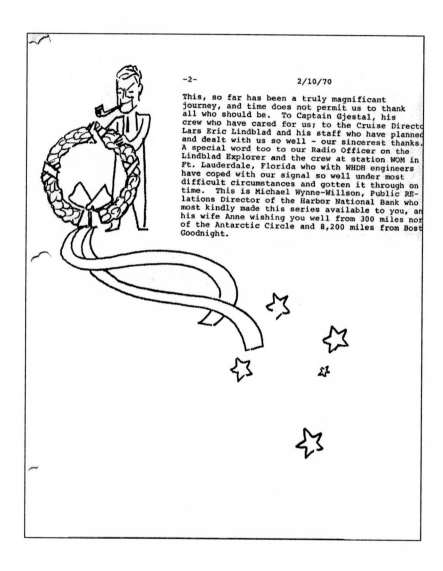

-2-   2/10/70

This, so far has been a truly magnificant
journey, and time does not permit us to thank
all who should be. To Captain Gjestal, his
crew who have cared for us; to the Cruise Directo
Lars Eric Lindblad and his staff who have planned
and dealt with us so well - our sincerest thanks.
A special word too to our Radio Officer on the
Lindblad Explorer and the crew at station WOM in
Ft. Lauderdale, Florida who with WHDH engineers
have coped with our signal so well under most
difficult circumstances and gotten it through on
time. This is Michael Wynne-Willson, Public RE-
lations Director of the Harbor National Bank who
most kindly made this series available to you, an
his wife Anne wishing you well from 300 miles nor
of the Antarctic Circle and 8,200 miles from Bost
Goodnight.

The ANTARCTIC CIRCLE

This is Michael Wynne-Willson from the Lindblad Explorer for Expedition Antarctica. We have been sailing north since leaving Palmer Station at 1:30 this morning and we arrived at Potters Cove at 5:30 p.m. All were ready to disembark as we dropped anchor and, as quickly as possible, went ashore hopefully to find elephant seals. Once ashore we were told to wait for all to disembark and not start our exploration in groups in fear of frightening any seals who might be on the beaches. During this period, the Explorers Club contingent took the opportunity to have their group photograph. At last all were ashore and the word "charge" was given. Maybe that wasn't the word exactly - but that's what it looked like and appeared. One hundred Red Penguins armed to the teeth with photographic devices - not to mention tape-recorders; tripods and binoculars - soon came upon the first of hundreds of Elephant Seals lying placidly near the water's edge. Bedlam reigned as all, it seemed, tried to photograph the first we saw - and 50% of the film taken was of the back of one eager red penguin trying to get closer than an other. Manners and tempers were forgotten in the faces of these huge oderous lumbering beasts. In short, their behavior was much better than that of ours at first.

After discovering that these seals were plentiful and in no hurry to take to the water, everyone relaxed and settled down to some serious photography and just plain looking. It is hard to describe the enormity of these mammals - spread out along the beach singularly and in groups of 5; 10; 50 and 80 which was the largest sighted today. Many were tame and sleepy enough to touch or even sit on and most had acute halitosis and bore scars of battle at one time or other. Whale bones of all sizes and shapes littered the beaches and, on the rocky promontories, grey and white baby giant petrel chicks sat on their rocky nests. Their parents wheeled attentively high above, making diving passes with agitated shrieks on occasion as we stopped to photograph them.

- 2

In the gold of the setting sun, the sight of
about fifty of these seals - average length
10 - 12 feet, weighing over a ton each, lying
close to and on top of each other - sleeping;
snorting; belching and bellowing, was unique
and exciting. They had little if any fear of
us people - and in the main, could have cared
less. By their size they intimidated us, and
this reporter felt grateful that they allowed
us so near and to photograph them. After 3
hours ashore - and as many rolls of film per
person for the Wynne-Willsons, we returned to
the ship and dinner. We were in considerable
awe of what we had been priviledge to see. As
we head now into Drake's Passage and begin to
feel the first signs of what will be a rough
crossing - this is Michael Wynne-Willson wishing all at home, 8,000 miles north, a good
night.

The ANTARCTIC CIRCLE

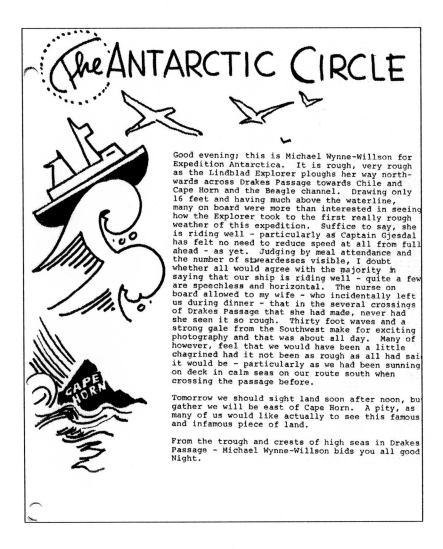

Good evening; this is Michael Wynne-Willson for Expedition Antarctica. It is rough, very rough as the Lindblad Explorer ploughs her way northwards across Drakes Passage towards Chile and Cape Horn and the Beagle channel. Drawing only 16 feet and having much above the waterline, many on board were more than interested in seeing how the Explorer took to the first really rough weather of this expedition. Suffice to say, she is riding well - particularly as Captain Gjesdal has felt no need to reduce speed at all from full ahead - as yet. Judging by meal attendance and the number of stweardesses visible, I doubt whether all would agree with the majority in saying that our ship is riding well - quite a few are speechless and horizontal. The nurse on board allowed to my wife - who incidentally left us during dinner - that in the several crossings of Drakes Passage that she had made, never had she seen it so rough. Thirty foot waves and a strong gale from the Southwest make for exciting photography and that was about all day. Many of however, feel that we would have been a little chagrined had it not been as rough as all had sai it would be - particularly as we had been sunning on deck in calm seas on our route south when crossing the passage before.

Tomorrow we should sight land soon after noon, bu gather we will be east of Cape Horn. A pity, as many of us would like actually to see this famous and infamous piece of land.

From the trough and crests of high seas in Drakes Passage - Michael Wynne-Willson bids you all good Night.

The ANTARCTIC CIRCLE

CAPE HORN

Good Evening from Punta Areanas, Chile. This is Michael Wynne-Willson aboard the Lindblad Explorer lying alongside the dock at our port of disembarkation. We did not see Cape Horn, but passed about 30 miles east of it. After sighting land - with trees growing on it for a change - we next saw a camouflaged pilot boat approaching - more submerged by the high seas than visible. After some three-way altercations with the Lindblad Explorer; Chilea and Argentinians, it was deemed advisable to avoid an International incident between these two countries and avoid landing at the most southern settlement in Argentinia. As both countries are prone to fight each other at the loss of a sheep; it seemed prudent for us not to go there with an Argentinian pilot and proceed to Port Williams in Chile and have him arrested on board. It was then that a Chilean navy pilot who was on board this tiny vessel which approached us - for some reason better known to themselves - on the windward side. Our Captain looked with considerable alarm and no small horror as the two of us got closer. With an audible crack, we came together and it was only with the luck of the Gods and no seamanship on the part of the pilot boat that its' mast and superstructure weren't taken off, as it shot full speed ahead by our bridge and turned smartly <u>across</u> our bow as we were too, underway! Our Captain's expression had to be seen to be believed. Eventual discretion being the better part of valor, the pilot decided to invite us into calmer waters - almost on the rocks it appeared - and then requested we send a life boat to pick him up. That must have been the fianl indignity! Once aboard, however, this Chilean naval captain was the last word in business and efficiency as he took sightings every five minutes as we sailed up the Beagle channel towards Port Williams - the most southern settlement and naval base in Chile. We landed there supposedly to see many rare birds and parrots - maybe some bird-watchers amongst us did - but not for us. We saw a lot of gun emplacements; soccer players and dark-eyed maidens peering out at us from their hut-like dwellings. The naval officers and their children who came aboard that night though could not have been more friendly and the stop was worthwhile.

-2-

We sailed late that night for the 20 hour, 300 mile trip, up the Magellan Straits to Punta Areanas.

The portion of the straits which we saw the day following under grey or broken clouds was a little reminiscent of a giant-sized Caledonian canal, or Scottish loch without ends! Particularly notice- able were the hundreds of birds who patiently per- sued our ship - and the many seals "porpoising" along nearby. Packing too many things into too few suitcases took over most attention as we approach our destination. This is Michael Wynne-Willson on the Lindblad Explorer for Expedition Antarctica, back in civilization again. Good night.

Michael F. Wynne-Willson

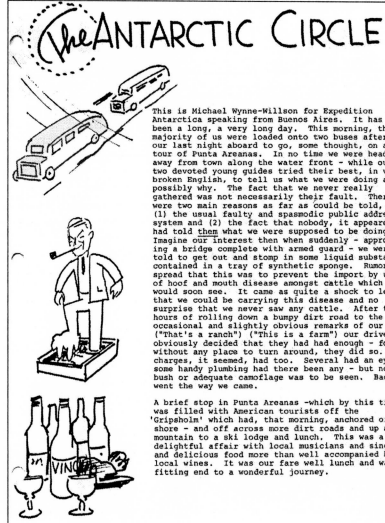

the ANTARCTIC CIRCLE

This is Michael Wynne-Willson for Expedition Antarctica speaking from Buenos Aires. It has been a long, a very long day. This morning, the majority of us were loaded onto two buses after our last night aboard to go, some thought, on a tour of Punta Areanas. In no time we were heading away from town along the water front - while our two devoted young guides tried their best, in very broken English, to tell us what we were doing and possibly why. The fact that we never really gathered was not necessarily their fault. There were two main reasons as far as could be told, (1) the usual faulty and spasmodic public address system and (2) the fact that nobody, it appeared, had told them what we were supposed to be doing. Imagine our interest then when suddenly - approaching a bridge complete with armed guard - we were told to get out and stomp in some liquid substance contained in a tray of synthetic sponge. Rumor spread that this was to prevent the import by us of hoof and mouth disease amongst cattle which we would soon see. It came as quite a shock to learn that we could be carrying this disease and no surprise that we never saw any cattle. After two hours of rolling down a bumpy dirt road to the occasional and slightly obvious remarks of our gui ("That's a ranch") ("This is a farm") our drivers obviously decided that they had had enough - for without any place to turn around, they did so. Th charges, it seemed, had too. Several had an eye t some handy plumbing had there been any - but not a bush or adequate camoflage was to be seen. Back w went the way we came.

A brief stop in Punta Areanas -which by this time was filled with American tourists off the 'Gripsholm' which had, that morning, anchored off shore - and off across more dirt roads and up a mountain to a ski lodge and lunch. This was a delightful affair with local musicians and singers and delicious food more than well accompanied by local wines. It was our fare well lunch and was a fitting end to a wonderful journey.

-2-

In great spirits we bussed to the airport to board our chartered jet to Buenos Aires - but found on arrival that it was two hours late. Misery. Unbeknown to anyone, the local travel agent in charge took one look at our assembled luggage - mountains of it - and must have had a stroke on the spot. Without ticketing or checking it and without anyone traveling with it, he ordered half of it to be sent to Santiago in Chile. At random, suitcases, etc. were removed and put on a plane about to leave - with no check at all. Thi incredible lapse in air traffic etiquette, unheard of on any airline ever, had the most ghastly repercussions which lasted for the next four days. It wasn't long before the word got around that some thing was grossly amiss and soon all were up in arms about either ,1,2,3,4,5,6 or 7 of their pieces of luggage which had vanished into Chilean air.

Eventually- lack of heavy luggage regardless, we embarked on our chartered jet for the 3 1/2 hour flight to Buenos Aires. It was hard getting an average of five or six pieces of hand luggage onto and stowed on the small jet - but nigh on imposs ible to get it off an hour after take off at a border airport which should better remain nameless. Sometimes there are reasons for things - visible reasons - but this Argentine fiasco was incredible. Dumped in the middle of a hot airport - and then ordered to take all luggage out - then bussed to the 'terminal' for customs - and the performance repeated was too much. It was an operation designed to test the patience of all - several of us barely passed.

For those who returned to Buenos Aires - either wit all; some; a little or no luggage - life was anything but humdrum for three days. Nobody, but nobody, at first knew where our luggage was and it almost seemed as tho' nobody except we cared. Calm, quiet and soft-spoken men and women became tyrants; calling on anyone from Lindblad; their local agents; Lan Chile and Aerolineas Argentinas to do something. The Foyer of the Hotel Presidente was somewhat akin most of the time to Grand Central Station when the Long Island Rail Road strikes or can't run.

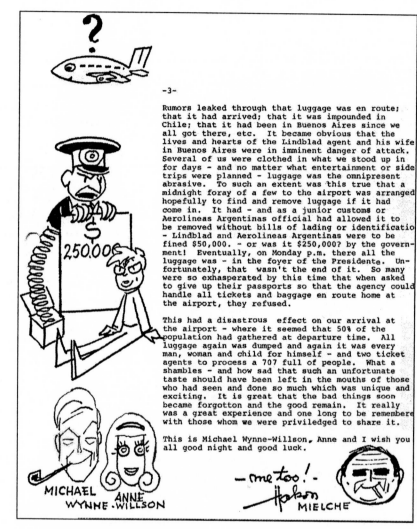

-3-

Rumors leaked through that luggage was en route; that it had arrived; that it was impounded in Chile; that it had been in Buenos Aires since we all got there, etc. It became obvious that the lives and hearts of the Lindblad agent and his wife in Buenos Aires were in imminent danger of attack. Several of us were clothed in what we stood up in for days - and no matter what entertainment or side trips were planned - luggage was the omnipresent abrasive. To such an extent was this true that a midnight foray of a few to the airport was arranged hopefully to find and remove luggage if it had come in. It had - and as a junior customs or Aerolineas Argentinas official had allowed it to be removed without bills of lading or identificatio - Lindblad and Aerolineas Argentinas were to be fined $50,000. - or was it $250,000? by the government! Eventually, on Monday p.m. there all the luggage was - in the foyer of the Presidente. Unfortunately, that wasn't the end of it. So many were so exhasperated by this time that when asked to give up their passports so that the agency could handle all tickets and baggage en route home at the airport, they refused.

This had a disastrous effect on our arrival at the airport - where it seemed that 50% of the population had gathered at departure time. All luggage again was dumped and again it was every man, woman and child for himself - and two ticket agents to process a 707 full of people. What a shambles - and how sad that such an unfortunate taste should have been left in the mouths of those who had seen and done so much which was unique and exciting. It is great that the bad things soon became forgotton and the good remain. It really was a great experience and one long to be remembere with those whom we were priviledged to share it.

This is Michael Wynne-Willson, Anne and I wish you all good night and good luck.

MICHAEL
ANNE
WYNNE·WILLSON

— me too! -

Hakon
MIELCHE

Now that you've had the chance to see Hakon Mielche's talent, you should know that Anne and I had an instant rapport with this charming and often hilarious Dane and we became, as I said, the firmest of friends on this and subsequent trips which I'll mention as we progress.

So what were our main impressions on returning home from our Antarctic Adventure? Without any doubt, we had never had the opportunity to see such incredible and, to us, unique beauty which luckily we were able to capture on color slides and motion picture films. The contrasts, the starkness, the vastness, the omni-present danger of fast-appearing storms, the wildlife and the fact that, surprisingly, we received barely a covering of snow on the whole trip, were all to stay in our memories. Additionally, we were a rare bunch and life was never dull, for sure! It was most interesting to note that there were some with us who were well used to enjoying a good intake of liquid on a daily basis. The further south we sailed toward the Antarctic, it became apparent that the stresses and strains of daily life at home fell from their shoulders and they began to enjoy and mix with their fellow travelers. Sadly, the reverse occurred after we reached our most southerly destination and the boat turned north again heading for home.

We noticed, too, that before boarding, the media were still bothering Mary Hemingway and forever fussing her about her husband's death and the reasons for it. Due to this, we all greatly respected her privacy during the voyage. At one base that we visited Mary became a bit stuck on some rocks while approaching a penguin rookery and seemed in minor trouble. Anne, who was nearby, hastened to assist and thereafter she kindly gave the two of us, and Hakon, the opportunity to get to know and enjoy her. She was great fun, easy to talk to and enjoyed a voracious appetite for information that the various lecturers on board imparted to us daily about the Antarctic and all that it contained. She helped me with the distribution of the Antarctic Circle and after we all returned to Buenos Aires, gave a magnificent dinner-dance for many of us at her favorite restaurant. She most kindly invited Gerry and Sam Gray, our previous hosts, before sailing and with whom we happily stayed again on our return. For some reason best known to her, Mary gave us a very nice gift of a set of steak knives, a constant reminder to us since of a charming and warm-hearted lady.

Anne and Three Living Elephant Seals

Anne wanted me to bring this whale rib home!

If memory serves me correctly, Anne and I took over 1,500 color photographs and slides on the trip and well over a half-hour's worth of movie film. Divorce almost reared its ugly head as we struggled for hours selecting the very best exposures for personal and lecture display! On my return to the Aquarium a display was arranged there and Dave Taylor asked that we show the photos to the Globe staff there at a luncheon. This we did gladly but we were so enthusiastic and grateful for the Globe's assistance that we went on showing photos of penguins, seals, albatross and goodness knows what-all for far, far too long and greatly over-extended our welcome. It really said something for the somewhat sophisticated staff that sat there for slide after slide, and none got up to leave! Doubtless, many never again wanted to see another penguin!

Our Christmas Card—1970

Annie's Birthday Sketch by Keith Shackleton

Lamaire Channel Aboard "The Explorer"

Sometime after this, the Globe fulfilled its promise and did include a few pages in their Sunday 'Rotogravure' section of several of our photos. Many were kind and said our photographic coverage of the adventure was great but, let me add hastily, that was probably due to the scenery and the weather. It was usually warmer where we were than at home and it was nigh on impossible to take a bad picture surrounded as we were by almost unimaginable scenery!

In all, the voyage was a never-to-be-forgotten one. We were lucky indeed to be given this great opportunity and will be forever grateful to those who helped us so generously to go! It was, without doubt, the first of our 'trips of our lifetime'.

THREE
1970 - 1972

Our New Home—For 31 Years Ahead!

This was the year of Antarctica, as you've seen and now, in August, it is the year of our move. For a while, Anne and I had been thinking that a move might be in the cards because it really seemed that many of Jackie's and my old friends in Hamilton really didn't know how to cope with her! That hurt her, let alone me! Suffice to say, it was a tough time. It was one that we didn't need and was most unfair on Anne but that's the way it was, so I suggested that we move. After searching, with minimal success for several weeks, we fell upon a delightful, sunny and newly decorated house in Westwood which seemed made for us and as time has told we were right on the money! It even had a small swimming pool! Mark, who was 16 at this time and had just won a Latin Prize at St. George's, just couldn't believe that when we told him and was overjoyed.

The move to Westwood was quite traumatic for Anne because, like most such events, it was like trying to put two pounds of candy into a 1 pound bag! I remained packing up and helping the movers in Hamilton while she was eagerly awaiting their arrival at #29. In the event, the phone rang and it was Anne in tears crying that nothing, but nothing, was going to fit anywhere. It did! We found Westwood to be welcoming and life seemed a good deal simpler. I hasten to add, however, that the people of Hamilton had, for 21 years, been more than hospitable, kind, generous and helpful to Jackie and our family, and they will always hold a warm spot in my heart. It is, I think, the loveliest part of Boston's North Shore. Many years later, Anne and I returned there regularly to see our old friends who, unsurprisingly, had gotten to know Anne well and welcomed her as a long-lost friend! I knew well that she would win their affection eventually, but it was sad that it took so long and was so rough on her at first.

Our very first guest was Toddie, Lady Wills! For those who read Book I, she was the wife of Sir Gerald Wills, the adopted son of Ronald, who was sent to my father's school in England to learn and get into one or other of the military schools or a university. It was he, also, who became a big wheel in Britain's Conservative party and was knighted for his work as an MP and Chief Whip. Anyway, Toddie who was recently widowed, came and spent a week with us before we moved and then went off to visit friends on Martha's 'Vineyaaard' as she insisted on calling that island, and then came back to us for another week in our new house!

Over the years we've found that those who are not family members, coming to stay with us from overseas, do tend to stay for a while! A week or two was not unusual, but then in the old days, if one came by boat, which took at least five days on average, it really wasn't worthwhile to make a fleeting visit and that was understandable! Now that it takes but a few hours to get here, things haven't changed much! That old adage about fish and guests smelling after three days was unheard of back then, but it seems to be a saying borne on this side of the ocean, rather than the other. Don't think for a minute that I am not going to hear a lot more about this in the future and probably from the U K but it is, honestly, borne of experience. I repeat. This, of course, is in no way a family matter!

Among our best Christmas gifts in 1970 was Tinsel, named rather obviously and given to Anne, thoughtfully, by my daughter, Wendy, as a replacement I'm sure for Minus. A Yorkshire terrier aged 6 months on Christmas Day, Tinsel was quite a new type of dog for me to have. I had, stupidly, said that I didn't think I could ever cope with a small dog hinting, I guess, that it looked a bit feminine. What a lot of horse-feathers! Tinsel romped his way into our hearts in no time and it was the best gift that Wendy could have given Anne and we were so grateful.

As you'll see, he was with us for 16 ½ years and a great addition to the family...and spoiled rotten like all our animals, by me says my better half!

While I was still enjoying doing the PR for the Aquarium and Harbor National Bank, Anne and I took off for a weekend and visited the somewhat lonely island called Monhegan off the coast of Maine. Ron Wysocki, a staff reporter for the Boston Globe, had called me previously to say that he'd heard from Chuck Miller, who used his home on the island as a one-room schoolhouse, wondering if Ron, via the Globe, could find a most reasonable place for his ten charges to stay if they could get to Boston. On hearing this, I jumped at the chance of offering to try to arrange a week for them in Boston so they could 'see the sights'. Our enthusiasm for this project was greatly enhanced when we met all the children, who ranged in age from six to 14, and Chuck had found out that the one place that they all wished to see was the new Aquarium! As I was more than fearful that the we might be accused of exploiting these kids for our own advantage (publicity), it was great that I had Ron on whom to lean in the publicity department, and to know and be sure that it would be done right and in the best of taste.

On getting off the ferry at Port Clyde and driving home, Annie and I both said almost simultaneously that it'd be the greatest fun if we could, somehow, invite them all to the Aquarium so that they could actually see that incredibly popular attraction firsthand. It wasn't too long before we realized that that was going to take some doing, however, as funds we were told were by no means flowing on the island and that, therefore, sponsors would have to be approached and signed!

Wysocki had Chuck's letter printed in the Globe and fifty letters and many 'phone calls were the result from those wanting to help. That gave me considerable courage to go out and try to sell the idea...and soon found that none was needed! The results were as follows:

On their arrival by car from Maine, they were fed and housed for the night by the Holiday Inn on Cambridge Street in Boston. The following two nights they actually slept in the Aquarium on camp beds, the first ever to do so! Included in their program and at their request were:

- A visit to the Berklee School of Music to see and hear a Synthesiser:
- A visit to Barnum & Bailey's Circus who happened to be in town
- A tour of The Museum of Science and, of course, the Aquarium
- A Red Sox game

- A ride to the top of the Prudential Center
- A visit to Logan airport and a tour of one of Alitalia's new Boeing 747s
- A flight over Boston and Cape Cod
- A visit to the Zoo
- A tour of Boston and of WGBH.

Chuck allowed how, at the end of their stay, that it was all beyond the wildest dreams of the kids with enough memories for a lifetime and a love for Boston and its hospitality! Was I ever proud of Boston, too! Only one individual turned me down for an offer of something, and that was, sadly, no surprise. Suffice to say, the person in question was in the catering business and had been a bit of a pain back then and I doubt if, since, has made any effort towards improvement in manners, generosity or bearing over the intervening years!

Shortly after this heartening experience, I found that the bank for which I toiled while with the N E A, was about to sever relations with me due to financial cuts. This was saddening, but not to worry, our association had always been very pleasant. Soon thereafter, Boys and Girls Camps of Boston took me on as their program development person. In fact, it had a thoroughly inflated and over-rated title for the job that I hesitated to use! It was a well-worthwhile task for underprivileged kids, but my association with the chap that ran it left much to be desired! Anyway, I remember one event that delighted the kids at one of the camps on the way to Duxbury. I was able to talk the Traffic helicopter pilot for radio station WBZ into flying down for the 'Christmas in Summertime Day' which he most generously did dressed as Santa Claus! He landed right in the middle of the camp and was immediately swamped by admiring campers! Why I was having a Christmas in Summertime Day, goodness knows, but Santa's arrival made it all worth the planning and doing!

It was during the last year, or two, that I'd gotten to know well the Regional Manager for Alitalia Airlines, Giandrea Montanarella, and we greatly enjoyed his and his wife's company. He came to realize that I was doing a great deal of lecturing, not only for and at the Aquarium but, also, at clubs, schools and many other organizations throughout New England on our Antarctic adventures. Let's face it, we were two of not too many back then who had ever been there! With this, perhaps, in mind he most generously invited Anne and me to go on Alitalia's Inaugural 747 flight from Boston to Rome direct. There were a number of travel agents and media people invited, of course, so it was a very cheerful group who flew off with most knowing each other. What a great time we had, not only in Rome but, also, it had been arranged that the two of us could fly to England from there and visit family and friends. We were indeed lucky and grateful to have been given this opportunity and, hereafter, we became good friends of the Montanerallas, as time will tell!

On our return, we received the upsetting news that Don DeHart, was leaving to join Dusty Howland in his investment company. It was Dusty who put Don at the N E A originally, I always thought. We, who had been on the staff, were a bit unnerved by this news because we knew, understood and admired Don, particularly as he had coped so well with so many of the growing pains and problems since his appointment. Little did we know, or imagine, what we were going to get in his place!

Sadly, my daughter Wendy was having her problems and had had since her mother died in 1967 when we were living in Hamilton. Suffice to say her Mum's death shook her greatly, as well it might and did us all, but I think it affected her by far the most. It was the dreaded '60s then when everything, everywhere, seemed to come unstuck and nothing that Anne, nor I, could do was in any way acceptable to, or reasonable for, her. She ran away from school which set the cat among the pigeons because my old friend, Aileen Farrell, was head of it in Lenox and she was furious and told us that she didn't want her back. Wendy, walked into the Aquarium the day she left and told me that, as she had no money, she talked a taxi driver, at 7.00 a m in Lenox, into driving her to Boston on the Mass Turnpike. The only identification she had was a nametag on one of her socks! Quite a feat! In the event, she went to the Hamilton—Wenham Regional Public School, less than a mile from our house. That, of course, was just where she hoped to be as her horse, Piglet, was stabled just down the road. Life can be really complex at times, can't it?

Mark was winning prizes at St. George's, and didn't even seem to be getting caught too often when carrying out some of his atrocities! As far as I can remember, he had a delight in climbing up the chapel tower in darkest night and tolling the clock bell...at least that was what I was told! One thing happened to him that I thought strange and unnecessary. He got caught covering for an Afro-American student friend after the latter had gone in a taxi to Newport to buy some booze that was, unsurprisingly, a supreme no-no. For this the Headmaster sent him home for a week as punishment. This proved next to nothing and a total waste of everyone's time. I didn't help at home by occasionally offering him a beer. This time he refused and admonished

me, quite rightly, for doing this due to 'his punishment!" It was lucky
that he was on the Dean's list most of the time he was at S G.

As you can guess, these crises were not all that easy to cope with for
Anne, but she did well and refused to let things get her down. As for me,
I fussed and stewed and felt hopelessly 'in the middle' very often and
should, probably, have been far stricter with Wendy than I was...even
though we were, and Jackie and I had been, known as quite strict
parents. One good thing happened before the year was out, however,
and that was my appointment to the board of The English Speaking
Union in Boston. I had always hoped that I might be able to work for
that organization and to try and assist in Anglo-American relations,
which had always been a cause very close to my heart.

I really should tell you about one really scatter-brained idea I had
right around this time. It won't take long, I promise you! Somebody,
somewhere, decided to make sticky-backed, linen, miniature figures of
all kinds that could be bought for a song. I came across these when a
friend, by the name of Charlie Heartfield, showed up with a whole batch
of different ones. At once I suggested that he and I go into business
wholesaling these to all and sundry retailers and call ourselves, PRESS
ON REGARDLESS, Ltd.! Surprisingly, he fell for this and so P O R Ltd.
was born! Shortly thereafter, Charlie and I were joined by Peter Payne,
and we went roaring around sticking these things on the lapels of every
salesperson we could find in every conceivable store that might carry
them! The craze was more then short-lived, but we made a buck or two,
as far as I remember, and had great fun while we were at it!

Among other things, this was the year of the 'GET OUT THE VOTE'
campaign at the Aquarium.

I'd been searching around for a good and cheerful publicity campaign
for the N E A as the tremendous amount of publicity, we had gratefully
received when new, was inevitably beginning to wane. One day at lunch
a friend mentioned that he wondered what was the most popular exhibit
within this institution. I replied that I didn't have a clue but would ask
the Education Department, headed then by Carlo Mosca, and see if I
could give him an answer. That started something! On driving home
that night, I started talking to myself about having an election at the
Aquarium so that, by popular public ballot, we could determine the most
popular inmate...not necessarily the most popular exhibit. Living things
would be much more fun and interesting than just an exhibit! So! The
idea of the first vote for an aquatic creature in an aquarium was born on
my commute home from Boston.

The result of my somewhat crazy thinking was as follows:

We dreamt up the following candidates for election of the First President of the Underwater States of America. They were:

- Hoover Harbor Seal
- Homer Lobster
- Ichabod Cabot-Cod
- Thalassa Turtle

The sponsoring organization was, of course, the Aquarium. Everything went along swimmingly (whoops!) until a lady of some considerable and deserved repute in the world of flowers and gardening, took immediate and exceptional umbrage at the partial use of her name, Thalassa. She made this more than apparent to me by letter on the day Thalassa Turtle announced her candidacy in a release to all branches of the media. She was, most noticeably, the only female in the race...T Turtle, that is. All's well that ends well, however! Thank heaven, I found out that Thalassa is a Greek word for seaweed and that couldn't have been more appropriate in this case. After that explanation to Mrs. Crusoe, the day and my neck were saved! Thalassa Henken Crusoe was a good friend of Cam and Peggy Patterson, my in-laws, and Anne got to know her well, too, when growing up during the summers in Marion.

The late Mrs. Crusoe, known then by all and sundry who watched Channel 2 in Boston, was a charming English lady whose knowledge of her favorite subjects was boundless. She, also, mixed few words and said just what she thought! I got to know her thereafter and enjoyed her greatly. Never did I mean to embarrass her publicly. However, I have to admit to a little surprise at her initial umbrage!

The 'polls' were open at the N E A for the month of August for the thousands of votes cast. At the kick-off lunch for the campaign, the Globe quoted me as saying "I read from a letter from Peter P. Penguin...It has been brought to my attention that my name was mentioned in the upcoming election. I must make myself perfectly clear that I am *not* a candidate, nor do I intend to become one. I have stated that, 'If nominated I would not serve, and if elected I would not serve'." It was then that we received a telegram from Mrs. Burton Brown, President of the Miami Seaquarium, stating that her institution was going to hold an election also, which would embrace many other than Yankee fish including Hugo, the Killer Whale. It seems that my response to her was that we would have to consider this additional competition very carefully because, with a Killer Whale running, the Mafia might well be lurking in the depths!

I have little remembrance of who was the eventual and winning candidate (how could I be so callous?) but believe it to have been, unsurprisingly for the state of Massachusetts, Ichabod Cabot-Cod. His slogan, 'COD CARES' and his oft-repeated remark, "You have to put your faith in Cod. If you don't trust Cod, we could all go down the drain." was highly quoted and equally successful.

What a hoot that promotion was! It was the combined product of many, both at the NEA and the Globe, who recorded the daily happenings and scores with delightful tongue-in-cheek! In retrospect, the differences now in PR, with the things one could, and did do, that were apparently acceptable back in those days, are major! Never, I'm sure, could I have gotten away with, let alone persuaded the marketing manager of a company, to let me put mice and a huge loaf in the windows of a bank; have me sent to the U.K. to cover, on radio, the arrival of the Queen's baby! I mention only a couple of examples from a more innocent time and reckon that public relations was so much looser and so much more fun in those days! I really can't quite see having Boston vote today for "Cod Cares" and "In Cod We Trust," can you?

After Don resigned new management took over and the situation changed dramatically. Pink slips abounded! Three or four of us did our best to persuade the trustees that all was by no means well regarding internal communication with the staff, and I may have led the pack. Why? Because I got Jane Shannon, the talented and decorative seal trainer, a spot on the popular and national TV program, 'What's My Line?' But a decision was made to prevent my taking her to appear in New York! I had to go then to Paul Helmuth, Chairman of the Board, to ask if he would over-rule this nonsense. Having heard the story from both sides he, mercifully, did just that and, as expected, it was a great success and got the Aquarium much more national and local publicity.

SAFARI #1.
OCTOBER 1972

As I mentioned previously, we had gotten to know the Montanarellas well and liked them very much. I, also, saw eye to eye with Giandrea who was doing much for Alitalia Airlines as their New England representative. One day he mentioned to me that, as I was doing so many lectures to clubs, schools, etc: about our Antarctic adventures, he'd like me to help him put together some trips using his airline. He'd provide the transport if we'd get a group together to go with us. Where on earth would we like to go?! Can you imagine such a question? It blew Anne's and my minds! At first we said, after considerable thought, that we'd like to go to Abyssinia, since named Eritrea. Why? Because it seemed that no one knew anything much about the country and, certainly, there was no tourism there from the USA. We were judged to be pretty good photographers since our Antarctic adventure, so felt confident that we could return with a good photo-story for the media, locally at any rate, not to mention a lecture.

As the Italians had gone to war with Abyssinia during the Mussolini years I thought, misguidedly as it turned out, that quite a few living in this country might be interested in going there on our return. Also, the ex and late king of that country, Haile Selassi, a k a the Lion of Judah, escaped to my home town of Bath in Somerset and we used to see him, in his brown suede shoes yet, walking down Milsom Street just before WW2! Ever since then I'd been interested to know where he came from and this seemed like a good chance to find out. No way! When the government there received our application to go and shoot film and photos, there was no doubt from the response that they had no wish whatsoever for the W-W's, or anyone else for that matter, to go snooping around!

Annie and I had always had a longing to go on safari in Kenya, or Tanzania or both, so we suggested that as an idea. "Great!" agreed Giandrea," let me know when you can go and I'll arrange it all for you, first class!" We did ask, however, that we would like to make our own arrangements with a safari company because we had to be certain that we had what we felt was the best and most reliable, as the trip we'd take later would be our responsibility. This sounded all very good sense until we found out what the cost would be for the two of us to go off alone for ten days with a personal driver/guide! I nearly had my second heart attack! "Not to worry! It's only money! We can't take it with us, so let's bite the bullet," said Anne. I, of course, agreed! Giandrea was quite amenable to this so we went ahead and contacted Abercrombie and Kent who were, we felt and had been told, the best in the business. They arranged to meet us in Nairobi with the driver assigned to us, Philip Nunga, who would be our guide and know-it-all throughout the safari with one worrisome exception, as will be seen shortly.

Some may remember that my late wife, Jackie, and I were hosts to Joy Adamson of BORN FREE fame, when she visited Boston for the U S premier showing of that movie, when I was involved with the Boston

Zoological Society. At that time, she made us promise that, should we ever go to Kenya, we were to stay with her. In the event, I wrote to her and told her that we were, indeed, coming and promptly got a warm reply and further invitation. On October 6th, my Mum's birthday, we left home on this considerable adventure and flew off to Nairobi. Guess with which airline! Alitalia, naturally!.

Philip Nunga met us as promised and, forthwith, drove us from Nairobi's airport straight to Joy for what she insisted be a five day stay at her lovely, big, bungalow on the shore of Lake Naivasha. As soon as we drove up Joy's driveway and got out, we both knew that some crisis was afoot, for she rushed out in alarm and whispered that 'someone was desperately ill in the house and that we were not to make a sound'! Who 'he', or 'she' was we hadn't a clue, but we knew that it couldn't have been George, her husband, for he hadn't lived under the same roof as her for years and had his own camp with his lions a long way away from Joy. Philip, feeling the tension, decided that this was a good time to take off, so left us on our own to cope as best we could...which never, previously, had been easy. After the initial panic and she had calmed down, Joy allowed that her eight-week old female baby leopard named Taga, which she had recently acquired from the Orphanage for Animals in Nairobi, was very sick she thought and that's why we had to be ultra quiet! As it turned out, most sadly, the poor creature couldn't stand Joy at all due to a nervous condition, and frequently tried to bite her. She was all over Annie like a tent, however, and allowed her to play and cuddle with her constantly.

Joy Adamson and Taga

In addition to Taga, for whom Joy had built a king-sized 'boma' or enclosure, in the garden in which to keep her, she had several really beautiful Colobus monkeys which lived 'way up in the palm trees which edged the lawn and lake and a couple of Verraux eagle owls who would fly to earth at her call to be fed. They are extremely handsome birds and, on the ground, stand about 1 1/2 to 2 ft.

To be brutally frank, our stay with Joy of 5 days was about 4 1/2 too long. This sounds most unkind and ungrateful, but she had recently endured a bad car accident that prevented her from doing any of the things she usually did, such as paint and draw brilliantly, so was forced to use her left hand only. Consequently, this made her highly irritable and nervous, in fact, more so than usual. Added to this her servant, Joseph, the only other resident in her home, was just as creepy and unnerving as anyone we'd ever met. He never spoke nor made a sound and would suddenly appear, unheralded, behind one or other of us and scare us witless! Unsurprisingly, we were not all that sorry when Philip drove up to get us and take us on the first leg of our safari. Unbelievably, we heard later that Joy took Taga to the vet in Nairobi later and left her in the car where she, somehow, got into a plastic bag and suffocated.

Taga and...Me

On the two occasions during which I got to know Joy quite well, once in Hamilton, MA and once at her home on Lake Naivasha near Nairobi, I came to this conclusion. She was the most persuasive, talented, unpredictable, difficult, determined and selfish person I'd ever met. On top of this though, she had moments when she was funny and thoughtful but, sadly, they were few and far between. Mark you, some of my problems with her may have been my fault as she spoke so rapidly and with a slight Austrian accent, that I may have gotten the wrong end of the stick occasionally! It was painful indeed for us though when eventually we heard, years later, that Joy had been found murdered by a servant of hers. Nor did it come as any great surprise after more years, to hear that George, her husband of many years, was killed by one of his lions. After Joy's death, one of Boston's radio stations called to ask me to comment on our association. I found that, sadly, difficult to do with either warmth or affection.

Our driver came to fetch us again in a mini-van with an excellent sliding roof in the back that was ideal for us as we were armed with much motion and still photographic equipment. This was on October 20th 1972 and our safari route was as follows; we started in Keekorok, in the Mara Game Reserve in Kenya and then on to the Seronara Park Game Reserve and the Ngorongoro Crater in Tanzania. It was here that we ran into a bit of a problem with our driver/guide Philip who, without warning, decided he'd leave us and go off somewhere or other on his own! What came over him, heaven only knew, but he took off for two days and left us in a hotel over-looking the crater. The staff here were Tanzanians who, then, had little or no use for Americans as we, generally, used Kenyan safari tour operators, rather than their own due to Abercrombie & Kent being based there.

During this time Anne and I, somewhat nervously as it was a bit scary being left on our own miles from anywhere in a country with then quite unfriendly people, waited to see when, if ever, Philip would re-appear! All we could do each evening was to ask other guides as they came in whether, or not, they'd seen him. Always the answer was the same, "No!" We were told that this wasn't all that surprising as it was a fairly regular happening among guides then and, consequently, they would cover for each other if asked. We did hear though that Geoff Kent, son of the founder of Abercrombie & Kent, was on tour with a group and that, probably, we'd meet him as we progressed. I couldn't wait for this as I was rapidly acquiring a real spate of bad language to describe my feelings about one of his best drivers and his sudden disappearance!

Eventually, a tour came in and we were told that Philip was lying next to his van barely a mile from where we were. We found him pleasantly passed out, face up in the sun, without a care in the world! When we woke him we gathered that he had had been on quite a bender!

85

His story of having the van pushed over by an elephant and being knocked senseless by it and then spending the night under it was too much to take, particularly as he didn't have a clue as to how it happened! After pulling himself together and sobering up, he joined us in the hotel and started to weep and wail saying that the whole affair was God's will! With little understanding at the time, I put the fear of that deity into him by saying that, unless he straightened out, I'd report him to his boss, who, as it turned out, I was to meet very shortly. That worked and there were no further problems.

Some days later at Fort Ikoma Lodge, in Tanzania also, and surrounded by the Serengeti Plain we met Geoff and his small group. He, kindly, invited us to meet him at the end of our safari so that we could enjoy the then unique experience of a tented safari and not in lodges as we'd been doing. This we did and what a super experience that was!

Geoff's mother and father, who owned A & K then, were with him. Why the name A & K, we asked? Because Mr. Kent Sr. wanted to be at the beginning of the alphabet in directories and because, then, Abercrombie & *Fitch* were well-known and popular outfitters and clothiers of safari and other hunting items. A would go with K just fine!

We were lucky indeed to have taken our first safari at that time (1972). The wild animals were everywhere and in vast numbers and could be viewed by us when no one else was within miles. Now, sadly and years later, it is all very different due to the animals being far more scarce and, with walkie-talkies, tourists can be rushed within minutes to any sightings with resultant overcrowding to, and aggravation of, the wildlife let alone some of the tourists.

On completing our safari we headed by car for a few days to Ocean Sports, a delightful, small, quiet and unsophisticated beach resort on the Indian Ocean. We returned the car to Mombassa and then caught the overnight train from there to Nairobi, 300 miles northwest, which was quite an experience! Stops and starts all the way, probably for wild animals on the track; a delicious dinner on board and a most interesting, spotlessly-turbaned and polished Indian gentleman with whom I had a long talk before we got moving. He had a real Oxford accent and it transpired that he was the engine driver!

There follows a story that I wrote for a Boston paper after returning to Nairobi on that train:

"While in Kenya recently, having just returned from safari, I received a letter from my brother-in-law who is headmaster of a boys' preparatory school in London. Would I go to a place whose name, like so many in Swahili, was, I thought, unpronounceable, Starahe Boys' Center? There, he said in his letter, was a young boy called Joseph Ntaiya whose education and upkeep his school was sponsoring for a year. Little was known about him and, due to the distance involved, no one from London had ever seen him, nor had anyone had any firsthand visit either to him or his school.

"One morning, with my wife at the hairdresser, I grabbed the opportunity to visit Joseph and his school that, phonetically, sounds something like 'Starayhee' and means 'help' in Swahili. In ten minutes by taxi from downtown Nairobi, I found myself at Starahe's impressive gates. Moments later I was seated with Mr. Geoffrey Griffin, its Director, founder and guiding light since he started the school in 1959, and what a heartening story he had to tell me!

"Early in '59, Mr. Griffin started to raise funds for a private venture to help care for abandoned, orphaned and homeless boys between the ages of seven and thirteen. He wished to draw public attention to the enormous social problem of juvenile vagrancy, so prevalent then in Nairobi. Soon Shell, then one of the world's largest oil companies, gave him financial backing and, on a tiny site, two tin huts were erected to serve as sleeping quarters for the first boys brought in off the streets. I found these huts, still in occasional use, as I started out on my tour of what is now a ten acre site on which 1,150 boys from seven to twenty years of age live and learn, taught by a staff of sixty from many nations of the world.

"Primary education and simple trades were taught at first and, as international support was forthcoming, a secondary school with its own Arts, Science and Commercial classes followed. Next, a Technical School and a 'school leavers' hostel were added. Here, those who have graduated and are finding their confidence in their first job can live among friends for this period.

"Starahe students now come not only from Kenya but from other African countries and are from all conditions and levels of society. Many who can well-afford to send their children to private and more expensive schools, now send their sons there, due to the excellent tuition and morale. The Center still abides by its charter, however, in that the less money and resources a boy may have the more likely he is to gain admission.   From this, it can be well understood that the roads to Starahe are via the Rescue Centers; the court -houses; police and by word of mouth.   No boy has ever been denied entry through inability to pay and, as Mr. Griffin proudly explained, there has never been a budget, for never has he known what the next year would bring in donations. Without them, Starahe would close immediately, but never has!

"Companies with well-known international names are in evidence due to their sizeable gifts. For instance, I found myself walking down Colgate Palmolive Avenue! A street here, a dormitory or science block there, are named for their benefactors. A fine dining hall, seating 450 and serving 1,650 meals a day; a clinic; sick-bay; workshops and labs: have all been donated over the years, and it was with little wonder to me that both boys and staff had such obvious pride in belonging.   The behavior, manner and smart appearance of both had to be seen to be believed.

"I asked Mr. Griffin if, due to our own problems, America has shown interest in supporting this truly worthwhile home of learning.   He replied that he had had little success in the States because he felt so few had heard, or read about, their work. He asked if I could help, being in the Public Relations field.   He asked, too, if I knew that the cost of tuition and board for a Starahe boarder for one year was one hundred dollars? I did not, nor could hardly believe it.

"It was then that Joseph ran up to be introduced to me. At once I noticed his proud bearing and considerable height and shouldn't have been surprised because his father was a Masai. Aged twelve, a Catholic and standing rigidly to attention, Joseph told me his father was killed in a tribal battle in 1967 and his mother was left to bring up five children as best she could on the product of five cows, her total wealth and inheritance.   Dressed in his smart red and blue uniform, I was hard pressed to realize that, before me, was the son of a nomadic warrior who has been reared in a mud hut and whose staple diet had been milk, meat and blood.

"Joseph knew about my brother-in-law's school providing him with this opportunity, and asked specially that I send him his 'extreme' thanks. He wished me, also, to say how much he enjoyed the work he was doing; how proud he was of Starahe and what wonderful friends and opportunities he was enjoying. Finally, as he was about to join his fellow students at the daily flag-lowering; prayer and bugle ceremony, he asked shyly if I could find some people in Boston, USA, who might sponsor some other Masai boys who badly hoped for the chance to learn at Starahe. "It costs seven hundred shillings, which is an awful lot of money," he said, ($100.00) "but look what you get...look at me!"

"Well! I just wonder if I might be able to persuade some schools, clubs, or just solid citizens to sponsor a boy like Joseph for a year? Joseph's funds are raised through the school chapel collections of the three hundred boys at Colet Court prep: school in London...and I'm told it is THE collection to which every boy kicks in. Starahe's school motto is 'Natulange Juu', or 'Aim High' in English. I think that is just what I must do for Joseph Morompi Ntiya, the Masai boy from Narok."

FOUR
1973 - 1974

Prior to leaving on our first safari, I approached the powers that be at the Aquarium and asked if, at last, it'd be possible for me to work full-time for it, rather than having to share my business life with The Harbor National Bank. I was finding this increasingly difficult, particularly as the former was getting the lion's share of my efforts and was beginning to cut into the time I could allocate the latter. Luckily Dan Needham, still boss of the bank, was most understanding of my problem and was most helpful.

Suffice to say that on my return from safari, I found that no decision had been made about my position so, in a fit of pique and without too much sense in hindsight, I cast around for another, single, P R position. Quite shortly, one Casimir de Rham, President of the Board of Trustees of Mount Auburn Hospital, asked me to join that fine hospital in Cambridge as their P R Director. Dan Needham was also on the Board, so that was where that idea started, I reckon. As the salary was better I accepted, again without all that much conviction that I was making a first-rate move. After all, and as per usual, just what did I know about hospital P R? Not much, if the truth were known.

Things were fine at home with Anne coping well. Mark graduated in September from St. George's having been on the Dean's List for ages and had taken up sky diving during his summer vacation. Anne took him to Orange, MA to do this and I have a feeling that she was much more scared of the procedure than Mark! President Lyndon Johnson died. Peace had broken out in Vietnam and Wendy was, bless her heart, doing her own thing. I was able to take Anne for a week, or so, to Bermuda which was, as always great, bar an unfortunate scene at the airport on leaving. While shopping one day at Triminghams, I spied a delightful and smart blazer, bought it and decided I'd wear it on the way home. We'd bought a couple of things there, as most do, but never gave a thought to declaring anything as nothing was of sufficient value and was 'worn goods'...we thought! U S Customs, back then, operated at the Bermuda airport, don't ask me why, but when Anne and I saw everyone checking with them, I suggested that we approach a charming and attractive-looking young lady, who I was sure would smile benignly at us and wave us on. No way! From a cute-looking popsy, she turned instantly into a tough, all-searching, monosyllabic matron. Everything was searched and you can guess that there were a few things that we'd 'forgotten' we'd acquired which she just happened to notice, as she tore our suitcases apart. Then, with a contemptuous smile on her face she lightly said, "That looks like the most delightful and expensive blazer which I'll bet you bought at Triminghams!" 'Oh yes!' I replied smugly, "but as you can see, I'm wearing it and have been all day, so it can't possibly be for resale, or given away when I get home and it is just for my use." "Nonsense", she replied, "you obviously don't know the law!"

At this, unsurprisingly, my whole attitude changed like lightening and I started to produce any manners I could muster, thinking that she really wouldn't hold up such a charming, well-turned out, young couple. No Way! Three hundred dollars later, we parted company having lost the battle every which way. Ever since, I've been terrified of Customs officials the world over, particularly attractive-looking ones, and always head towards the toughest male official in sight!!

I see from the incredible photo albums that Annie keeps that I wrote a letter or two to the papers this year! Why I seem to have a penchant for doing this, I don't know, but I used to do it regularly so, after checking them out first with my chum, John MacDuffie mostly for, I hoped, his amusement, I'll include these, just for fun! Additionally, I see that I gave one of my legion of lectures about our Antarctic adventure from a notice sent out by The Brookline Country Club (known universally as The Country Club or TCC). The price of dinner AND my lecture was $7.25 per person! You can tell that you got what you paid for in the entertainment department in those days!

The Country Club, and that is its full name, by the way, is in Brookline, MA. It got its name because when it was founded it was the only one! Whether or not the Myopia Hunt Club in Hamilton, MA, would agree to this, I doubt. But not to worry, they are both great institutions.

We are nuts about birds and shamefully feed them throughout the year which I gather is a definite no-no. Anyway, here's a note I wrote to the Globe in January of '74 and which, amazingly, they printed. It must have been a 'no news' day!

BATTLE AT THE BIRDFEEDER

It could be logically supposed that with the ever-increasing crunches and crises and more snow and ice than seen in ages, no one in their right minds would let birds bother them—particularly when the sun is brilliant and sky cloudless.

But our bird bother is too damn much! All the cute little tits and sparrows, finches gold and purple and our very own cardinals have gone, or been driven next door and we are left with starving, stuffing, starlings.

Twelve of these pot-bellied, bombastic and bad-mannered bullies are, as I write, visibly lowering the level of food in a 12 inch by three-inch cylinder. This, plus a smaller one containing more highly priced delicacies, hangs from my own extra-specially constructed about-to-be patented birdfeeder hanger. So far, this prototype device has cost me twelve dollars, excluding food dispensers!

Saturday was a dead loss; barging in and out refueling dispensers and shooing away starlings, in addition to several visits to hardware stores and supermarkets to acquire more seed and suet, not to mention peanut butter and a special bit with which to drill holes into my most precious birch log which has graced the Living Room fireplace during the summer for many seasons. Now it hangs, poised ready to break the kitchen window with the first puff of wind; the mixture of peanut butter and suet now frozen solid in the indentations within it, a mass no self-respecting feathered friend would approach.

My wife, normally a charming and clean-mouthed Boston-bred beauty, has suddenly developed a vocabulary relative to starlings that Playboy would be ashamed to print. As for me, I'm faced with no Saturday dinner, near financial ruin and the acquisition of a 12-guage shotgun unless an answer to the question, 'what the heck can we do about these **** starlings?' can be answered by some concerned, starling-loving, reader.

M.F.W-W.
The Globe

In this year, too, it seems that a certain Congressman was having a spot of bother with one Fanne Fox by name, and this was all receiving far more attention than it probably deserved in the media, I thought. In fact, this was perhaps, the start again of a litany of carryings on by those in public office. Determined, it seems, not to be left out of these proceedings, I find that I whipped off a note in misplaced high dudgeon to TIME magazine in December that, again most surprisingly, it printed.

It referred, obviously, to Senator Wilbur Mills, Chairman: of The Ways & Means Committee. I wrote,

"The extracurricular ways and means of Wilbur Mills defy belief. His latest Foxe hunt through Boston's combat zone is a blot on the escutcheon of every Arkansan who voted for him and all who hope to see the return of honest and respectable government.

M.F.W-W. Westwood. MA."

My Mum, circa 1947

My Dad, circa 1935

In hindsight, why I was so wee'd up and holier than thou about this matter, I can't imagine!

It was in this year, too, that my better half excelled herself for The Vincent Club in Boston, when she achieved First Place in the sale of 36 contracts, the most advertising contracts for the well-known and read program for The Vincent Show. Years later as I write this, that doesn't look like too much money, or too many contracts, but it certainly was then! She has worked so long and hard for this ladies' club that raises large sums of money through putting on a musical show yearly (for three nights and a matinee) for The Vincent Memorial Hospital, the GYN arm of Mass General Hospital. I tried hard to do P R for them as a volunteer, and have always had a great interest in all their fine fund-raising efforts. The money they raise through the show and program these days, years later, is incredible! Around $300,000 + is a figure I remember for last year, ('01, the year that Annie won The Mary Ann Vincent Award for Volunteer Service!). Such husbandly pride!

I can't let this year go by without mentioning that this was the year we lost my Mum in England at the ripe old age of 98. She was born on October 6th 1876. As, maybe, you will have gathered, I'd seen her far too infrequently for my liking since I came to live in the USA in 1948. The occasional visits of mine to the U K and a couple, or so, to this country by her when much younger, were all I had face to face. We did keep in close communication with letters, however, until she found writing too hard. My sister, Betty, kept me well informed thereafter, however, and I'll always be grateful to her for helping in that respect. As I said at great length in my first book, Mum was special, very special, and I have a tremendous amount for which to be more than grateful, not only to her but, also, to my Dad who died so many years before when I was 17. They are buried together in the grounds of the charming little church at Chewton Mendip in Somerset, close to Wells. Most sadly, I was unable to be there for her funeral.

SAFARI #2
1974

It was early this year that Anne and I took off on our second safari, this time leading a small group from these parts and Long Island. We knew none of them really well and most joined us having only heard about us from the first couple that decided to go. The husband of one of the couples was a gentleman about whom I had heard frequently. From all reports, he was a tyrant in business and one who commanded instant attention and respect! As you might guess, I was somewhat terrified at having him with us and was not a little concerned about how I would be able to manage him when confronted by any one of the huge animals that we might come upon in Kenya or Tanzania. I couldn't quite imagine how I was going to tell him to 'be quiet', 'sit down!' or 'mòve!' when and if the occasion demanded, even though that was not necessarily my job! To do that while on safari, we had, of course, a most charming and experienced guide who was with us to do just that and many other chores! Alan Binks was his name and was assigned to us by Abercrombie and Kent, our tour operators again, and lucky we were to have him with us. He was excellent and highly qualified. Earlier, he had fallen in love with and had married Mary, one of the guests for whom he was the guide several years before! At that time she was on a safari with her grandmother, Mrs. Scribner of the publishing family. Alan and Mary settled in Nairobi and, happily, we became good friends though haven't seen as much of them as we'd have liked over the years since.

Anyway, to get back to my 'tyrant' who continually checked his breast pocket railroad -watch to see if all was going with similar efficiency! I knew enough then to know that, if he continued to do this on safari, life would become unbearable for him and all of us as little, if anything, runs on time when involved in such an adventure. So! What to do and remain in one piece, taking into consideration the difference in our ages and business acumen? The opportunity soon presented itself as we flew into Nairobi and went for a couple of nights at the charming Norfolk Hotel. On seeing him check his watch on several occasions within a brief space of time, I knew that I had to do something, and fast. The next time he did that I was ready. "Sir", I said, "may I, please, suggest that you put that watch away permanently until the end of our safari at least, otherwise you, your wife and all the other guests, my wife Anne and I, will have a miserable time and you will ruin a great opportunity for all of us!" As I finished, I just knew that I was about to become the 'late' tour-leader!' No way! He looked up, smiled and said, "You know, Michael, maybe you're right, that's just what I'll do!" From then on his pet saying throughout the safari to all involved was, "I just can't believe this! This is the greatest!" and I never saw his darned watch again! Happily, he and his wife became good friends of ours for many years thereafter. We were devoted to Buck and Pit Dumaine and we miss them both.

As safaris to Kenya and Tanzania have become as common as trips to London or Paris, this time we saw far more game than is possible today we're told, (2001). More is the pity. One of many high spots was a special, chartered, flight given us by one of our guests in gratitude for what we'd done for her and her husband on tour. This involved a few of us in a flight from, and back to, the private airport in Nairobi. We flew to and around Mt. Kenya in the north and then southward to and around Mt. Kilimanjaro enjoying perfect weather and views of the terrain below. For lunch we landed at Kilaguni Lodge, but not before quite an excitement!

There's an old saying that 'when you've got to go, you've got to go!' Such was the case with Anne who, somewhere between Mounts Kenya and Kilimanjaro, realized she was facing this crisis. This news she managed to let me know, but with difficulty as I was sitting in the second pilot's seat in front of her. I passed it on to the pilot, but without due concern on his part, I felt, particularly as he had once had the embarrassment of letting the starboard engine, on my side of the aircraft, stop as he had omitted to switch the gas flow from one tank to another! Bad show!

After quite a while and far too long, I felt, knowing that if Anne was in trouble, real trouble, something should happen almost immediately, we came into sight of the Kilaguni strip and guess what, there were zebras and heaven knows what all over it!

More, desperate, delays as we had to circle several times to make room for our arrival by scaring off the wildlife! At this juncture, I didn't dare look behind me to see how my dear bride was faring, though I knew the answer! Those seated around her had gotten the message clearly by that time and were offering prayers, I'm sure, that relief should be immediate, though it looked nigh on impossible, as the strip was a fair way by jeep to the nearest loo. In the event, our landing was made and the passenger's door opened before, I'm sure, the plane came to a full stop. Out leapt my beloved and, 'without further ado' as the saying goes tho' why, God knows, she nips under the fuselage while the props are still turning and completes the greatest relief of all time! None of the six passengers seemed to know much about this operation, nor did they relate their previous concern to me but, like I am so often, I was dam' proud of her for her self-control. I never, ever, thought she'd make it!

We shall always be most grateful to our friend, the late Louise Marshall, wife of John Marshall Sr., for this most generous and memorable gift and flight.

While at Mt. Auburn Hospital as P R Director, I started a news magazine for its constituency, by the name of 'PROFILE'. After returning from this safari, I included in it a story I wrote regarding a group of girls I met over there! It went like this:

They sound as if they are from Japan, but they are from a small town in Jkenya, East Africa. This is the story of Seven Sisters of Nanyuki and how I came to meet them recently.

Some time ago, Mount Auburn Hospital had a project going with a hospital in West Africa. Our used textbooks were shipped over for the education of African student nurses. Luckily, I had the opportunity to return to Kenya this year, and so began to wonder if I could find a hospital, or clinic, with which Mt. Auburn could correspond, exchange ideas and, perhaps, provide some funds or articles which an African hospital might well lack, but which we might take for granted.

Seven Sisters of Nanyuki

I wrote to two hospitals asking if there would be any interest in establishing a relationship, but the mail was so slow that by the time I left for Nairobi in March of this year, I had received no reply.

Still interested in visiting a hospital, I called the one at Nanyuki when in Nairobi, but conflicting accents and languages were not conducive to freely flowing conversation!

In due course we arrived at The Mount Kenya Safari Club, and there I discovered that Nanyuki, a small country town, was but five miles down the road. In no time I was off in one of the Land Cruisers, again with our original driver, Philip Nunga, as interpreter.

When we arrived at The Mary Immaculate Dispensary, (similar to an out-patient clinic), we received a welcome as warm as the climate. Sisters Mary Eliana and Mary Markina took the greatest pains to show us everything of interest and to introduce us to all who are involved in this tiny, by our standards, but important and very necessary clinic.

The Mary Immaculate Dispensary is the off-shoot of a hospital in Nyere and is funded by whatever fees the patients can afford to pay for the medical and dental care received from the Sisters. There are seven of these who tend to the needs of the outpatients and operate a teaching facility for thirteen young ladies who live and learn on the premises.

After a nice chat over a cup of tea we visited the medical clinic—a sparsely furnished, but spotlessly clean room with a small cupboard of very basic medicines and antiseptics. The hot water system worked well even though it was heated by wood. Next door is the dental clinic. My surprise at seeing a modern dentist's office, with all the usual paraphernalia was obvious to Sister Mary Markina, whose enthusiasm had prompted a wealthy and benevolent American tourist to supply the unit some time ago.

In a most charming and uncritical voice she said to me, "It was so kind of him, so generous, but no drills or tools came with it!" She was very happy, though, just to have her patients have the luxury of a dentist's reclining chair.

All the Sisters till the red, fast drying, soil in which they grow staple vegetables. With pride, they introduced me to their recently donated cow. Her ribs were more than noticeable, but she was doing a sterling job of providing a little fresh milk and, on rare occasions, the Sisters made butter from it.

The young students, between the ages of 16 and 20, live in one room filled with bunk beds. Some of the girls, I learnt, are mothers. Some are already divorced which I found hard to believe.

Their kitchen is a smoke-filled corrugated steel hut where they prepare the staple of their diet, 'porridge'. I could barely see this yellow, mealy liquid bubbling away because of the smoke that swirled from the wood stove.

All had been working for months on the construction of a 'maternity ward' which is highest on the clinic's list of priorities. I found it to be a big, empty room with a tin roof and cracked stone floor. It seems the money for completion ran out some time ago. I enquired how much it would take to finish the building. "I'm afraid it is a lot of money," Sister Mary Eliana replied, "at least three thousand shillings."

If only we could build a maternity ward at Mt. Auburn Hospital for the equivalent of $500, I thought, and theirs is already half finished!

My last stop on the tour was the classroom in which there were ten vintage, pedal-operated Singer sewing machines. These are used to teach the students how to sew and make the very simplest dresses for children and adults. The machines lay idle most of the time, however, because material is expensive and hard to come by.

Never have I seen such continuing smiles of kindness. Never have I been made to feel so welcome, and seldom have I seen such use made of so little. As I was leaving, everyone gathered at the front door that faces beautiful Mount Kenya in the distance. It was then that they presented me with the most exquisitely carved walking cane I have ever seen as a gesture of pure and spontaneous friendship.

I wish that others could meet the gentle Sisters of Nanyuki and see the wonderful work that they do. It would be fun and stimulating to develop a relationship with our hospital and The Mary Immaculate Dispensary. If anyone would like to learn more about the clinic, and would be interested in helping, please let me know.

For several years after this article, I received regular, long and delightful letters from the two Sisters, Mary! Happily, Dr. Calisti a neighbor, read the article and he was both a dentist and one who was involved with a large maker of dental equipment. He sparked a large shipment of equipment to the clinic, for which the Sisters were more than grateful and delighted, as was I of course!

101

FIVE
1975-1978

Our Danish friends, Hakon Mielche and his young bride, Suzanne, kindly invited us to join them on a journey from Italy to Denmark and Sweden in their Volvo station wagon. In his usual manner, Hakon christened this journey "The Mielche (as in Milky) Way"! We managed to find the wherewithal and time to do this, so promptly agreed to meet them in Milan, where we flew from Boston...by Alitalia Airlines naturally! Here they met and drove us to Hakon's beautiful house on Lake Lamone for a night and then started out across the Alps for Switzerland, Austria, Lichtenstein, Germany, Luxemburg France, Belgium, Holland, Sweden and Denmark! The only problem was that spring, which we were supposed to be following, flatly refused to do its usual thing and the weather was, for the most part, miserable! In fact 'they' said it was the worst for 100 years! Not to worry though, it could have been much worse and it was a memorable journey.

Our first excitement was not long in coming, however. As we drove over the comparatively low Alps, between northern Italy and Switzerland, we encountered two avalanches. The first occurred a day or so before we arrived, so we were not held up. The second happened a few minutes before we reached that spot and totally blocked the road before us. Luckily, there were no cars beneath it, but had we been a few minutes earlier, we would have had a more than interesting time trying to survive under ton upon ton of crushing snow.

Perhaps the most interesting and unique parts of the whole journey for Anne and me were our visits to the American and British WW1 War Graves as we wended our way westwards from Salzburg. Never had we seen such meticulous upkeep and that was both exciting and relieving. Particularly I remember the scene at Verdun with the remains of bayonets attached to rifles that were sticking up through the ground, steel helmets and barbed wire etc. To me it brought back horror stories of what my Dad coped with, if not actually at that battle, during WW1, let alone the monstrous waste of army personnel and equipment.

In Paris, the four of us stayed at a flat that a friend of Hakon's owned, while he was away. This was just as well because getting the four of us bedded down in there was as close as I've ever been to a sardine being stuffed into a tin! As there was only one bedroom, Anne and I slept on the floor because Hakon couldn't have made it there getting up and down! He, whose girth had not decreased with age, was breathing about once every five minutes, hopefully not to keep poor Suzanne awake all night due to his snoring! Somehow, Paris in the spring wasn't all that it was cracked up to be for me that year, probably because we did not have the time fully to explore the places we either remembered or about which we'd read and learnt.

Some of you may know the Kukenhoff Gardens in Holland. Annie and I had never been there but, if you haven't, do plan to visit these incredibly beautiful gardens at the time when tulips are in bloom. The weather was not all that sunny when we were there, but regardless, the colors, carpets and fields of these beautiful flowers—in all directions— were unforgettable. Our journey ended in Copenhagen on May 1st. where Hakon was to be the honored guest at a gala dinner on the opening of The Tivoli Gardens for the year. It was during this meal that he regaled us with more of his incredible adventures the world over. Not the least of which was when he and a small boat full of shipmates became lost and had to land on an uninhabited island in the Pacific and were given up for dead before a Japanese ship spotted and rescued them three years later. As a result of this adventure, his book, 'There She Blows' was widely read and was published in the U K in 1952 and was among 35 such books! Another was when he was in Copenhagen during WW2 and was doing all he could to direct RAF Mosquito aircraft pilots towards buildings that he and his companion Freedom Fighters felt should, and deserved to, be bombed during Nazi occupation. Then he recounted his lifelong friendship with, and admiration for, Victor Borge, who outlived Hakon by many years. Victor was an artist, we all decided, who could bring tears of laughter to our eyes at any time, anywhere and on anything! And, finally, how he, Hakon, and his much younger wife, Suzanne who was with us, met for the first time at Tivoli Gardens when she was a policewoman there a couple of years before! As I've mentioned on previous pages, it was Hakon that we met on the Lindblad Explorer when his publisher sent him to Antarctica to have his photograph taken in tails, surrounded by comparably dressed penguins!

On this trip, it was Hakon who made all the overnight arrangements, almost invariably at small hotels and Inns where he was more than well-known and admired, both as an artist and writer, not to mention a radio and TV personality of repute, so we were always basking in his fame! Then there were our picnics for lunch almost every day in the countries we drove through. Simple they were, which was just the way they should have been, but invariably with hard-boiled eggs that had been delightfully painted appropriately with the flags of the nations we were visiting! What fun was this chase of spring!

So! Welcome to the Bi-Centennial Year, 1976, and the exciting goings on! Why don't we take a minute, first, to take stock and check on what's happening to whom in the family? I'm 56; Anne is 35. Mark is at Tufts and seems to be getting on finely, though we don't hear much from him, which was par for the course in those days! The same goes for Wendy, from whom we hear less if at all. I guess she has made the decision not to be a part of the family. Our livestock in Westwood include Duchess our ageing but greatly loved Sheltie, Perky our massive marmalade cat and a colorful and constant panorama outside our kitchen window of Cardinals, Goldfinches, Doves, Nuthatches and Tufted Titmice. I'd love to call the latter Titmouses, but that would be socially gauche, I fear! As expected, we miss Minus, that dear, wonderful dog, who had lost his tail before he came to live with us so I christened him that. As I am so hopeless about such things, Anne most kindly coped with the trauma of having him put down about two months after we'd moved from Hamilton to Westwood. I was still at the Mt. Auburn hospital in Cambridge, trying my best to cope with the several and dire managerial problems that beset it.

One of the better evenings in our married life was during one of three visits we made this year to the U K. This time we were with Peggy and she, some months before, read about a great show that was opening in London called 'Evita' and that she was crazy to see! Could I get tickets for the three of us! No problem! My sister swung into action, most kindly, and came through with three good ones! How we all loved that show and what a huge success it was around the world!

**With Peter Tunley,
Manager, Stanwich Club, Greenwich, Connecticut,
2001 President of The Club Managers' Association of America**

105

It was in '76, too, that, somehow or other, I was made a member of The Country Club Not long afterwards I was made a member of the House Committee there and Mr. Huber was the Club Manager who was about to retire and a new one sought. In his place came Peter Tunley, a Cornishman. It was on this committee that I got to know Peter and, straightaway, got the feeling that he would do a fine job for us all. I did feel though that he might have been a bit in awe of his new surroundings, in contrast to those he had known previously at Bermuda's Coral Beach Club where things, probably, would have been a bit more relaxed, so reacted in rather an unusually stern manner. I later found out that he thought I was a real stinker, which was sad, but it all worked out well in the end!

Not too long after his taking the job, he was visited by his Dad and Mum and I thought that he'd have a hard time showing them around this part of our country due to his work, so offered to do this myself that all thought a good idea. I had the best time taking them around Newport and St. George's and, of course, around my old haunts on the North Shore such as Rockport, Ipswich, Hamilton and Gloucester. Unsurprisingly, I got to know them both well and enjoyed our tours more than they did, I'm sure! Most sadly, we lost Peter's Dad not too long afterwards, but we have kept an eye on Jeannie in Cornwall and on her considerable travels ever since and with the greatest pleasure! More about Peter, probably, as we progress!

With Peter and His Mother Jeannie

CS and Jackie Lee

In February, with the kids away, we took off on a swing around the south mostly by air to places we'd hear about a lot but never had had the chance to visit. Our first stop was in Austin, Texas. Here, we were entertained by Jackie and her husband, 'C S' Lee. Jackie was a good friend of Anne's, and still is today as is C S! Jackie's mother, Rommy Vaughan, who took Anne under her wing when the latter lived in Hamilton, was most kind to her when she really knew no one there, lived two doors down from us in Hamilton. Her husband, Norman Vaughan, used then to alert the neighborhood by charging around the village with a bunch of Eskimo dogs pulling a two-wheeled device of some sort, and him! This was in preparation for the Iditerod Races in Alaska that, if memory serves me correctly, he did for several years at an incredible age! He, much later, made a considerable name for himself by climbing, Mount Vaughan, the mountain, named after him by Admiral Bird on his travels to Antarctica, back in the 'good old days'! On this occasion, he was 89 years young, and he forthwith wrote a book about this considerable feat.

Next stop was the town of Daphne, hard by Mobile, and the home of Hamilton and Jamie Wright. Jamie was a school chum of Anne's. That territory was new to both of us and once we learned the language, we never looked back! I'm kidding, of course, but what with my 'harf and haff; Anne's 'Boston' and Jamie's 'Southern' accents, it took a bit of concentration to know who was saying what to whom! Add to that, my hearing was beginning to fade a bit due to that crazy doctor, who 'administered' to me at my prep school, (Book I) and flying between two engines in WW2, so there was never a dull moment! We, also, had the fun of flying to New Orleans in our hosts private, twin-engine, plane that added a great deal of interest to me, as you might expect.

Flying on to Tampa/Sarasota you may remember Louise Marshall, the dear and generous lady who came with us with her husband, John, to Kenya on our second safari. They most kindly wanted us to stop to see them in Boca Grande on Florida's southwest coast. Here we were, yet again, spoiled rotten by Louise as we were given their guest cottage on the grounds of their home on the beach for a couple of days, or so. Very high-powered living that was, we thought! Finally we made our way by air, again, to Savannah and then on to Beaufort, South Carolina, to stay a day or two with Dolly and Dan Sawyer who had moved there from Hamilton. They had been such a part of my life in the USA for so long and as Dolly was Anne's Aunt we found, we had to look in on them and see how they were faring. Happily they were in good, though ageing, fettle and it was, sadly, the last time we saw them both. Such good, kind, generous and helpful friends they had been for so long.

Around this time, I particularly remember picking up a fortune! I was walking down Broad Street in Boston and spied a piece of paper upside down in front of me on the road. Being inquisitive and it being roughly, I thought, the size of a check, I bent and picked it up. It was made out to Cash, signed by the person whose name appeared upon it in the top left hand corner and was for the amount of one thousand dollars. I would be totally dishonest if I didn't think, at once, that this was my luckiest day because, let's face it, the check was drawn on the U S Trust Co. on the very street I was walking down and all I had to do was pop in and cash it! My infuriating conscience rose yet again, however, and I found myself walking into The Camera Center on State St. to ask my friend, the owner, Ted Brody, if he knew who the original owner was. He did, dam' it! In his usual calm and pleasant way, Ted took the check from me, promising to return it to the original owner. That was the end of my dream, except that I thought, perhaps, when Ted met the individual with his check and giving him my name as the finder, I might hear from him and he might be disposed to buy me a beer or something...if not a good dinner! No such luck. It does take all kinds to make a circus, doesn't it?

ST. GEORGE'S SCHOOL

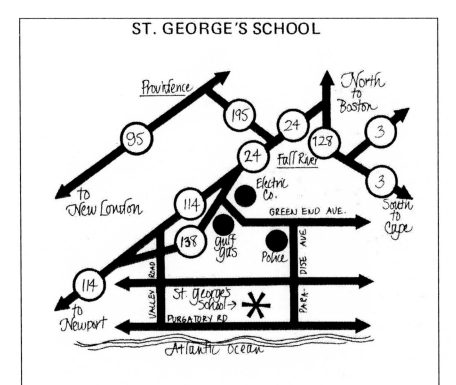

Address: Purgatory Road
Middletown, Rhode Island 02840

Telephone: 401-847-4649

Game Information: All games are played on campus.

In case of emergency:
School Infirmary 401-847-0091
Newport Hospital 401-846-6400

Nearby Restaurants:
Johnny's House of Seafood, Middletown
Canfield House, Memorial Drive, Newport
Chart House, Bowen's Wharf, Newport

It was fairly early this year that I got an idea which I hope would put Noble and Greenough in the spotlight within the whole area of New England's prep: schools. I found that endless parents got lost en route to games played away at other schools and were invariably late to see their prides and joys do their things against 'the enemy'! With this in mind I approached Anne Robb a proud parent and talented artist as well, and asked her to form a small group who might barnstorm the idea of providing information which would help parents get to where they were going and on time and get it published with my doing the ground work! Mostly happily and graciously, Anne agreed to this and "AWAY GAMES", An Independent School Travel Guide Book was born! The Dedication reads as follows:

"This guidebook is dedicated to all loyal and supportive parents who became lost or late in the pursuance of games, music, art or drama...and to all present and future parents who support their children at such events.

Henceforth, may their routes be accurate and their arrivals both safe and timely."

M.F.W-W

It was added: "Sponsored and created by the Noble and Greenough team, "AWAY GAMES" is designed for the benefit and use of all the 39 schools it includes". It was, of course, 'A Noble Production'!

At the risk of being overly proud of our combined efforts, this publication met with considerable success and was either given away, or sold, by all the schools included. I am still, umpteen years later (20+), asked regularly if copies are available, which they are not. A sad sequel is that a friend of mine not unknown in the scholastic business, John Ross, and I thought of republishing this work again years later, but to no avail. We found that so few parents can visit their kids' games, in comparison to the great numbers that did in 1978, due to two parents work-involvement etc, that there would not have been the sponsorship we sought fully to pay for it. I include a sample page within its pages so that you can see the result.

I'm sure many of you will remember a CBS evening show called THIS IS YOUR LIFE. Many of my age used to watch it once a week, due perhaps for lack of anything better on the box! It was around four in the morning one day that the 'phone rang and, on answering it just about in my sleep, I heard a very, very British accent say in trill tones: "Is this

110

Mr. W-W? Jolly good! This is Debbie Black at THIS IS YOUR LIFE at Thames Television in London and we'd like you to come over!" At that hour, this seemed a bit much to me, but I hung in there anyway and answered her questions with as much enthusiasm and good manners that I could produce at that ungodly hour. It seemed that the good lady had been told to try and find me and to invite me to fly over to partake in a program dedicated to my old chum, Cyril Fletcher, of 'ODD ODE' fame in the U K. My Radio Operator and I met Cyril and his wife Betty Astell at the Midland Hotel in Manchester during WW2, plum in the middle of a sizeable air raid! Here they insisted on sharing their dinner with us, two highly scruffy looking RAF types, who'd taken shelter from bombs dropping outside at that time and the Maitre d; had refused us entry to the about-to-be-closed dining room!

It was a tricky 'phone call to answer due, a, to my being highly dopey at that hour and, b, because those of my native land, to me anyway these days, are inclined sometimes to speak so fast that I'm lost from the word go! However, I became alive enough to say that I'd be happy to do this, providing I could bring my better half with me and that, at least, some of our expenses would be paid! Praise the Lord! It transpired that all was paid, from Boston to Boston! The program, in honor of Cyril, was scheduled for Wednesday, March 9th and, as you might guess, it was great fun and well worth it all the way! Thames TV did us proud and the others participating in the program were well worth meeting. Sir Alexander Korda, his wife Dame Anna Neagle, both most well-known in the U K and U S film business at the time, were among those friends and admirers of Cyril's who appeared and Eamonn Andrews, the very well-known M C, did his thing with usual efficiency and professionalism. We, also, were able to visit my family and have fun with them and, particularly, on a visit to my cousin Bill W-W and several of his family who had all gathered to be with us, most kindly, at his home at Henley-on-Thames.

On February 7th I took the plunge and resigned from Mt: Auburn Hospital in Cambridge as its P R Director. Without too much thought, and due to many months of frustration with management, I found myself telling Larry Witte, my immediate superior and assistant to the Director (I think that was his title), that I'd had it up to my gills and wanted out! I'd been offered the job of Director of Development and P R at Noble and Greenough Prep: School, about three miles from home and had a feeling that, as all my immediate male ancestors had been in the scholastic business, I might have a place there myself. It wasn't too long before the Headmaster was announcing to all and sundry about my new position. As it turned out, it was a considerable error both for him and me. As it was a long and painful and unnecessary passage of time and tribulation for the two of us, and as it has all paled into oblivion as things like that always do, and should do, that's enough of that! Suffice to say, however, that the President of the Board at that time, five years later and now a good friend and neighbor, approached me at a party at the Somerset Club in town and apologized sincerely for the treatment I received at that time. I accepted this with considerable gratitude, also saying that what a shame it was that the Headmaster, whose wife allowed that she had a crush on me when I was a kid at St. George's in 1936/37 and who was the daughter of one of my teachers there, couldn't himself have made this simple gesture five years previously when it happened! What grief it would have saved quite a few of those involved, but I guess he forgot.

This year, between Mt. Auburn and Nobles, Anne and I had planned to lead another safari to Kenya and Tanzania with Abercrombie and Kent, as usual! When all was just about settled and the necessary and small number of people to join us had been obtained, a family of five had to withdraw due to illness. The planned safari was scrubbed, most sadly, due to that and the economy being terrible in 1975.

While in Boston one day, we met on the street, a good friend of Anne's, Lee Sprague. As she was as brown as a berry, I asked her where on earth she'd been! "Barbuda", she said. "Bermuda", said I? "No!", she replied, "That's what everyone thinks!" "Barbuda! Where on earth is that?" I asked. "About 12 minutes flying time north-east of Antigua", she replied. To cut a long and most interesting explanation short about Coco Point Lodge, the small, simple, group of cottages on the 3-mile beach, Lee filled us both in on what, to us, sounded the most perfect place to visit for a holiday. It was, and still is, the most perfect, calming and unspoiled place to be found almost anywhere! One particular reason for our being drawn to it then is that one paid for everything in advance. Regardless of what we ate, drank, did and felt like tipping, it was all included in the price paid per day. That even included flying you from Antigua airport, landing on Coco Point's private, grass, strip and returning there at the end of your stay. No surprises! There were none with their hands out for anything, and only an emergency short wave 'phone was available for such calls. No safari was possible, so off to Coco Point Lodge we went for ten days. It was all for which we had hoped and still is so many yearly visits later! We're either in a rut, or else we're in love with the place!

On our return from Barbuda, via San Juan always these days, we struggled into a major snowstorm that knocked the sunburn right off our faces. Shortly thereafter, #1 and only son Mark graduated from Tufts University on May 27th and well at that! Of course, Anne and I and his godmother, Moody Ayer from Hamilton and the one, the only, Bette St. Laurent and her husband, Charlie from Ipswich, were on hand to give support and congratulations! Bette helped us at our home in Hamilton for years, and referred to the kids as 'her children!' Naturally, his Dad was as proud as a peacock of him, but a little worried that he decided uniquely that he was not about to wear a shirt and tie underneath his gown! It wasn't all that hot either! Not long thereafter he bought a Jeep and headed west to, of all places, Las Vegas! Just the location his old, conservative, Dad would have chosen, naturally! You can imagine the enthusiasm that we felt when it dawned on us that we were going to have to go to Vegas for Thanksgiving with him! He'd gotten himself a job in the warehouse of Circus Circus, one of the Casinos on The Strip, as you're probably aware, and informed us that he'd made reservations for us for Thanksgiving Dinner at The Dunes hotel/casino!! There was never a dull moment with Murphy, as I often called him, for some obscure reason! Actually, that went off well and it was an experience, for sure, and not quite that to which my Ma-in-law, Annie, nor I were used!

Coco Point Lodge, Barbuda

The following day Mark allowed that he'd like to fly us in his 4-seater 'plane to The Grand Canyon. Now, at this juncture, I knew that he had about 70 hours flying experience and could remember, just a little too well, how proficient I was not, when I had that experience, years before! It seemed that neither Peggy, nor Anne nor I, had the guts to say we'd rather not go, nor hurt his feelings, so off into the wild, blue, slightly terrifying yonder we four flew! After being airborne for a few minutes, both Anne and I realized that this was it! 95% of the family were encased in this minute plane and, should we, for any reason, disappear no one would be any the wiser! Not to worry! With his Dad sitting in the jump seat and the girls in the back we pressed fearlessly, at least not so anyone would notice, forward to the Canyon airport. On landing I noticed that our pilot, my good son, didn't ask that the plane be filled with gas for the return flight, an essential operation 'in my day'!

Our visit was a great success, it being a perfect day, and before leaving, we enjoyed a delightful meal in the El Tovar hotel's restaurant overlooking that vast, deep and Grand Canyon. Back to the plane, take off and the knowledge that it was getting towards sundown which we could see easily as we were flying straight at it, just about due west. As we did this, we became less and less talkative, which is not unusual on such a return trip, but it did provide me time to do a little calculating due to the position of the pointer on the gas gage! It appeared to be going down towards empty faster than our coverage of the impossible land on which to make any form of landing below! The shadows of evening were upon us and not even the considerable glare of Vegas was anywhere to be seen. Mark was totally silent. I was nervous and that, too. The girls were ignorant, thank goodness. It really did seem that we were on fumes when we made our approach to land. The fact that my son had beaten Sir Isaac Newton and his law of gravity and the fact that we were just about out of juice, brought about a joy of living within me which had been unknown since the RAF in 1943! In a typically paternal way, I did mention on the way to the hanger, having parked the aircraft, that *not* filling up with gas at a destination prior to return was one of the great no-nos of all amateur and, I think, all service flying. I think he listened as he is still with us, thank God, though he did eventually sell his plane! I may be wrong, but I think that may have been due, or partially due, to having the engine cut-out over the Strip when at 1,000 ft., or less, on one occasion! In a typically paternal way, again, I must be honest and say that that may **not** have been the real reason! I think it was because he did not have enough use for it, so it was an unnecessary expense.

Great sadness overcame us prior to Christmas as we felt we had to put down Duchess, a k a 'Duchy'. A more gentle and affectionate Sheltie would have been hard to find and it was only due to her almost total

114

blindness and lack of orientation that we had to do what we did. I don't know about you, but losing a beloved four-feet is one of the very worst things that can happen; worse, perhaps, than losing a relative.

The year 1978 was Anne's and my 10th anniversary. It was, also, the month of January wherein her father, Campbell Patterson, died on the 31st. at the age of 84. His funeral was at the Church of the Redeemer in Brookline. This was followed by *the* blizzard of '78 and Anne's birthday both on the 6th! A dear and gentle man, Cam more than made his mark at The Country Club in Brookline and in the world of golf there, not to mention his service for his country and the shipping industry. Anne herself was 38 and I wasn't getting any younger, just for a change. In no time we were having one of the BIG blizzards of the decade, if not longer, and it was 5 days before we could dig our way off the hilltop where we lived. One considerable problem we had was letting our animals out to do what came naturally. We kept on losing Tinsel as he disappeared under feet of snow! And both he and Perky got stuck with iced up and lumpy feet and paws, rendering them next to immobile!

In July of '78 we had a king-sized heat wave, just to balance the storm earlier in the year to prove that 'If you don't know what's coming in New England, wait awhile!'

We were off to Mark again that Christmas in Las Vegas and the Flamingo Hotel where he'd booked us. My memory of this stay isn't, surprisingly, all that vivid. However, I do remember Mark taking us to a Christmas Eve service, at our special request, and it was colorful in the extreme! When I asked him how he chose the church, as I'm ashamed to say, Jackie, my late wife, and I may have left undone many things which we should have done in regards to his and his sister's religious up-bringing, he replied "In the Yellow Pages, Dad!" That's my boy! This reminded me of the Easter before Anne and I were married and Anne, in church, asked Mark if he had any money 'for the plate'? Mark answered her, "What plate?!" Oh to be eleven again!

Peggy, Anne and I left thereafter for Hawaii as her guests with the idea of helping Peggy get going again after the death of Cam, her husband, much earlier in the year. As rotten luck would have it, Peggy had gone to an agent who had as much idea of what she would have liked in travel as the man in the moon. The flight there was uneventful but, as soon as we landed, we were hustled into buses and taken to have our first meal (with one complimentary drink per person) and to listen to a chap by the name of Don Ho. As we were in a large group, and Mr. Ho seemed to want to greet each of us personally, he did nothing but scream

'ALOE—HA!' (phonetically) at the top of his voice. In no time, actually it seemed like hours as we were pooped after all that flying from L A to Hawaii, we were taken to our hotel on the beach for the night. The next morning, we were rousted out of bed and rushed off for 'a day on the beach'. The snag was that other enthusiasts had gotten there earlier than we and there was, literally, a piece of sandy property the size of our small beach towels for each one of us, and no more. Never, in the field of human travel, have so many vied, to the accompaniment of the overwhelming and sickening aroma of coconut oil, for space on that beach! After Coco Point Lodge in Barbuda, where if you passed three people on the three mile beach you'd be amazed at the crowd, you can tell how our noses were a bit out of joint and how spoiled we two were!

From the foregoing, you can tell that Peggy's agent was not doing too well with her, nor us, but we'd never been to Hawaii before, so we had no right to complain, Mr. Ho, or no! The ultimate high spot of this performance of five or six days was proudly billed as 'The Flight to the Islands' and again, we were all yanked out of the sack at cocks' crow and were bussed to the airport. Here we were introduced to what appeared to be a squadron of antique aircraft, lined up as if to 'Scramble' in Battle of Britain days. In groups of 15, or more, we were ushered into these aircraft, just as if we were going to make the jump over Normandy on D Day. The only difference being that, at every moment, someone, or other, was yelling "ALOE—HA! This was repeated louder and louder, with almost all responding in unison, at every stop on every island 'til utter exhaustion took over around 4.00 p m. and we returned to base, thank heaven! Off to a Luau that evening with many more you-know-whats and quite a few pigs with apples in their mouths looking their very worst for wear, poor things. After many swinging hips, indigestion and sad songs of departure, we bussed off to the airport and flew off home the next morning, for hours and hours and hours! Quite a performance all told, one that we will never forget! Before we move on, however, here's an insight into a small crisis we three experienced at the L A airport en route home.

We left Honolulu very late, 5 hours late in fact, but made up the time due to tail winds by the time we'd reached L A. Unsurprisingly, we had next to no time to scramble across the huge L A airport to make our connection back to Boston, so I saw to it that my two charges, Anne and her Mum, were primed to hustle on arrival. That was not to be, however! On arrival, my mother-in-law allowed that we had to go to the Baggage Claim area, God only knew how far away, to pick up her pea-picking pineapples that she'd bought for her friends back in Chestnut Hill. Most miserably, she had not seen to it that they were ticketed

directly to Boston! Now, I usually made it my business to get along with
Peggy, who had her moments, but this time I nearly lost it and said so.
However, this was mere child's play vocally to that of my dear, lovable,
bride, who blew it on the spot and made one of the better scenes, I felt,
ever witnessed in this hub of the west coast! It was the first time in her
life that I'd ever heard her talk back to her mother! She was 38 at that
time and the intrigue and faces of those hundreds who passed by had to
be seen to be believed...in fact there was a veritable traffic jam! I was
not amused! Much to my surprise, we did make the connection having
added that dam' package of pineapples that I had to drag, with many
other cases of this and that, for the several miles involved!
Unsurprisingly, yet again, the conversation between the girls in the
party was non-existent from L A to Boston and, if memory serves me
correctly, I don't think I uttered a word, either! Remember! Getting
there, or back, is half the fun!

It was in September of '78 that my sister, Betty and her husband,
arrived for a few days and that was on the same day that Anne went for
an operation due a cancer scare. Thank heaven we got the news
promptly that the results of her cancer surgery were benign. No doubt
you can imagine the state we'd both been in since she'd gone into Mass
General. Speaking personally, I'd been out of my gourd due to having
lost Jackie to cancer in '67 so it was anything but an easy time, though
the relief was unspeakable for us both when it was over! Now I come to
think of it, the arrival of Betty and Henry at that time must have been
quite a shock for them both, as well and neither they, nor Mark, were
ever told about of this up-coming surgery.

SIX
1979 - 1981

1979 in the early stages still had me fuming away at Nobles until I could leave and then started to think about what the heck I was going to do for a living. At that time, like any other more, or less, it wasn't a breeze getting a job at 60 years of age that I was. After trying hard to pick up my somewhat flagging self-confidence, writing to all I knew and some who I didn't with ideas, suggestions and plans, I waited, and waited and did that again. After all that, I decided to heck with it! I worked for myself when I first came to this great country, so I might as well start again and did with Anne's usual and heart-warming encouragement. Not only did she give me all of that generously. She allowed as how, since I'd be getting no benefits, which would include insurance, she'd go back to work and obtain these for both of us. Most typical of her, bless her warm and great big heart! So to Talbots she went with General Mills' benefits!

What was I going to do, you might ask? Well! We were both known, we were told, as being pretty darn' good photographers having shot some pretty good stuff over the world and even given talks with accompanying color slides. You may remember the silver scare around this time when a chap called Hunt set out to corner the Silver Market, forced up the price to about .50c per ounce, and had people all over the country melting and selling this commodity? Also, there were many who became somewhat scared of owning this and many other *objets d'art* in their homes and who decided that they needed a Visual Inventory of their treasures to back up any Insurance Schedule they might need, or have already. With this in mind, I wrote to all who I knew around New England, and was shocked to find out what a cost in stamps and paper etc: that was! In the letter, I suggested that if they wished photos to be taken within their home of their treasures, either take the photos themselves or, as they knew and, hopefully, trusted me after 'all these years', they hire me to do that professionally for them. I, also, begged them not to invite anyone they did not know to do this. It was shocking how many did just that at this time, and who were right royally ripped off as the result.

I was delighted to receive many requests to fulfill my suggestion and off I started! Soon thereafter, while at a Museum of Fine Arts lecture on "Photography of Important Museums and Homes ", wherein the lecturer suggested that all involved go out and buy Polaroid cameras if they didn't have them, and do the job themselves! This wasn't the greatest idea as far as my new money making project was concerned, as you can guess! So! I jumped up and suggested that this was by no means the best and most economical idea at all! Hiring a professional was far better! Afterwards, a lady sitting next to me, one Dale Pollock, stopped me on the way out and said that she was a good Jewelry appraiser and would I, on my travels, consider referring her to appraise things wherever I went? I asked her to go away and find out all about me and that I'd do the same about her and then we'd talk. We did and with this idea in mind, The Appraisers' Registry took its initial and continuing shape for, at least, the next 23 years with, eventually, 24 member appraisers. I must, without doubt, give credit to the person for the name of the company that I founded then. His name is Paul O'Friel and a kinder, more concerned friend would be hard to find. I met him during my crisis with Nobles and, previously, he'd had a spot of bother in the TV business, so we were kindred spirits, I guess!

May was a family crisis month because we had to put down Perky, our marmalade cat. Sad to say, he'd been mauled by a neighbor's dog and the only humane thing to do was that. Cats sure are cats, but Perky gave us much tolerance over the years and we were so grateful for his attention, his personality and occasional affection.

In August of '79, Peggy, suddenly allowed that she'd like to take us to the U K! I think her reasoning was that she wanted, badly, to visit and see all the places we'd been to and about which Anne had talked, such as the Palace at Wells, where my Uncle Basil was Bishop and my sister and I'd spent so much time as kids, not to mention the really beautiful and famous cathedral next door.

This announcement of Peggy's was a bit of a shock coming out of the blue, but more so when we learnt that she wanted to do this one way on the supersonic Concorde! All of a sudden I became more than enthusiastic and I wondered if her most generous offer was tinged, a wee bit, by her desire to be the first in Fairgreen Place, hard by The Country Club in Chestnut Hill, to travel on this exciting aircraft, then in its comparative infancy. Maybe that was unfair, however! Her wish was that we should take her to London on Concorde and return, first class, on a BA 747 and she'd got it all organized! As soon as she asked us to join her, I wrote to BA and asked, as I'd written quite a few stories for the press over the years, if they'd allow me to sit in the jump seat behind the pilots of that plane from New York to Heathrow. Much to my surprise and delight, they agreed. They let me be there after we'd reached cruising altitude over Cape Cod, until we started our descent possibly, if I remember correctly, over Southern Ireland. The whole flight took about 3hrs: 20 minutes, I believe. As you can guess, this was a most exciting experience for this old RAF-type. It enabled me to write a comparative story of my flight back from Dorval airport, Montreal, in a Liberator bomber converted for passenger carrying in 1943 to Prestwick in Scotland after my 'rest' in eastern Canada. If I can dig it out I'll include it in this litany and I believe the Globe in Boston was brave enough to print it! Suffice to say, it took us longer to get into London than it did to get to Heathrow from The Big Apple. On the return home, Peggy had a ball with a cheerful fellow 'upstairs' on the 2nd. Floor of BA's 747 to Boston! Annie and I will never forget that flight to England and, now I come to think of it, maybe Peggy won't on the return flight either! It was a great treat and, certainly, a unique experience.

Great! I've found the article that was written, I see, on Sept: 13th. '79 in the Daily Transcript, and not the Globe. It appeared in the "IN FOCUS" section and I quote:

Concorde flying at the speed of sound.

By Michael Wynne-Willson
(Special to the Transcript)

N.B.—Author's license has shortened and made occasional alterations for this use.

How time does fly...and Concorde! It was 35 years ago that I made my first west to east crossing from Montreal to Prestwick in Scotland.

With a British Overseas Airways crew of four a few of us R A F pilots, were squeezed into the converted bomb bay of a Liberator aircraft where we sat on canvas backed, upright, metal seats. WW2 was beginning to end, but this journey was still considered an adventure. I remember well wondering what the next day, or so, would bring as Capt. Poole lifted the huge, lumbering, 4-engined plane off Dorval airport's runway at 11.00 a m to land at Gander, Newfoundland, four hours later.

After a welcome cup of very hot tea, because the cabin heating consisted of a six inch diameter pipe through which warmish air flowed into the 'bomb bay', and an essential visit to the bathroom as no such necessity was on board, we set off from Gander on the final and most dangerous leg of the flight to Prestwick in Scotland.

Then, 9 hours and 45 minutes later, at 2.00 a m local time we landed frozen, and almost stiff, yet delighted to be home again. We had been airborne 14 hours altogether flying at 9,000 ft. at an average speed of nearly 210 m p h to cover 3,000 miles and we never saw a German aircraft, thank goodness! It was two weeks ago that I made another west to east Atlantic crossing. from New York (JFK) to London (Heathrow). This was every bit as much of an adventure as the one just described. It was made in a BA Concorde at supersonic speed. My wife and I had been invited, most generously, by my mother-in-law to escort her to England to meet my family and visit the places where I was brought up in the Cotswolds and Mendip Hills.

Our flight originated early in the morning from Logan airport and, after a brief flight to Kennedy, we were ushered into the Concorde Lounge. Over Champagne and *Paté de foie gras* sandwiches...at 10.30 am no less!...we found ourselves really close for the first time to the needle-nosed and acutely streamlined machine which was going to take us across the water in less than 3 and ¾ hours. Fellow passengers started to arrive and a very definite air of excitement was noticeable, quite different from boarding a conventional aircraft. We noticed a would be rock star with his personal retinue including a photographer, a preponderance of business men as expected, several single women and a charming mother and daughter team. The mother, we learnt later as we talked together, is the editor and publisher of the Anchorage Daily News in Alaska and was making the brief stopover en route to England with other relatives. At 12.15 p m we were pushed out from the loading ramp and started the usual long, winding drive to the runway in use.

"Good afternoon, ladies and gentlemen, welcome to B A's Concorde", announced the Chief Steward, never "The" Concorde as we seem to refer to it here. By dropping the 'The" the British makers of this supersonic aircraft, with the French, appear to give it a little extra reverence!

Sitting two abreast either side of the aisle, half way down this comparatively small plane built to carry 100 passengers, it was strange to look out and see only about 10 to 15 feet of wing below. I had forgotten, momentarily, that this was a V-wing plane and that the maximum width was behind and towards the tail. Here, all four engines providing 36,000 pounds of thrust each are located; two on either side of the fuselage and under the wing.

Looking down at Nantucket and Martha's Vineyard islands to the west, we passed though the first of our two 'barriers'. The first being the passage through the speed of sound and then, twice that speed. Other than a very slight shudder produced by the surge of power, nothing other than the mach meter on the bulkhead in front of us, and the Captain's voice, told us that anything extraordinary was happening. Anyway, I guess exceeding the ground speed of 720 mph at 30,000 feet is pretty humdrum these days!

Shortly thereafter, the *Dom Perignon* champagne and smoked salmon sandwiches were served and then we went to twice the speed of sound and that was exciting! How blasé we have become! The mach meter shivered between 1.99 and 2.00 for a while as we reached 52,000 ft giving us a ground speed of 1,320 mph...23 miles a minute! At that point, I could not help but think back to 1944 when I was in the same general vicinity in the Liberator, staggering along at 43,000 ft below, at a speed 1,000 mph slower, dressed in layers of flying clothing and eating a dry ham sandwich and hard-boiled egg out of a cardboard box! If memory serves correctly, and that is a doubtful now, we had nothing to drink then; but that may well have been planned due to the lack of loo problem!

I'd been given to understand that cruising at such a height the sky appeared violet and that the curvature of the earth was quite obvious. For some reason on that day neither seemed a bit obvious and everything looked as much as usual.

Many stories, I know, have been written pro and con sonic and super-sonic flight. As I was lucky enough to have had this experience, I will not add to them. However, as an American, I was sad that the proud Concorde was not of our manufacture. As an ex-Englishman and RAF-type, there lingered a feeling of pride that the country of my birth did, in part, do the job.

In 1944, on our arrival at Prestwick, I was driven to Kilmarnock railway station to wait in a blacked out, deserted platform in snow, for a train that was 1 ½ hours late arriving. If Kilmarnock to my destination, at an RAF Receiving Station at Harrogate, was not abject misery and change of scenery trauma, to boot, heaven knows what is!

Not long ago it took us half the time of flying the Atlantic to go from London's airport to our hotel in town. Maybe time doesn't fly so fast, after all!"

Peggy saw a really good deal of the southwestern part of Jollye Olde. Our first stop was the Bristol Hotel in Mayfair, which used to be the famed Berkeley Hotel adjacent to the Square of the same name and tune. And then on to the Bear in Woodstock, near Oxford near where we visited Winston Churchill's grave, so simple in the grounds of a small church close to Blenheim Palace, his ancestral home, and then a big family lunch with my close cousin, Bill W-W and Pam his wife and their family. That afternoon we drove to my old 'alma mater', Radley College, near Abingdon and were delighted to show it all to my 'belongings'! From there I drove them to the Cotswolds taking a look at Lechlade and Castle Combe en route and to Alderley House, Wotton-under-Edge, my super home of many, many years ago. All the history about all this was included in my first memoir, by the way! The hotel we stayed in that night was The Priory in Bath where, as you might expect, we did quite a bit of sightseeing as Peggy had never been anywhere before in England except London. Finally to High Littleton House, another home we enjoyed as kids, to Chewton Mendip where my Dad and Mum are buried and then to the Palace at Wells!

Concorde Cockpit

I had always been fairly sure that Peggy, never believed a word of my true story that my Uncle, Dad's eldest brother was, among many other important positions, Bishop of Bath and Wells and lived in the Palace like dozens before him over the years! (Again, you'd better get Book1 and then you'll know what I'm taking about!) As I felt this was the case, I wrote some time before to the Bishop there at the time, the

Rt: Rev: John Bickersteth, and asked if I could bring Peggy and Anne to the Palace so that I might show them the private quarters in which my parents and my sister and I would often stay and, by so doing, persuade Peggy that I hadn't been fibbing through my teeth! Happily, I got a delightful reply from him saying that, regretfully, he had to be away when we planned to come, but Major So & So would meet us and be glad to escort us wherever we wished! That took care of that beautifully, thank you very much, and Peggy became a believer!

Speaking of Peggy, both Anne and I heard often that she'd heard, or read, about a great new Andrew Lloyd Weber show that had just hit London's West End, 'Phantom of the Opera' and she'd love to see it with us, if my sister Betty could get tickets for it. She did this for us once before with Evita, if you remember, with great success! I went to work promptly and Betty, again, came crashing through with enough tickets so that we could take my family as well, a night or two after getting to London. How she pulled that off, as tickets were scarcer than hen's teeth, goodness knows but she did! She and her husband, Harry (a k a Henry sometimes) joined the three of us and we added their son Robin and his wife, Veronica, (a k a Pooh usually!) and their two sons, Edward and Jamie. What a magnificent and colorful show that was, especially as we were there for the night of a performance just before it opened officially, and Andrew Lloyd Weber was sitting just in front of us checking it with his producer. As all know, it ran for years and played in all parts of the world thereafter! Following this, Harry had made arrangements for me to take all of us to dinner at his club, The Garrick, for dinner. Again as many will know, this is one of London's most famous and older clubs whose members, in the main, have been famous actors and the memorabilia and their signatures in the several sitting and dining rooms have to be seen to be believed! That was one of the very best and happiest nights we ever had with most of my immediate U K family enjoying it with us...and, perhaps, with Peggy enjoying it most of all!

At the end of October, we both were greatly saddened by hearing from Suzanne that her husband, Hakon Mielche, had died of a heart attack in Hamburg. It seems that the two of them were visiting the gravesites of some about whom Hakon was writing, when she turned around and found Hakon slumped over one of the gravestones. He had suffered a heart attack so, as swiftly as possible, Suzanne flew back with him to Denmark where he died on this 75th birthday. This was, after many trips and excitements we had shared with him and his resulting closeness to us both, an awful shock, but nothing compared to that of poor Suzanne who was, as I said before, 42 years younger than he was.

She had quite a performance getting him out of Germany and back home to Denmark where, previously, he had insisted upon being buried. In no way would he let her bury him in Germany. Ever since WW2 and the treatment both he and so many of the citizens of Copenhagen received at the hands of the Germans during the occupation, he couldn't stand being associated with them, let alone being buried on German soil.

This year and subsequent to my leaving Nobles under the circumstance that I mentioned previously, I worked off my anger and frustration by painting every room in our home in Westwood, MA! It was during this painting spree that some one suggested that I should seek help to rid myself of this anger and to try to recoup my self-confidence. That person suggested that there was a brilliant woman nearby who could do just this for a price. He'd had a problem and she worked wonders for him. Due to my ludicrous state, and obviously being pretty light-headed, I sought her out and signed up. Normally, the very thought of my going to someone for 'help' would have been the last thing on earth I'd have entertained...being a growing old, old, conservative ex Brit.! Nevertheless, off I went and tossed myself into the hands of this character who announced that why she charged so much was that 'she was so darn' brilliant' that I had to pay her umpteen bucks and to get on with it! The darnedest thing was that I did, and that shows you what a rocky state I was in! So! I went through the course, though how God only knows, and I was so shattered by the amount of dough that I'd spent on what I considered a totally useless course of 'therapy' that I emerged cured of whatsoever it was that ailed me! Maybe she did me a favor, though not in the way I thought she was supposed to! After this, my idea for The Appraisers' Registry business really started to make headway and, thank goodness, has never looked back!

For my 60th birthday on 9:13:79, Annie pulled together a super party for me at home. Tinsel greeted our guests in a quiet and gentlemanly fashion, of course, as he was not a yapping Yorkie! Among those kind enough to come and have fun with us were names from Book I such as Gus Shemilt, my RAF chum from Canada who was with me at RAF Station, Greenwood, Nova Scotia and was a guest at the wedding in Middleburg, VA in 1944 plus many other RAF types! Dave Taylor, Jeanie Putnam and Betty Buck from Milton all came, as did my friend and supporter during the Noble's fiasco, Dick Morse and his wife Clare, to mention but a few.

This cheery event was followed soon after by one of great sadness to both Annie and me. 'Uncle' Vaughan Merrick, my headmaster when I was at St. George's as an Exchange Student in 1936/37 and subsequent great and really special friend for many, many years died. His funeral was in Wakefield, R I. just a few miles from his home which Bea, his wife and he, gave to my late wife and me for our honeymoon in May '44. I was most honored by Bea and her family when she asked me to be a small part of 'Uncle' Vaughan's funeral service.

As I mentioned, Anne was concerned as was I, about working for myself as I'd have none of the benefits I got at Nobles and Mt. Auburn, so off she went to work at Talbots in Wellesley. This was the job for her, for her clothes sense is par excellence and she had just the right ideas for what clients should put on their backs! I should note that those who worked 'on the floor' there then were given what, to me anyway, were incredible discounts for anything they bought, so Anne was sure in the right place to get 'benefits'! I've always said, and dozens of our friends have agreed over the years, that she should have become a ladies personal clothing consultant because she has such an incredible eye for color, mix and matches etc:, both for herself and for others. No husbandly prejudice, just a fact! In fact, over the years, I seldom dress for an event of any kind without checking my choice of clothes and their color with her first! Of course, should I not agree with her I usually defer!

It was on February 6th '81 that a great event occurred at The Country Club! My much better half became 40 years of age...with little sympathy from me, I might add! In the event, my mother-in-law decided some time before against Anne's wishes, to give her this party to which, happily, a great group of her friends of all ages came. It was 'black tie', with all the trimmings, speeches, poems and, believe it or not, a Belly Dancer! In no time, all had decided that this was a definite first for TCC and, as it was a surprise both to Anne and, certainly, her mother, none of us dared look at the latter! Like Queen Victoria who was 'not amused,' it could have been that Peggy could have blown her stack! Mercifully, she took it all in great stride and, even though she thought Annie, or I, was responsible for this act in the first place, she laughed along with the rest of us and the more so after Annie assured her that it was a surprise to her, too! I was privy to the donor of this unique gift, at TCC anyway, and loved Page Osborn for perpetrating it so courageously, as did the good staff that rushed, regardless, to view the performance! Peggy really pulled out all the stops for her daughter at that party, however, at which I think every single person there had a ball!

**We get spiffed up for The Country Club's
100th anniversary**

In the summer of this year, my sister Betty (a k a Betsy in this country for some unknown reason!) and her husband Henry (a k a Harry etc:!) came over for a visit from London. Anne and I thought they'd like a change of scenery from our home in Westwood, and as they had suggested the possibility of finding a cottage on the sea, we did just that with the help of my old Wenham chum, Joe Robbins, and found them one right on the sea at Biddeford Pool in Maine. This they seemed to enjoy greatly, particularly as the weather was great, and they invited me to go and spend a couple of nights with them. Anne came with me but then returned home alone for work the next day. Anyway, after we'd had tea one day and B and I had gone for a lovely walk on the beach, I went to my car to pick up something and, stupidly, left the key inside and it locked. With a bit of embarrassment I went in and explained my dumbness to my brother-in-law who could, on occasion, be pompous! Sadly, he chose this moment to be that and, in school-masterly fashion, started to give me the word about what I should do about the matter. This was all to do with what had to be done in the U K, which really didn't help much, besides I'd already called AAA who said they'd get to me, even though it was Labor Day week-end! Sadly, Henry refused to believe this and told me I didn't know what I was doing, and he did! As I had lived in this country, and had done for many years, I disagreed, vehemently. Had I been sixteen, I probably would have listened and done what I was told. The trouble was then that I was a whole darn' lot older and still smarting over the Noble & Greenough ruckus. And here I was faced with yet another headmaster giving me a bunch of advice that I really didn't need, and for which I did not ask!

Sad to say, all at once, I lost it totally and a flush of venom exploded from my mouth regarding just what I thought of prep: school masters and their conviction that they were God-sent and knew so much that they could afford to throw it away! In other words, I blew my stack at my unfortunate brother-in-law, in front of my sister, and told him just what he could do with about everything for several minutes without repeating myself. My sister was, unsurprisingly, in tears as she'd never heard such vitriol directed at her husband, let alone from her little, always much younger, brother! All involved were upset, and it was not a chatty evening, nor was breakfast the next morning as can be imagined. Let's face it, by that time, I was almost feeling guilty as Henry had never, ever, had anyone speak to him that way and he was looking and feeling hurt beyond measure.

It so happened that we were leaving the house that morning at the end of their stay there and heading for Westwood where we were picking up Anne and then going on to Marion where we were all going to stay a night, or two, with Anne's parents. When we got to Anne she bounded out of our house with her usual warmth and greeting, but it took her only a split second to realize that, sometime before, a few things had hit the proverbial fan! By the time we got to Marion, things had improved all round and, I did write to Henry after he'd returned to the U K and say how sorry I was and that I was at fault. Many months passed, however, before we were on a moderately even keel again, regardless of my apology. Happily, after that outburst, I regained my sanity and got on with life and forgot, 99.9% anyway, about all the Noble's nonsense. Enough already!

It was early on in this year (1982) that Aileen Farrell, one of my very oldest friends, died at Lenox in Massachusetts within the grounds of her prep: school for girls, Foxhollow. Some may remember page 1 of 'BEFORE I FORGET!' Book I, wherein I wrote about my falling into a boiling bathtub, literally, at the age of 2, or so, and it was Aileen that pulled me out! In fact, the first sentence of that book was, "I love girls, I always have and always will, and my first memory is of one!" That one was Aileen! She and her 'school for Little Darlings', where I first met Jackie my late wife, were all through my first book and I had always been very close to her, except when Wendy ran away from that school and things were a bit tense then for awhile! That didn't last long though, happily!

All my adult life I'd wondered why Aileen had left my father's school in England, in what seemed a hurry, only to come to this country to teach at a girl's school called Foxcroft in Virginia. This was something that seemed to stick in my craw, however, so on one of Anne's and my frequent trips to and from Lenox to see and try and cheer her when she seemed so ill and not to last long, I decided to take courage and ask. You see, I'd always had my feelings about this, again as an adult, but had never mentioned it to a soul other than Anne. So! I said to her, "Dear Aileen, I've always wanted to know something and never had the courage, nor felt that I had the right, to ask you. Why was it that you left Dad's school in England to come here when it seemed that you were so happy there? We've known each other for years and years and though the question I'm about to ask you is none of my darn' business, was the reason because you fell in love with Dad?"

In a very small and somewhat muffled voice, I was just able to catch her reply. "You're right Michael! I often wondered if you knew!" Shortly thereafter she died and we went, of course, to her funeral at the Roman Catholic Church in Lenox. I always heard that she and my Mum got along beautifully, but then Mum did that with everyone. I've often wondered, however, if the outcome would have been the same had that affection been born many years later and with things being so different. Mind you I never had the courage to ask Dad what his feelings were about it all! As he died in a cricket match in 1939 and I was just back from a year in the States at St. George's, I was a bit young for that kind of a question, especially to my Dad!

Part Two

SEVEN
1983-1985

The first event that I seem to remember in 1983 was being awakened by Annie who was in agony in one of her shoulders! She'd been having therapeutic shots in them for two years and this sudden attack was something new in our lives and I hadn't a clue what to do about it. Her doctor at that time was a famous physician by the name of Henry Mankin, who happened to be Chief of Orthopedic Services at Mass General Hospital in Boston. Not being one to think lightly about calling such an august individual at his home when he is, presumably, tucked up snugly in bed, I hesitated. This brought about increased yells from Annie that banished any qualms I might have had, so promptly she called him. Unsurprisingly, he wasn't too thrilled by her interruption, but said, anyway, that I was to take her forthwith to MGH where he would meet us. It was neither a quiet nor comfortable ride at 5.30 A M!

True to his word, Dr. Mankin was on hand at 7.30 A M to meet us in his office and immediately went to work on Annie's shoulder with explosive results. It seems that she had amassed a horrendous amount of calcium in a joint and that was the cause of her misery. Calcified Tendonitis was the medical terminology. After three nights in the Phillips House at MGH she came home highly relieved. That was my introduction to this kind and greatly admired doctor and, in spite of our shocking and untimely introduction, he has become a dear friend and has looked after us both for years and years and without his TLC we would have been in a mess, as you'll gather later on. Annie got back home from MGH on February 5th. On that day I decided that everyone was, and had been, getting far more attention than I, so I threw my back out for good measure! I was not a happy camper, I assure you! It seems that that wasn't quite enough to do the trick, so in May I was taken to Mass General's E R for a Hernia operation. I got little mileage and precious little TLC for that performance as far as I remember, as it wasn't nearly dramatic enough.

It was during this operation, for which I had a spinal injection done this time by Dr. Bill Wood, I gathered that I would not be knocked out and that he and I could keep up a conversation if the spirit moved. Mercifully, due to a sheet placed vertically between me and my tummy, I couldn't see what mayhem he was creating with my interior, but I could see a most gorgeous blond standing doing nothing, I thought, behind me and to my right. Intrigued as to her function, I asked her what her purpose was for being there and she replied cheerfully, "I'm just seeing that everything's going all right!"

"Not on my time at these prices!" I allowed. Then, and for some unknown reason, I lurched into a story that I thought might amuse my friendly, highly renowned and competent surgeon and his 'assistant', the blond bombshell doing nothing behind me...on my time yet! It was the story of how I got shot for a fox when lying, most conservatively I might add, in the hay with a girlfriend during a brief leave during WW2, near Broadway. (Book: 1!) Half way through his job, I noticed my eminent sawbones trying his level best not to shake with laughter, even though I couldn't see what he was up to beyond a green sheet between him and me.

"For heaven's sake be quiet, Michael!" He said, "I'm trying to tie up a few bits and pieces back here and I can't possibly concentrate and do a decent job if you continue this crazy story!"

This I did, of course, but not until the blond gorgeousness behind me sidled over and made me promise to tell her the end of it when I got into 'recovery'! Having her stand over me attentively while I 'recovered' seemed full of possibilities, I figured!

Our annual time at Coco Point Lodge this year was memorable in many of its usual ways, but especially because a very famous lady appeared among us. Miss G came as a guest with her niece and this was the first of several visits she made in subsequent years. Her arrival was shrouded in a bit of mystery and, as you can imagine in such a marvelous place renowned for its peace and relaxation, gossip was all the rage! We soon, however, could see for ourselves that Miss G, as she liked to be known, was Greta Garbo. Understandably, Martin Price, then the new manager of Coco Point Lodge assisted by his charming wife, Caroline, both from Norfolk in England, asked all of us guests to treat her with the privacy which was her due. I must say that it was a bit of a temptation for some of us of advancing years who'd enjoyed some of her spicier movies to stand or sit and gawk at her, dark glasses, floppy hat and all!

Annie, being Annie, at cocktail time when we all gathered in the open air bar for a quick one, or two, before dinner, would often walk round with the hors d'oeuvres which, usually, were on a central table for all to reach easily. Miss G, however, would invariably sit with her niece as close as she could to the beach looking out to sea. Often, Anne would go up to them and naturally wanting to be welcoming, offered both of them what she carried. In this way they recognized her when walking the beach the following day, as they (and we) did each day. This season we got as far as "Good morning," or "Good afternoon," and that was that for this year. As, obviously, all had been asked not to photograph Miss G anywhere at any time, I took a photo of her obvious foot prints in the sand, as we followed one day far behind her! Very brave I was! As it happened, as the years went by we did get to be quite chatty and she loosened up considerably with a few of us.

Our most memorable time with her, however, was as follows. The Rizers, Betty Ann and Dean, who had for many years joined us at Coco Point, were having their 30th wedding anniversary while there and Annie and I decided we should have a party for them. What to do? I then got the idea of asking the owner and founder of CPL, Bill Kelly, if it might be possible to move the sizeable yacht up to and opposite the main buildings and just have the party on board. It was then anchored a bit further down off the beach and was there for guests to charter as they might wish. I had noted that the yacht had been there for a while with no one chartering it, so suggested to Bill and Martin that if guests were able to get on it and see how nice it was, more business might be done! Happily, they thought it a good idea and so we set about designing an appropriate invitation to be sent to many of the guests a few days before the event. Should one be sent at breakfast to Miss G and her niece, we wondered? We surely would have felt terrible to exclude them altogether, though we were certain there was absolutely no chance of their showing up! Just in case, we did warn them that they would be receiving an invitation the following day.

On the evening of the party, Martin and the staff, had rigged a 'jetty' on the sand opposite the yacht so that any guests that came could board the boats which were to take out the guests without getting wet feet! After a few were transported and the Captain of the yacht was greeting people warmly, who should be spied walking up the beach from their cottage, but Miss G and her niece. None of us could believe our eyes! We got her safely on board and, after introducing them to the Captain, I turned to Miss G and announced that, even though I was going to photograph the evening's fun, I would promise her that none would be taken of her by me, or anyone else. That was fine by her, she allowed!

Suffice to say the cocktail party on board was a great success and thoroughly enjoyed by all and certainly by Miss G! I went and sat with her and Anne after landing her safely before dinner and it was then that she said to us that "she hadn't had that much fun for 25 years!" Happily, we found that the Rizers felt just the same way and that it had made a special time for them. Miss G, like a few others who were aboard earlier, slept pretty darn' well that night, I figured! Not a single photograph was taken of her, either!

In June, Annie and I enjoyed our 15th anniversary (they said it wouldn't last longer than six months due to our age difference!) by driving down the Mass Turnpike and heading north to the Arlington Inn in Vermont. We were looking for a quiet time in old-world surroundings with fine food, and we hit the nail on the head! Not long after, in about a month, we were off again, this time with Peggy, my ma-in-law, and six other friends to Scotland for a few days and then onto The Illyria for a North Cape cruise starting at Leith, the port for Edinburgh. "Follow the Vikings" was the theme for this trip and this took us to the Orkneys, Shetlands, Norway's fjords, Bergen, Oslo and Denmark. We were blessed with good weather for most of the journey other than Scotland, which was lucky. We loved it and learnt a lot including that the Kattegat can become unholy rough and did nothing for Annie! She came to and made her entrance into the dining room just as Cherries Flambé were being borne in on high at the Captain's final dinner and we were entering Copenhagen's harbor!

On our return home, there was much work that had piled up for The Registry though, as usual, I had left the handling of business things to Martha Richardson, one of T A R's Painting Specialists, who always coped efficiently. Tinsel, who had been staying with Elsie at her New Pond Kennels, while being spoiled to bits as usual, was awaiting us with customary enthusiasm and licks on our return home.

Speaking of my Registry, which had been going along slowly and fairly surely, it was right around this time that a good friend, Henry Doerr, who we'd met at our regular and favorite watering hole, Coco Point Lodge, invited us to fly up to Wayzata his home on Lake Minnetonka hard by Minneapolis, to meet some of his friends in business. At that time, he was the President of one of the Twin Cities prominent banks and, more than generously, he thought that I should meet some of his associates in his and other institutions who might well be interested in The Registry with a view to franchising. Off we flew, full of enthusiasm and hope and stayed with him and his charming wife for the best part of a week. Not only did he take me into his office daily in Minneapolis, but Ann, his wife, operated as my secretary, taking calls etc: for me each day! Henry worked miracles for me and in no time I was being introduced, not only to bankers, lawyers and civic movers and shakers but, also, to many of the Cereal Barons, and their staffs, whose homes were on the lake as well! As I flew home, not only was I incredibly thankful to the Doerrs for all that they had done for me but, for my part, I was convinced we had really struck oil and that in no time there would be an Appraisers' Registry in Minneapolis-St Paul! Believe me, I am not, and have never been, one to count my chickens before they were hatched but this time I really felt it was time that they were! Every person I met in business and to whom I was introduced and spoke about The Registry, thought that that idea was great and their enthusiasm bubbled over for the project!

For weeks after I returned I heard not one blooming word from anyone there! I wound up, after a month, or more, of total silence by writing to Henry to ask if he had any clue as to why this might be? He replied to say that he couldn't understand it, but not to worry, I'd made a good impression!

What happened and why you may ask? Ages later, I was determined to find out the reason so looked into the whole visit again. It seems that the powers that be there decided that what I'd started back in 1980, or so, really was a great idea but who needed M.F.W-W to run it? Why couldn't an old prune of his age, 60ish back then, be found locally with his enthusiasm and years' worth of friends and associates, who could put the show on the road? Anne and I figured that that made sense, regardless, so I moved on!

1984 saw my old Royal Australian Air Force and Radley College chum, Jum Falkiner, and his wife Anita, for a visit to us in Westwood in April. Some of you may remember our antics from Book I! Anyway, it was Anita who wrote eventually, after my years and years of trying to track Jum down in OZ, that they wanted to come and visit us while on a junket around this country. Some friends in OZ had won a prize of a trip here, which they were unable to take as their kids were either too young or at school, so they'd asked Jum and Anita to take their place! Great excitement! As I set off down the drive to go to Logan airport to meet them, I suddenly thought, 'what if I don't recognize Jum? I shouldn't have worried, there was that tall, handsome man with Anita waiting at the curb for me, and I knew him immediately! He looked different facially, of course, but not so that I allowed myself to notice!

As we knew we would, we had a great time all together and, as a 'house' present, they gave us a three foot high baby cherry tree which we ceremonially planted on the lawn in back of our house. From then on it was always known as The Jum Tree and now, umpteen years later, it is enormous and gives forth masses of edible cherries about every three years! Sadly, our beloved birds devour them long before we can get at them and they are ripe enough for us to eat!

137

Michael F. Wynne-Willson

It was on June 26th that our beloved Yorkie, Tinsel, that Wendy gave Anne for Christmas 14 1/2 years before, had to be put down. I, as usual, was a basket case due to such an event. Dr. Roger Prescott, a charming and excellent vet, had looked after Tinsel with kindness and talent for 14 years and it was to him that we went for the last of Tinsel's visits. We had heard that the best way of doing this miserable performance was to be with the dog and hold him when injected, so that he should not be unduly scared. Annie elected, with usual kindness and guts, to do this while I stood by, chicken that I am at such occasions. As awful luck would have it, for once Doc Prescott miscued and didn't hit one of Tinsel's tiny veins. The result was shattering. With Tinsel screaming and Anne doing the same asking if he was dead yet, I lost it completely and started using disgraceful language at the unfortunate Doc, who was, probably, more upset than we were as he'd grown to love him, too, and he was one of his first patients. Enough of that but, oh! Lord it was awful...for all concerned.

Three days later, most guilt-ridden but bored with being a basket case brought on by the loss of Tinsy, I acquired, without Anne's knowledge, another Yorkie, a pup that Anne named 'Radley'. He threw-up all the way home in the car from the North Shore where we bought him! Roger Prescott started to look after him a few days afterwards and did for years until he, Roger, died suddenly and most sadly. You'll hear, unsurprisingly, lots about Radley as we progress, no doubt!

It was in October that I did something that I just couldn't believe I would ever do! Radley, our new Yorkie, was being a king-sized pain! He refused to become house-trained and perpetrated other horrors frequently which began to drive us nuts and we were getting frantic to know what to do about him. This was upsetting since we'd been told by the breeder that he was house-trained! Nothing was working for us, nor for him! Somewhere along the way I'd heard about a local dog psychiatrist! An old, conservative, ex Brit such as me even thinking about psychiatry was nigh on impossible, of any type, let alone one who talked to dogs! Not to worry! A Dr. McSorley duly arrived, invited to our home one evening and, in all truth, I thought I must be dreaming! Anyway, he sat us down and talked to us and to Radles and told us bluntly that, poor dog, he was battling against filling Tinsel's shoes and that was almost too much for him...or words to that effect! Additionally, he gave us several other suggestions as to how we could help him straighten out, not the least of which was to have him altered! I think when he heard that one he piddled on our best carpet, yet again!

After I'd given the good Dr. his check for $60.00...and that proved to myself that I was nuts...he left and the three of us went to bed, somewhat chagrinned. I have to tell you, however, that this doc was a dog-send, honestly! From the next day on we never looked back, all three of us, and life soon became bearable specially for Radles who, for the rest of his life, led a charming, beloved, if sexless life! I did apologize to him for the latter matter, I promise, and he was most understanding and never held it against me, ever!

It was in December of this year that I flew to England to meet a man who ran a cottage rental business in the Cotswolds. Why? Because a good and charming friend, who owned one in the beautiful village of Burford, Russell Ford, said that I really should meet Peter Ansdell, the cottage chap, because we'd get along fine and I might be able to help him! We decided that Annie and her mum should follow a few days later, which is what happened. On meeting Peter in his office in Little Farringdon, we did indeed hit it off and before I left he asked me if I could help him line up some business in the States for him. Never having been one for passing up an opportunity I said that I'd certainly give it a try! As usual, what I knew about renting cottages etc: long-distance was next to nil, but it sounded like fun and, for once, I would know what I was talking about relative to the locations of his attractive rentals. He took me round to see quite a few and, as expected, they were delightful. In no way, I figured, would it conflict with The Registry which was going along slowly, but certainly surely, by then.

Radley in Christmas Mode

CASTLES, COTTAGES AND FLATS

So now I had two jobs going at the same time from my 'study/office in our nicely finished basement. The two of them went together well, and when I was building one I found the other was complementing it because so many were interested in cottage rentals at that time. This was due to the prices of hotels abroad and in the U K, being very high then, particularly for a family holiday.

At first, I just talked up the idea with friends and associates and found that the chances of obtaining a few bookings for Peter were not at all bad, but as usual, I had to do more than chat to chums! For many years, as those of you who have followed these ramblings of mine, will know that I'd been on the borders of the advertising business for years, and certainly had been my own P R man. Couldn't afford a professional! Consequently, I still had, even after all the years, quite a few good and loyal friends in the media and advertising fields. One such person was Jerry Morris, the Travel Editor of the Boston Globe. He, both kindly and generously, wrote a long article about Castles, Cottages and Flats in his weekly column and my efforts to get the show on the road. Little did I know what results that would have! A few weeks later, letters began to pour in from all over the country, Canada and Hawaii, wanting to know all about us, prices, what and where were the cottages which might be available, and when! I had completely forgotten, if I ever knew, that Jerry's column was held in the greatest respect and was copied in newspapers everywhere! Homegrown panic was forthcoming as I was totally incapable of coping with such mail promptly, even with Annie's help and that of several other good friends. All I could think of, respectfully to answer all the enquiries that ran often to 20 to 30 a day through the mail anyway, was to have some post cards printed telling of our immediate problem and asking for patience for a few weeks! Beth Ladd, nee Williams, Annie and I spent hours and days addressing postcards that, thank heaven, cost only10 cents to mail then! The investment in the newly formed company was, as you might guess if you read Book One, minimal in the extreme, so that was a bit of a problem as it cost heaven knows what to mail anything to Canada then, and still does!

C, C & F grew and grew over the next few years with ever-increasing coverage not only in the U K, but Ireland and elsewhere. This involved one or two trips to the U K to meet owners and one to Ireland to look at Castles and to meet their owners. Annie and I toured from Waterford to Ballybunnion to Limerick and spent nights in several castles, and looked at many cottage colonies en route with a view hopefully, and by request, to write a report on our findings. This is where I got stuck and, sadly, didn't enamor myself to some of the owners I heard later. In comparison to what was offered in the U K and from the point of view of the American traveler who might be booking such places, I found it impossible not to be a bit critical of some of what we saw. I tried my hardest to be helpful, rather than critical, but it wasn't easy. I guess I never should have circulated the report, for nothing changed much for a few years thereafter for whatever reason though I hope it has!

We made many friends, however, not the least was a good lady I met who ran a successful cottage-renting business in Scotland, Jill Bristow, by name. Through and with her, I managed to get a group of around twelve cottage-renters in the U K to come to London's Grosvenor House Hotel for a conference. My nephew, Robin Collis, had good contacts there and graciously made all the necessary arrangements for us to have the room and facilities.

Several years later, I arranged for another such gathering at the most delightful cottage called The Rose & Crown House that Annie and I rented in Chipping Camden. This was owned by Patrick & Fizz Laycock, who also rented other and most attractive cottages in the Cotswolds. As problems changed very little in this business between operators in the U K themselves and, also, between them and us in the U S, nothing of too great import ever seemed to be forthcoming at these meetings, but many lasting friendships were made, anyway!

While I continue our journey in these pages, C, C & F went along well, though like other efforts of mine in the business world over the years, it didn't make the money it should because there was only so much money the average traveler would pay to rent a cottage per week, and there was only so much C C & F could charge on a commission basis! The net result was that I found myself getting up and into my office at home around 5.00 A M daily to retrieve 'phone calls from the U K, plus faxes, and then up to 10.30 P M or so to do the same from Honolulu! All that thanks to Jerry Morris at the Globe and the great article he wrote about us and the vast coverage it got overseas, as well as at home! Still, never mind! I greatly enjoyed trying to help people find what they sought in the beautiful Cotswolds and elsewhere in U K, though it did get a bit hectic when I'd get a call like this:

"This is Mrs. Upsquash calling and you'll remember speaking to me about six weeks ago about the 4-room cottage we want in the village of Filkins? Well! I was wondering if you have ordered the cot we need for Tootsiebell, our baby, and for the car which we'll probably need, but don't want to order this far in advance, you'll understand".

"Have you decided when you need the cottage, Mrs. U?".

"No, not really; you see, we hope to have Tootsie in four months, so it's very difficult for us to decide when, where and what we want when we get there right now!"

I exaggerate just a little bit, but you get the point! At 12.00 midnight in Westwood, it was only 9.00 P M in San Diego, so that was quite a normal time, and cheap too, to call C, C & F!

Before forging fearlessly forward, why don't we take a glimpse at some of the things about which I lurched into print, either for fun or frustration!

Firstly. There's always been the problem of my name which my first and late ma-in-law could never pronounce due to her French upbringing. Eventually, after several years of trying, she settled on it phonetically as follows: Mykal Will Winsoll! That and many other efforts over the years prompted me to push off a letter to the Boston Globe that, much to my surprise, was printed. It went like this and appeared in early '87:

HYPHENATED NAMES ARE A COMPLEX MATTER

"As one who had had one longer than most...67 years...and dragged it along when I came to live in the U S in 1948, I'd like to sound a note of caution to those considering doubling up. You'll never stop explaining the reasons for doing it!. A Wynne (female) married a Willson (male) a couple of generations ago and, no doubt, insisted on nominal representation at the altar.

"Nobody will ever spell it correctly; and often it is written in incorrect sequence. This is unsurprising, with two 'Ws', three 'Ns' and two 'Ls'; Wyn F. Wilson Michael is not infrequently received through the mail.

"A hyphenated name will, probably, be too long to fit on a driver's license, credit card and other identification papers. Worst of all, each year, as a new computer operator at the IRS records your vital statistics, she or he will display ingenuity by spelling your name the way he, or she, thinks it should be spelled. As this, most likely, bears no resemblance to your correct name, the real fun starts.

"Letters and phone calls start coming in with regularity from the IRS, each with a name variation stating that you owe thousands of dollars and that you have, apparently, not paid Uncle Sam since 1966!

"I wouldn't change my name for anything because I've fought for its accuracy for so long and, as my headmaster said to me years ago, 'Boy! You bear an honored name, smarten up!'

"However, I do give thanks that I was not blessed with two hyphens in my last name at birth, like some were in the U K back then! One Old Radleian was blessed with the moniker, Cedric Hammond-Chambers-Borgnis! (The last name, of course, was pronounced 'Borny'!)"

Jan Hanley (See Book I)

April 1987, The Boston Globe.

"Of the many disadvantages of having a name such as mine, one tiresome and wasteful one is that in almost every mail delivered to us, there are usually several duplicated catalogs...one to Wynne and the other to Willson and, frequently, three with different variations of our name. The appalling waste of paper, wood pulp, let alone money defies imagination.

Now that our lives have been made so much simpler (?), more accurate (?) and better (?) with computer devices, you should know how brilliantly they react when faced with my name on an address. I am, and have been I promise; Wilson, Michael Wynne with any variation of ns, I am Waynewilson; Wilson; F. Mikal; M Wilson-win; Wilson F. Michaels and, perhaps the most interesting of all, the Chinese version, M. Wilson F. Wy!

Let's face it, on an address I'm a mess and am, just about always, last in line! Not to worry though, as long as I'm around, I'll always be: M.F.W-W with 2Ls, 3Ns, 2Ws, and a hyphen!

In retrospect and looking through Annie's photograph albums for photos to insert here, I came across this one of Jan Hanley, taken at our home in Westwood...by Anne I might add! Hanley was her surname at the time. Those who may have read my first memoir may remember her and how my late wife and I met and how she allowed, frequently, that she made the *world's worst* bologna sandwiches! We have been friends for years, even tho' she lives in St. Croix and is a hopeless communicator, and if I didn't have a photo of her in this book I'd never hear the end of it. So! Here it is!

EIGHT
1986-1989

Just about the first thing I remember about this year was shocking. Annie and I were driving, sadly, to be at Kitty Clark's funeral in Hamilton. You may remember Kitty and Tim Clark our neighbors on Bridge St. in Hamilton who were good friends to us 'way back in '48 and the '50s/'60s at Mendip Cottage. For some forgotten reason we drove there, listening to the radio, via a place called Lynn on the sea north of Boston. As we were driving along the road next to the beach, the next thing we knew was that we were listening to the Cape Canaveral blast off of the Challenger spacecraft. You remember the rest, no doubt. It was January 28th, and this was a long and disturbing stop, a sad day indeed and a memorable one for our country.

In February, our dear and longtime friend from St. George's, Marge Wheeler, suffered a leg amputation in a Newport, R I hospital. Her husband, the late George Wheeler, had coached me when at S G in 1936! Ever since then both of them had been close and dear friends. After George died, Annie became very close and devoted to Marge and kept a close eye on her through countless tough, medical, problems; many due to her long, but eventually discontinued, battle with smoking. Many was the time we drove down to Newport hospital to check on her and, invariably, she would be cheerful and showed incredible guts. As I wrote before, she and her husband and his father before him were pillars of S G for years and were beloved by dozens of classes over the years. Their circle of friends and admirers was akin to a ripple from a stone, ever enlarging, as well it deserved to be.

May was a miserable month, too. My old and admired friend, Wallace Pierce died. As boss of S.S. Pierce, Fine Grocers, he helped me beyond measure when we started making marmalade and other products when we got to Hamilton in 1948! What fun he was and a very real gentleman! It was he who let his friend, Lord Palmer, know that a young marmalade-maker was coming to England who wanted to know how Bath Chocolate Olivers, the best biscuits ever created in his humble estimation, could be imported to the USA! This resulted in my being given an extra special tour of Huntley and Palmers famous biscuit factory in Reading (naturally pronounced there as Redding!)! Sadly, other than being able to buy them for ourselves, in very small quantity due to expense, we were never able to bring them in in quantity as we'd hoped. Fortnum & Masons in London stock them we found not so long ago, but take a few 'quid' along if you want to pick up some. They are not cheap!!

Speaking of Wally, he was always thinking of useful and helpful things for us to do! One time he had invited Mme Bollinger to Boston, owner of the famous French champagne bottlers that bears her name. For some reason, he insisted that I meet her, too, though why, heaven knows for we sure weren't in her league for dinnertime drinking! When I met her, but briefly, I asked a dumb question:

"Why, Madame, do you have so many bubbles in your champagne bottles?

"Ah! Michelle", she replied in her delightful accent, "so that you Americains can spend more time stirring OUT the bubbells!" I should add that it was around this time that many jewelers and specialty shops were selling silver and gold swizzle sticks, as it was deemed socially chic to remove the bubbles in those days!

Next came my dear friend, Anne Doerr, whom I mentioned when writing about my non-productive visit to Wayzata and Minneapolis for The Registry, and what a great help she was. We had a good chat with her on the night of May 24th. She died, suddenly, the following day. What a shock that was.

Prince Charles and Princess Diana were married on July 23rd., to write about cheerier things! Annie and I left for England a few days later and picked up a car and drove directly to Norfolk. Now, I don't know about you, but I am constantly amazed at how those flying either way across the Atlantic are allowed to get straight into a car and start driving, often with no clue about the workings of what they're in, nor of which side of the road is the best side on which to drive! On this particular trip, we hired a car at Heathrow and I, as usual, 'because I've been doing this for years and am SO used to driving on the *wrong* side'; took off aiming for the big road, then under construction, heading roughly northeast towards Cambridge and/or Norwich. Traffic, usually bedlam at that hour of the morning, was that and more and, because I was so used to knowing where I was going, headed straightway on the M number whatever it was. After driving for about 20 minutes with everything passing us at about 90 mph. on the wrong side, naturally, my dear bride, quietly and inconspicuously, as always, mentioned that she'd just seen a sign for Guilford and she'd been there before and thought it was on the way southwest opposite to where we were headed. This, of course, I found nigh on impossible to believe, BUT! It was an even quieter ride thereafter, for 16 miles anyway as we retraced our steps!

Eventually, we got to Melton Constable in Norfolk though how I'm not too sure! Annie had been awake since we left Boston, when we had our minor discussion as to whether, or not, I was going northeast or southwest after starting from Heathrow! Added to our problems, the M road as they're called in England on which we hoped to be traveling, wasn't by any means completed and that complicated my life more than somewhat, as Annie was sleeping soundly on my left hand side in the *passenger's* seat and being no help at all! On arrival we stayed with a dear couple, the Diggens, who spoiled us and, among other things, took us horse racing at Newmarket where Princess Anne was riding. She was much smaller than we thought! It was with Bridget Diggens, by the way, to whom I spoke constantly making bookings, via 'phone from Westwood, when I started to work with Peter Ansdell and C, C & F. Happily the four of us, that included her husband David christened by me as 'The Lodger', have remained good friends ever since although our paths have crossed all too seldom.

While there I drove Annie down to Little Snoring, a name you might just remember from Book I. My late wife and I had rented the most charming, old-world cottage there in which we lived when I was stationed at RAF station, West Raynham, with my squadron at the Central Fighter Establishment just after WW2. Strangely, I could barely recognize it due to the fact that in the intervening 40+ years everything had grown up around it so much! The aerodrome nearby, on which we used to drive around at night then shooting rabbits to increase the food supply, I hardly recognized at all, even though small single-engine private planes still flew from there. By the way, the adjoining village, in rather typically English fashion, is known, or was then known, as Great Snoring, not Big!

From Norfolk, we then retraced our steps and on to my sister Betsy's and Harry's house at the Glebe close to the Long Man near the beautiful village of Wilmington south of the Sussex Downs. En route we passed Lakenheath air force base that is practically on the main road! We stopped here to watch American fighters, and bombers as far as I can remember, taking off...in peacetime for a nice change, but awe-inspiring nevertheless! It is one of the big aerodromes in England allocated to the USAF. After a happy time with my sister and her husband for a night, or two, we drove to see Robin, my nephew and his wife at Plaistow. We even went shopping in Guilford by which we had driven days before, just to make Annie happy!

In about 1934, or '35, Betsy and I crossed the Irish Sea from Fishgard to Cork overnight in a super, though very small, cross-channel 'liner'. I think it was called the M V "Ballybunnion", but am suffering from a Senior Moment on that one! Anyway, this time we flew from Heathrow to Shannon and it wasn't half as much fun! On arrival we picked up a car and drove to Drumoland Castle nearby for lunch.

After fortifying ourselves well, we drove three hours to Enniscoe House near Crossmolina on the northwest coast. I'm tossing in the names because I think they are so delightful, as is the countryside. Here we met up with the 'Four Old Bags' that A and I would drive all over the place! It was one of them, Bodine Lamont, who wished to be called that, by the way, and insisted upon it! I'd never have dared to be that rude! We had gotten to know Bo better since we first met her in 1984 and thereafter with Jackie and C S Lee on Vinalhaven. She is a most interesting and well-read lady who recently wrote her own memoir, and we have enjoyed several trips with her abroad. We have also frequently had the pleasure of staying at her two adjacent houses on that island. One has a view of the sea and coast, which blows the mind each time we see it.

She rented the cottage adjoining Enniscoe, and Anne and I and the 'Old Bags' were there with her. Additionally, there were Helen Wheelwright, a charming, slightly myopic friend of Bo's from VT and CA; Ann McNulty another friend of Bo's and Dorothy Howard from North Haven. Also, there were Bo's son, Sandy Lieber, and his wife Curly who rented Enniscoe, with their great chums, Kathy and Ken White, plus children, At that time the Liebers and Whites were living close to each other in New Haven, CT, and they joined up with us at the end of our tour before we flew home to Boston from Shannon. All told, it was a most amusing and cheerful junket with good friends through wonderful scenery. Annie and I greatly enjoyed 'pushing the Old Bags around' and there were few dull moments and we were only away from home for 16 days.

Due to the Cottage business, the Rizers and Henry Doerr, whose wife sadly died so suddenly, decided to rent a lovely cottage from me near Goring-on-Thames at the end of September. This was on the proviso that Annie and I joined them as their guides and then took them around some of our favorite haunts in the Cotswolds. What a chore! As you can guess, we didn't take much persuading and we were off again. I won't bore you, I hope, with our itinerary again, but suffice to say Henry drove all the time which kept him busy under the circumstances, which was fine for Annie and me who were able to show them some favorite stopping places en route. There was The Palace at Wells and the Cathedral next door where we found the painting and burial place of my Uncle Basil. Then we drove to Radley College near Oxford, where I was during my 'formative years' of 1933 to 1936, prior to going as an Exchange Student to St. George's. There was a RAF station at Kemble that we passed that had a full scale Gloster Meteor jet as a station symbol at the entrance, at which of course we had to stop and look! Quite incorrectly, but most pleasantly, Dean Rizer was determined to believe that, as I flew one in WW2, this was my very own 'personal' one and, wherever he went thereafter, always referred to it that way! At first I was horrified...just a little...but eventually got used to it and decided to leave it all where he wanted it! Let's face it. It'd have been most rude to contradict such an eminent physician! As a finale to the journey we had a 'cruise down the Thames in a rented motor cruiser and a big gathering of my family at the lovely rented house we had, owned by Lady Anderson, the wife of Prime Minister Winston Churchill's Chancellor of the Exchequer during WW2. You can tell why I was tickled to bits to have started C, C and F sometime before, can't you? Tough life!

"My" Gloster Meteor Jet—
According to Dean Rizer!

The year of 1987 was not, one way and another, the best of many. Dear friends left us, sad to say. However, a couple of things bear mention, perhaps. Annie upped and left Talbots in May. Her back, never strong by any means, started to give out from working on a thinly carpeted cement floor so, sensibly, she quit particularly as we seemed to be making some sense with my ever-growing Appraisers' Registry business.

As I said a minute ago, among the departures of friends, three were very special to me. The first was 'Aunt' Bea Merrick, 'Uncle' Vaughan's wife. You may remember that he was my Headmaster at St. George's, a gentleman whom I admired greatly and to whom I was devoted along with Bea for many, many years. I was most honored by her daughter, Little Bea, who asked me to read the lesson at her Mum's service at a church hard by her home in Matunuck, R I. Secondly, there was John Taylor who, together with his cousin and my chum, Dave Taylor, was running the Boston Globe. John and Dave were among the first to help my late wife and me at the start of our Marmalade business in 1948! Finally, there was Dolly Sawyer who, with her husband Dantan, rented Jackie and me our very first home in Hamilton, MA. in '48 and, later, found us our second, Mendip Cottage and, later again, sold us their lovely house, also in Hamilton!

On October 19th, 1987, many will, most likely, remember that the Stock Market did a spectacular dance and dropped considerably. At that time, we were staying on Nantucket with Steve and Susan O'Brien and they and Anne had just come in from scalloping. I, for some reason, had decided not to join them. Anyway, I had the radio on and was vaguely, but vaguely, listening to the news after the Market closed. I've never been one to listen too closely to the ups and downs of this, as you may have gathered from previous, obvious and dreary reasons, so I didn't take much notice that there'd been, for all intents and purposes, a major crash!

When they came in, I happened to say in a bit of an offhand manner to my close chum, Steve, a man well aware of, and highly competent in, the world of finance, "It seems there's been a lot of fuss on the Market today and a lot of misery seems to have set in. I guess it dropped something like 500 points."

Now, I've known Steve for many a year and have seen him blush, on occasion, but I had never seen him go white as milk before, nor move to the 'phone more quickly! An hour or so later at about cocktail time, he returned and had what he needed and were they ever stiff ones! I was left with the acute feeling that I didn't make him aware of the news too thoughtfully, I'm afraid! Now I come to think of it, the reason we were there was to celebrate his birthday. Some present!

Finally, in 1988, my sister Betty and her husband flew in for Christmas on 12:19, followed by #1 and only dear son, Mark, from Reno. All had left by December 28th. However, the only notation I can find about it in either Anne's, or my, records, is Anne's to the effect that she served 107 meals in two weeks starting on the 19th!

Anyway, we were still in Westwood with me working hard at The Appraisers' Registry and C, C & F, with the latter taking more time than it should have done, really, for the income it produced after all was said and done. Annie was giving much time to her volunteer work at Mass General and the Vincent Club and Radley, our Yorkie, was becoming more spoiled and adorable by the day!.

On Jan 11th '89 Bodine came to stay and the next day we three flew off to Miami and on to Quito, capital of Ecuador. I'd managed to have awful 'flu for a day, or two, prior to leaving and there was really some doubt as to whether, or not, I'd be able to go. All was well however, though it probably didn't help much with what follows! As many may have experienced, when we disembarked from our Eastern Airlines flight, I began to feel like death with the worst headache I'd had in years, as did Anne. Why? I'd quite forgotten that we were 9,000 feet higher than at Miami and that was playing havoc with our sinuses, as it does to most people I found. It didn't take too long to become acclimated, however, and off we went by bus to the Otavalo market, one of, if not the largest and most colorful markets in South America. It was an eye-opening and fascinating experience and one that gave us, promptly, a good look at the bright and interesting people who live in the countryside there.

Susan And Steve O'Brien on Barbuda

Bodine Lamont

Soon we found ourselves on a bus again, passing through exciting, mountainous country, en route to Guayaquil, pronounced phonetically 'Wyakeel', which, of course, you knew! This took three nights, I think, with stops en route at small hotels and Guayaquil must have been the hottest place on earth! On the next day, the 17th, we flew off due west over the Pacific for six hundred miles to the Galapagos Islands. This was about a two hour flight and then we landed on a tiny strip on the Island of Baltra, with only about one building thereon, and were immediately transferred to a small most comfy ship named The Isabella II. She accommodated 34 passengers and was to be home for only 20 of us for the next seven days as we explored this incredible group of islands made famous by Darwin in the mid 1830s.

It is not my intent to tell you all about what we saw and did on this journey. That is for others far more versed in it all than I, but do seek some information yourselves, please. Suffice to say, I really wasn't all that keen to go originally though why I'm not really too sure. I could not have been more off base, however. I/we loved every single minute of it. The warm and tropical climate; the literally unique birds; tortoises, iguanas, huge turtles and other animals of land and sea; the flowers and people, they all left a lasting impression on me and I so hope that if you have never been, and get the chance, do go. At one island we visited, Annie and I swam around with some seals, tickling their tummies that they seemed to enjoy! It's a heck of a long way to get there from here, but oh! so very worth while, and I wish we had the ability to show you all our photos and slides. Such color!

On leaving the airstrip at Baltra again, we flew back to Guayaquil, the port for Ecuador, and then on to Quito and Miami. The reason we were made to take a bus to do the Quito to Quayaquil leg at the start was, we understood, due to the wish of the moderately financially strapped Ecuador government's effort to gain some tourist income by having us stop at pleasant hotels en route and, of course, do some shopping! Annie did her fair share, unsurprisingly! As an antique flier, I was most interested to notice that, for a runway near the port, I saw fighter aircraft tethered along the side of the straight main road! Never a dull moment for those pilots! We got home to Westwood on the 26th, immediately picked up Radles from Elsie at her kennel where she spoils her guests so well, and on the 1st of February it was a near record 66 degrees F. On the 3rd. there was an ice-storm. Welcome home to New England!

Annie worked mightily then for sundry causes, one of which was the Vincent Club in Boston. Every year the club puts on a theatrical show and makes much money for the hospital of that name within Mass General, not only via the show but, also, by selling advertisements in the large program. This year the powers that be at Firestone & Parson, legendary Jewelers of Boston, had her photographed drenched in jewelry for their full-page ad:! They could have made no less appropriate a choice, for this girl is insane about the stuff...ask any friend of hers and they'll agree! For the ad: she was arrayed in $300,000 worth of baubles, and things haven't been the same since...if you get the picture! I have to say, however, and without bias, that if anyone should wear jewelry, Annie should; but then, she could have married a yacht just as easily as a rowboat!

In July, we faced a considerable sadness as Bettee, i e Betty St. Laurent, our right arm at Mendip Cottage where we lived from 1949 to 1965, died quite suddenly and at far too young an age and was buried near her and her husband, Charlie's, home in Ipswich. The day after, I flew out to Wyoming where I met Mark in Jackson Hole for a five-day boy's toot. It is not often that he and I have had such an opportunity, but it was great as we toured the perfect scenery there and went all through Yellowstone together. Mark flew to meet me from the house he'd built in Reno near where he works. It has a great view over the city and he is near where he can enjoy his greatest enjoyments, climbing and skiing. In doing both, Annie and I are convinced that he is fearless and loves to live dangerously! In so many ways I am proud of him, not the least for starting at rock bottom of his company in Las Vegas, which has a franchise with Circus Circus casinos in Vegas and Reno, and is now holding a managerial position in the latter city. We had such fun together, but our time together was all too short, for me anyway!

Another happy time we had this year was a return to the Maritimes and Bodine joined us again. We drove all the way, starting on the car ferry, Scotia Prince, from Portland, ME across to Yarmouth N S and then on northwest to Greenwood A F B in the heart of the Annapolis Valley. It was here that I was stationed 'on a rest' while in the RAF in '43 for a while. How it had all changed and for the worst, I thought. I could barely find anything that I recognized and this was proof to me that, perhaps, one should think twice about going back to places one thinks one remembers from long ago! Anyway, we had a great drive through the provinces of Prince Edward Island and New Brunswick staying at delightful and colorful places that our good travel agent, Mary Wyman, had set up for us in advance. One thing which struck me most forcibly was how very much alike the Cabot Trail on the western shore of N S is to the comparable Scottish coast. We returned home all the way by land via the Fundy National Park and President Roosevelt's summer home at Campobello then down along the rugged coast of Maine. A trip well worth the taking we all felt.

It should be mentioned that Radley, our Yorkie, was with us all the way! It was hectic at the start because we found that we were not allowed to have him with us in our cabin sailing by night from Portland to Yarmouth! Disaster! How could we possibly leave him in the car which seemed like miles away from us in the bowels of the ship along with hundreds of others and, we assumed, in pitch darkness with the ship rolling viciously? Let's face it, he'd never been to sea before! Torn apart be misgiving, all we could do was leave him there and spend the night worrying about him and nursing a feeling of acute guilt! Not to worry, he was fine when I eventually found the car with him peering out of the windows as he had been, I bet, for five hours or so. What a good dog and what relief for us!

At the end of the year '89, during which we suffered 20 days with temperatures above 90 degrees F, I flew back to the U K to go, for the first time ever, to my old school, Radley's, annual 'Old Boys' (Alumni) Dinner in London. I'd often thought of going, and wanted to, but this time my nephew, Robin, who went there too, persuaded me that it was high time I made the effort. So glad that I did! I met many good friends of my 'era' ('33 to '36) who, at least, made it look and sound as if they remembered me, and it was high nostalgia standing to drink a toast 'To H M The Queen, God bless her' and then sing the National Anthem! It made me wish, at that time, that we in the U S had a bit more patriotism going for us. I felt that that had been lacking for much too long. In all I was there working and playing for ten days and was happy to be there for my great-nephew Edward's 20th birthday celebration, which made two great occasions for me to enjoy!

NINE
A SPANKING NEW DECADE! 1990 - 1995

Not that this was all that important! The media made a big fuss about it, but things seemed to go on much as usual. My Registry and C, C & F were proceeding nicely and kept me busy and occupied. The thought of retiring, as I was 71 at the time, never crossed my mind. I doubt if I could have afforded it, indeed I know darn' well that I couldn't for one thing and still do the things that Annie and I wanted to do, such as travel and to learn from each exciting experience. More good friends of mine had lurched into retirement at 60 to 65 and looked to me as if they'd rapidly become bored, not only of themselves but, also, a bit boring to their nearests and dearests as they were constantly underfoot when not on the golf course. Now that we have so many ladies who are in business and becoming high up in their chosen professions, I shall be most interested to see how they will take to retirement, and their spouses to them, should that be a fact of life! So far, I have seen and heard little of this in the media, surprisingly, but I have a feeling that they will continue to be most involved, one way and another, don't you?

After our regular stay at Coco Point Lodge in Barbuda for a few "glorious days and fun-filled nights," as the brochures say, and as usual around Easter-time, we flew off to Denver in May with Latimer, sometimes called Tim, Gray and his wife Judy to Denver, and drove to Colorado Springs for their daughter Margot's graduation. Suffice to say we so enjoyed that experience and meeting a special group of Margot's friends and it was, indeed, like a breath of spring! I had always wanted to see that beautiful part of the country and Tim and Judy showed us just the way to do that beautifully!

Parting company with J and T, Annie and I went for a night or two at the Broadmoor Hotel and then flew to Calgary where we rented a car and drove to Banff. This was the start of a more than special scenic drive, as it always seems to be, through the Rockies to Lake Louise and on to Jasper, stopping at the Columbia Ice Fields. Frankly, my mind and sight were boggled at what we beheld in the way of scenery, as this was my first visit to anything like it. The closest I'd ever come was to the comparatively flat Jura mountain range in France in 1946/7 and a view of the Alps in the distance.

After a good look at Jasper and the scenery around it from the top of a nearby mountain, we boarded a train for an overnight ride to

Vancouver. This was something that had been on my wish list for years and, luckily, we were able to fulfill it. We had a sleeper cabin built for two but not as you'd notice it and, due to frequent stops, 'sleeper' was a ridiculous exaggeration! Additionally, we had seats in the carriage that had a glass dome for a roof. This enabled us to admire the scenery for several hours before darkness and, again, in the early morning as we descended into Vancouver from Kamloops. The inclusion of that town's name is utterly superfluous, under the circumstances, but I love the name so, I just had to include it! If you ever get the opportunity to take a trip from Calgary to Vancouver, do take it, please! I gather that the train service has improved tremendously, so that will make it just that much better.

Just to continue this travelogue for a minute, in Vancouver we stayed at the Wedgewood Hotel which we found by recommendation and it was delightful in every way, as well as being centrally situated. A steamer ferry to Victoria Island followed so that we could see the Busch Gardens and, of course, have tea at the Empress Hotel. Why 'of course'? Because everyone who is anyone does, we were told. What a bunch of sheep we are!

Actually, we bought a good deal more than tea! On our way through Canada and at the Banff Hotel, we happened across some truly beautiful and striking bird and animal sculpture by a most talented artist by the name of Lyle Sopel. We were so impressed with this unique talent that we did something we hardly ever did...we bought one at his studio which we visited in Vancouver! Happily, he was there and kindly took us all through so that we could see the complete process, from large rock of dark green jade unique to north-western Canada to the delicate carving. What's more, we even blew it and bought another one at the Empress hotel! Annie would tell you that I was having a minor fit about doing anything so wanton as buying TWO pieces of sculpture ever, let alone within a few days of each other...but this was minor compared to some I've thrown!

Speaking of fits brought about by finance, it brings to mind a bit I wrote about around then for use on the radio. This one was called, 'WORRY ABOUT MONEY!'

"What on earth is there about old prunes like me that has so darn' many of us worrying about money and its use? During most of my life, I've noticed that those of us when we pass 65 start, if not sooner, to panic about the lack, or the possibility of running out, of the stuff. I noticed it about fifty years ago in others and now I am 'into' it, with bells on, so my dear and younger wife tells me!

"I think it a maddening habit and it has become such a regular one that I can well-understand how it could drive anyone around the bend who is closely involved. Like peanuts, it is a hard nut to break, I find, and I really don't know why. Many others I know, that are of about my vintage, seem to notice everything relative to the dollar and its expenditure. We flap if the price has gone up, which it always has; whether or not advantage was taken of every sale of everything, discount, two-for, or free sample, whether needed, or not. We stew, or at least I'm prone to, if a tap has been left dripping, if lights, heater, or computer have not been extinguished at most moments of non-use, or if soap has been left to disintegrate in a sink or bathtub! It is a malaise of which I am anything but proud and, frankly, it infuriates me and always has done, so goodness only knows what effect it must have on others!'

"Speaking personally, I like to think I have my own answer to this problem. That is that during WW2 in the U K, everything, but everything, was in the shortest supply. Everything had to last 'til it wasn't any more. I remember always attaching silver foil to the bottom of a bar of soap, which increased its life greatly; squeezing and flattening a tube of toothpaste 'til nothing could come out at all and, of course, saving everything and never throwing anything away which was reusable. I think this introduced me to the problem now, but watching and hearing about family members of others who are getting on, it seems, almost, a universal one. So often, it is quite an unnecessary trait. Let's hope I can lose it, in moderation, p d q!"

While I'm at it, I think I'll drop in another radio spot I wrote and broadcast entitled:

"...AND MUCH, MUCH MORE"

"What is there about us that, apparently, we can never get enough of anything? In recent years in most advertising that we see and hear, just about everything has the suffix...'and much, much more'! What on earth this 'more' business is, is left to our imagination, probably because the writer has drawn from every superlative about which he, or she, can think but is still driven to extol the virtue and necessity of whatever is being advertised. Glance at your paper, or blink at your TV screen, and I'm fairly sure you'll see to what I refer.

For instance, this caught my eye because of the trip my ma-in-law took us on the B A Concorde ages ago which was a fascinating and exciting experience...and much, much, more! It starts with 'WORLD'S MOST LUXURIOUS PLANE'. Now, really! By any stretch of the imagination, few could agree. The seats are minute and, probably, have less sitting space than any commercial airliner flying today, 'except for American Eagle ', said he from experience! This goes for the cabin windows, too. The seating is 'two either side of the aisle', the aisle being so narrow that passing an attractive flight attendant en route to the john is liable, perhaps, to become a too adjacent, if not an intimate, experience.

The ad: continues, 'You'll savor the Five Star gourmet fare set before you with impeccable service'. Now really, again! Five Star? I thought that Four Star in the Guide Michelin was for food that is unbeatable, but 5 star for a lap-served repast that was good, very good for what it was...no way!"

'CONCORDE PILOTS IN ACTION INSIDE THE COCKPIT'

...is the next lead.

The ad: says, "Fly London to New York at twice the speed of sound...and much, much more!"

Now let's get back to normal...and much, much more!

It was in October that I went to England on C C & F business taking Annie with me. One of the couples from whom we rented were the Laycocks, who had several. In this instance, I rented The Rose & Crown House on the main street of Chipping Camden where I planned, again, to invite as many cottage-renting agents who'd care to come and discuss plans and problems. It used, in years gone by, to have been a pub and had among others, a large and well-furnished Hall/Living room that was ideal for our meeting. Quite a few who rented not only cottages but castles and flats and cars, did come from all over the country happily, but as usual and sad to say, nothing too constructive and earth-shattering came of it. The many differing ways in which the English ran their rental businesses seemed, to me anyway, why we were unable to start any unified method of managing trans-Atlantic rental practices. As a result, we had to continue individual dealings with all involved until I, later, sold this business to another to run it.

1991 started off with a sizeable bang! Annie became 50 on Feb. 6ᵗʰ, that many refused to believe, and her mother was determined to give her a good half-century send-off at The Country Club near that date.! This she did in fine style though somewhat against Anne's wishes. She allowed she didn't like people making a fuss over her, as usual. However, Peggy and good sense prevailed and it was great fun! Many of her closest friends and admirers were there. Many from the Vincent Club were there to wish her well and great dancing music was supplied by Eddie Madden and his band who has played for that club for years and years and who never looks a day older!

In June we went to Glacier National Park for a week's holiday and picked up my son, Mark, en route. After saying good-bye to Mark who flew home, we drove to Kalispell and on down the Bitterroot Valley for a couple of nights at Triple Creek Lodge. We found this lovely and comfortable spot through the pages and excellent advice of Andrew Harper's travel bible, 'The Hideaway Report', that we have taken for years and have never, ever, been misled and we've given it tremendous and regular usage!

On to Yellowstone we drove and then to Teton Pines near Wilson, Wyoming. Wilson is just a few miles from Jackson Hole and while at the Teton Pines, another Hideaway spot, I found a wooden box full of special candies awaiting us, which we demolished in no time. They were so good, in fact, that I thought that they would be a good and unusual gift for my appraisers in the Registry come Christmas, so made a note to call the company later in the year to order. This I did, and that is how we came to know 1/800 Sue!

1/800-Sue was the name Anne christened the most charming and helpful lady who coped with me on the 'phone when I started, continued and finally ordered what I needed! I must say that the calls were numerous, probably more than were really necessary due to the fact that 1/800-Sue and I had great fun on the 'phone and, besides, the calls didn't cost me anything! Her name really was Sue Thompson who, I soon discovered, had a young son, Conor by name. The candies were a huge success at Christmas, I heard afterwards, so I continued to call once in awhile thereafter to see how things were going. One day, much later, we got a call from Sue saying that she was coming to New York for a Candy Convention. Whereupon I suggested that Annie and I go down to meet her as we all felt we knew each other by that time! In the event, we did and the three of us had a great dinner together with never a dull moment! Several years later and now working for Boise Cascade, and living in Idaho, she allowed that she was coming to Massachusetts, again on business, and asked if we could get together again. "Why not?"

we replied, "come and stay a night or two with us and we'll show you around our neighborhood." Along she came and off we went on a tour of the North Shore on a miserable, foggy, day including Manchester-by-the-Sea. Here she solemnly got out of the car and photographed the sea, or what she thought must have been the sea, but couldn't see, due to the fog! That was her very first view of something that we, perhaps, take shockingly for granted here I fear!

Goodness knows how many years Annie and I have enjoyed 1/800-Sue now, but we still communicate regularly by email and we both hope that it won't be too long before we see her cheery face again and, perhaps, meet Conor!

Sue And Conor of 1-800-Sue
Photo from a photo booth

Why did I tell you all this? Because you never know where, or when, you're going to find a dear friend on the other end of the horn! If it hadn't been for a box of candies we'd never have met. If I hadn't been courageous and extroverted as usual, I'd never have dared to suggest to Annie that we both go to the Big Apple to meet her! C'est la vie!

I have a feeling that, somehow or other, I have barely mentioned Julia Price. I think you should meet her now because she's been quite a part of our lives for ages. Julia is the only daughter of Martin and Caroline Price and it is they who have managed Coco Point so well and which I mentioned a page, or so, ago. We had a couple of years there before they came, but we got to know Julia and her brother Nick when their parents took over when they were very young and came out for holidays from England to be with them.

One year when Anne and I were there, Julia told us that she had decided to come to New England and be with friends in Boston and work here for a while. Quite a decision for a young teenaged girl, I thought! In the event, she came several years ago now, and found that a. she didn't have the job she thought she was coming to and b. didn't have a green card which she thought she could get so that she could work! Somewhat naturally, we'd said to her that we'd love to see her when she did come, so one day we received a call from her describing her woes and problems! Ever since then we have, most happily, referred to her as our 'surrogate daughter'! We lived through many of her happy times at an apartment with other girl-friends in Boston and helped whenever we could with the occasional meal and were delighted when she told us that she'd met and become engaged to a young man by the name of Chip Kern, whose family live in Connecticut.

To cut a long, and for us an important and never dull story short, Julia and Chip were married in Connecticut on July 20th of this year. Guests came from far and wide as expected and it was, without doubt, the hottest day I ever remember! It was 104 degrees! Julia's family and the Stringers, all six of them great chums from the U K, came which was great for Anne and me as we'd gotten to know and enjoy them all so much over the years at Coco Point. Their wedding was a great Anglo-American celebration in every way, in spite of the heat! My wife had a fit when I snuck off quite a while after the ceremony, and took off my coat and tie and put on my swimming trunks, which were suitably long and baggy for the occasion! It was either that or expiring, and many thereafter followed suit I'm relieved to say! (No pun intended.) Mercifully the generous family who enabled Jules to have the affair on their property, Jeff and Holly Ridgeway, with the Union Jack and Old

Glory much in evidence, had a big swimming pool thereon. As Julia, who had done all the planning and made all the arrangements herself, because she was away from her parents who had to be at Coco Point, had a 'hot' calypso band for dancing it can be understood that the pool became an essential part of the proceedings whether, or not, the later dunkings were planned, or just happened! It really was one of the best weddings in years! Ever since then we've been in constant touch with Jules and Chip who we now look upon as part of the family, so you'll be meeting them often, I suspect, as this odd pilgrimage continues!

I mentioned Holly Ridgeway just now. She has the dearest sister, Kitty, a close friend of Julia's and ours with her husband Jerry. Holly and Kitty's parents we've known and admired for ages! Hope Ford died in 2002 most sadly. Russell charges on regardless. He is much much younger than I am (three years, maybe) and is a fine exhibit of a true friend and Anglo-American.

We woke up to snow on Thanksgiving Day for the first time in 51 years, and were not surprised to find out that we were living through the coldest December in history.

Chip, Ben, Will And Julia Kern

Courtesy of Harding Glidden

Perhaps it is time for a check-up on what's going on with our family and where. The family in Westwood is comprised of Anne and me and, of course, Radley. Just about every day, he and I would go for a walk 'around the block' which takes in about two thirds of a mile, or else go to the lovely and spacious Hale Reservation which entails a walk of about two miles, or more. Most of the time, Radles takes me and stops at his predetermined places on the way around. Invariably, one or two neighbors stop to talk to me or, more accurately, to Radley—and he graciously gives them a few moments of his attention, always leaving them feeling happier and friendlier than before. He's about 56 dog years old now and invariably pays more attention to much younger, feminine, four and two legs than you would expect. Somewhat like his owner relative to the latter, some might suggest! He, Radley that is, does seem to be aging a bit though, and his eyesight and hearing seem to be beginning to fail a little, but not enough to cause too much concern, thank heaven. His carer, Elsie Wood, looks after him when we go away, but he loves her dearly so that's fine and, happily, the feeling's more than mutual!

Anne seems to be as busy, as always, doing good works voluntarily and, generally, running an excellent show here at home for us 'men' with the occasional dinner party to keep posted as to what's going on around us! Mark is working away, as he has done for years, for the small company that is associated with Circus Circus in Reno and seems to be happy with his life and progress as we are, certainly. Most of his spare time, which appears to me not to be too excessive, he spends either skiing or mountain climbing according to the season and usually dangerously! Like a fairly typical old father, I don't think I see enough of him, which is about twice a year at the most, but I have no cause to complain, though I do! He flies home every Christmas and keeps in good touch by 'phone etc. so I am lucky and have much for which to be grateful to him. He is a fine young man, great with Anne and me and I am most proud of him. I have a sneaking suspicion this may be repetitious but he deserves a double dose, anyway!

As far as 'business' goes, this is what's still happening. My Appraisers' Registry is going along well and referrals come in with regularity from the New England insurance companies who know about us and have had great confidence in us. I know this sounds a bit horn-blowing, but we are told we're the best in the business, so once in awhile it doesn't hurt to say so, does it?

Castles, Cottages and Flats is beginning to be a bit much with which to cope. Why you may ask? Because I run it myself without assistance and the 'phone and/or fax rings from 4 A M with people from the U K and, occasionally from France and Italy, wanting information or confirming/questioning bookings that are in the process of being made. Then in the evening hours the same is true from those in Hawaii and California, so sleep is short lived to say the least! This being so and with Anne wondering when, if ever, she'll see me for more than a gulped meal, I started to think about trying to find a buyer. Just for a change I'd never been busier, but due to the small mark up that I, the middleman, could add I wasn't making enough money really to make the extreme effort worthwhile. Happily, such a person was found with the help of a longtime friend and insurance agent by the name of Wally Sisson. I'd met him originally back in the Boston Zoological days, and that's a heck of a long time ago! The transition to Sally Potter, the buyer, was comparatively easy and was helped considerably by Julia Price, having worked with her, before her marriage to Chip, for some time in Boston.

I see from Annie's diary...where would I be without it/her?...that on February 28th there was a Needlepoint Kneeler Dedication at our church in Boston, Trinity Church. I remember this well because that dear girl of mine actually made me one that was dedicated on that day. This shook me up a bit when I first learnt that she was doing this for the church and me because I thought that that only happened when one was 6ft: under! No way! I was 'way behind the times as usual! The scene she chose for it was the Portcullis over the moat at the Palace at Wells, where my dear Uncle Basil did his thing as Bishop for many years when I was a kid. Additionally, it shows two swans pulling the cord of the bell that rang so that they'd be fed when hungry., and they still do it, too! Under this needlepoint picture is my name in full and the whole is mounted on a handsome wooden stand. Frankly, it was just typical of Annie to do something as special as this and I'm more than proud of it.

While on the subject of things ecclesiastical, we've been members of Trinity for a while. We started going, fairly regularly, to the church in which we were married in 1978, the Episcopal Church of the Redeemer in Chestnut Hill, a suburb of Boston. Then along came the gas shortage across the country so we switched, to save that commodity, to St. Paul's in Dedham, much nearer our home in Westwood. Here we had a young minister who sounded to me, when he entered carrying his staff at the beginning of the service and addressed the congregation that he had just hung up after having had a merry chat with the Almighty Himself! Let's face it, maybe he had and knew His number, but it all seemed a bit much to me, so we returned to The Redeemer.

After awhile, I was invited to be, and was made, a member of the Vestry. This was an honor but, due to the regular problems of a parish such as this, we got involved in as many as usual and I found it to be both exciting and frustrating at times. One such problem was that it was felt that there was not enough 'togetherness' among the people who did, and could, make use of the church...not a unique problem at all, for sure. To try and overcome the problem, I probably shook the good members of the Vestry to the core by suggesting that we have a dance. We should then toss everyone we could urge to it into a communal jig and supper to boot. Much to my surprise, the idea got going and our friend, Sally Hurlbut, and I were asked to get the show on the road, run it and prove that it could be done! Equally to our surprise, it turned out to be quite a success and, certainly, well attended by a good cross-section of the community. It was fun, too! Not long after this event, my time on the Vestry ended and Annie and I decided that we greatly admired the Vicar of Trinity Church in Copley Square at that time, the Rev. Spencer Rice. Due to my bad hearing, we started to sit right in front, 2nd. row on the right facing the altar, and have been there ever since! Seldom, if ever, had we heard a preacher who could, and did, command the attention of his congregation, which grew on each succeeding Sunday until there wasn't an empty seat available. It was in this year, 1992, that most sadly and for whatever reason, Spencer took his last service at Trinity on June 14th and he, his charming wife Harriett and daughter Gaylord, returned to Washington D C. and the search began for his replacement.

The Kneeler at Trinity

Just before they left, my afore-mentioned chum, Sally, gave a party for them and it was at this evening that we met, for the first time, a man who was to become a good and close friend to us as, we found, he was to half the country! We've never met anyone whom he didn't know! Anyway, he was The Rev. Canon Harold Sedgwick. From now until the day he died in our driveway at Orchard Circle on our way to hear his great friend, Spencer Rice, preach at St Aidens in South Dartmouth, MA, at which he was a locum for the summer, you'll be hearing more about this most interesting of men and his beloved alma mater, Harvard University.

As usual we went to Barbuda around Easter but then our dear, dear, friend, Marge Wheeler who, with her husband George and his family before, had been pillars of St. George's prep: school for ever it seemed, most sadly died and her funeral was held at that chapel on May 24th. I think I've written about Marge in both books, but she was one, great, lady and loved by class upon class over the years at that school, for which she did so much. I had known and admired her for nearly sixty years and Anne had for more than twenty.

I'd like to take you on a trip that Annie and I did this year with my dear and age-old friend, Moody Ayer via a report I wrote about it on our return. It relates to our first journey around the world and it goes like this:

A CHAMPAGNE TRIP ON A BEER INCOME!

When I asked my wife a couple of years ago what would really thrill her for her 50th Birthday present she, with characteristic excitement and hope said, "I think a round-the-world trip would be nice!" "Me, too", I replied, "better refer that to your next, hopefully rich, husband!" Regardless of how excessive that statement of Annie's was, however, it kept on recurring in my mind for the following two years. Let's face it, the idea bugged me in spite of it then being totally beyond the realm of reasonable possibility. For us, it was out of reach, irresponsible, irrational and, for me, irritating although I knew that Anne was only kidding when she said I'd always wanted to go around the world, somehow or other. Why? I'm not too sure, really, except that it is there and I haven't done that and you only go by once! In our 24 years of marriage we have, most luckily, been able to go to Antarctica, to Kenya twice; once to explore a safari service and subsequently to lead a group on one to Kenya and Tanzania and, also, to the Galapagos Islands off Ecuador. To put all this in perspective, you should know that we were usually sponsored on such adventures and funds were recouped by subsequent lectures. Additionally, we save like crazy and sneak off to Barbuda, hard by Antigua, for a few days annually of near paradise and once in a while return to England to see my U K family. From this, you'll gather that we are not your sedate and average stay-at-home couple, even though we think we are in comparison to some of our jet-set acquaintances!

Since 1991, the year my bride cracked fifty, the circular tour idea kept on regurgitating and always with the same symptoms, indigestion! What with a dismal economy and an indecisive business-sale possibility the idea, though gnawing, was regularly dismissed as out of the question. This was discussed, too, with friends and business acquaintances all hoping that their advice would be somewhat positive so that we'd think further about this major expenditure! No way! All said, "Go for it!"; "Get on with it!"; "Do it now or else you never will!"; and of course, "You only go by once, so go!" That, combined with the fact that Hong Kong was due to change hands in 1997, we'd always wanted to see it and my son, Mark, planning to be there in October of this year, did the trick! We would start to plan to go then, on October 10th 1992! We couldn't bill the trip as Anne's 50th birthday celebration, nor that of our 25th anniversary due in 1993. What then should we call it? 'A Champagne Trip on a Beer Income', I suggested, and was it ever!

Some sage once said, or wrote, that the planning of a journey was more than half the fun. He, or she, was right! Knowing that we should maintain a rigid budget, we promptly put that out of our minds and decided that, as it was going to be the trip of our lives, we must 'do it right'! How, only goodness knew, but that was how it had to be! Months before we decided to leave, we started hoarding brochures of hotels, airlines, tours and studying the expertise of potential travel agents. Additionally, we studied the two newsletters published in the States relative to far away places with exotic names that were relatively unknown. Books from libraries and friends relative to the Spice Islands, Indonesia, Malaysia and the Middle East were read avidly...all of which we found fascinating and most educational.

Where should we start? Should we go for a structured tour by a travel agency? Not if possible. However, I had always hoped that we might again enjoy at least a week, or so, on a very small ship which sailed to out-of-the-ordinary destinations. Such a one, I found, was the 'ISLAND EXPLORER' that plied back and forth with a small number of guests between Bali and Kupang in East Timor, calling at some of the Spice Islands between. Why don't we book on that ship, I suggested, for the October 19th sailing from Kupang to Bali, and then build our journey on that?

The travel agent we had selected with care. Mary Wyman, a lady of great experience and a longtime employee of Pan-American Airways during its prime, did the boat reservation for us, so we had a base on which to build. Additionally, she agreed to make all our reservations for us, flights, hotels of our selection and hers, car hires, everything necessary. This made all the difference for today individually planned trips are a rarity. The norm it seems is to join a tour and abide by its pre-designed route and accommodations.

How should we go? We had neither the time nor budget to go by sea to Indonesia so let's fly, we decided. "If we get that far and, probably, will never get there again, why not continue around the world? Perhaps it might be cheaper in the long run," Anne suggested. "With your miserable back, I can't see you flying in the back of the bus to Bali, and certainly not around the globe", I countered, "and I was hoping we could try for Business Class to Bali and back." It was right after I had said that, that our good friend, Moody Ayer, to whom we had spoken about our plan and who we thought might just come with us, called to say that Delta, Singapore Airlines and Swissair had offered a bargain price on a First Class round-the-world fare about which she had just read in 'The Hideaway Report'. Timing is everything, so how could we possibly not take advantage of such a bare-bones offer?! I was beginning to feel like a Las Vegas gambler who had blown his savings yet was determined to continue. "Not to worry, it's only money, 'deah boy", as a Boston *Brahmaid* was wont to say!" Actually, it was our dear friend, Moody Ayer, who said that, so we asked her to come with us and, unbelievably, she said she'd love to! As she was a wee bit convinced that she was *the* world traveler of all time, we really felt quite honored!

So now it seems we are beginning to convince ourselves that not only should we complete a rotation of the earth, but we should do it by traveling First Class in what many consider to be two of the world's best airlines anyway...and it'll be cheaper that way! With that supreme logic in place, we turned our minds to where we should go on this planned circumnavigation and where we should stay if, and when, we got there!

We knew we wanted to go to Hong Kong because Mark was going to be there as I've said and we had booked space out of Kupang in East Timor on the good ship Island Explorer! "I know a couple who live in Singapore. The husband teaches at the American school there, his wife is the daughter of good friends and Singapore looks as if it is in the right direction", Anne allowed. "Great idea!" I agreed, "it has always held a fascination for me, particularly as I had friends who were in the RAF there during WW11 when it was overrun by the Japanese and the Raffles hotel has always had a mystique about it, particularly for an ex-Englishman!" From Singapore to Boston looked like a forever flight, even if it were possible, so where to break the journey on our route home was the next question?

"I've always wanted to see the Taj Mahal at sunset...or is it sunrise?", Anne volunteered. On checking, we found this to be too time-consuming and expensive to take that in, so we dropped that one quickly! Additionally, we found out then that we had to keep going in one direction with no turning back, even though we could make as many stops as we wished within the four weeks we had allowed for this trip.

173

Cairo, Athens and Rome were all realistic stop-offs on the airlines we'd chosen, but we'd been to Rome on our honeymoon and both of the others seemed worthy of individual visits with more time necessary fully to enjoy.

Moody

I had always felt that there was something romantic about what used to be called when I was a kid, Constantinople. In fact, if I remember correctly, I think I can still remember the song about it and how it was spelled. Maybe you do, too! Anyway, it is now called Istanbul, as you all know. As I was more than curious to see the Bosporus firsthand, I suggested that we break our journey from Singapore there for three nights, or so. Happily, this met with wifely approval, as we figured we could fly back from there direct to Boston, or with another stop en route if it was too long a haul. Besides, we thought that the chances of our ever getting to Istanbul for a holiday were a good deal less than, say, Egypt or Greece which we had never explored together although Anne had visited the latter before our marriage. One day I'd love to get to Egypt particularly, providing I'm not on a walker by then!

As Singapore Airlines, who had come up with this great package deal, didn't fly into Boston directly from Istanbul, we turned to Swissair who did, but via Zurich, so we made plans to go there for our penultimate stop. With these vital decisions under our belts, where to stay when we got to these places was equally important and had to be decided. As I didn't have a clue and as we really wanted to be sure of our accommodations en route, I not only asked our good travel agent but, also, wrote to the Editor of HIDEAWAYS who, as you can guess from the name of his newsletter, was always quoting places to visit, or not, as he determined. His pen name is Andy Harper and, in retrospect, his advice has always been great!

"If you were going to Hong Kong, Bali, Singapore and Istanbul, where should we stay?, I asked him. His reply was prompt and we followed his advice to the letter. The Regent in Hong Kong; The Amandari in Ubud, Bali; Raffles in Singapore and the Ciragan Palace (Chiryan, phonetically) were his recommendations. Our travel agent suggested The Dolder Grand in Zurich. How lucky we were! Each was superb, colorful and beautifully situated and worth many stars in our book!

In the midst of all this planning, we suddenly realized that we were going to have to leave Radley the acknowledged head of the W-W household, for nigh on four weeks. This would be far too long a time to go to his regular country club of kennels, regardless of how much Elsie Wood spoiled him! With this realization, our plans plum fell apart, which will be understandable to those who have a family member such as Radley at home. He has, however, over his seven years, a most devoted stepmother who, on request, bathes, brushes, combs and generally spoils him rotten. It was Sharon Farnham in nearby Dover who completely saved this situation by, on hearing of our and Radley's predicament, announced that in no possible way could he spend that long in a kennel, regardless of how plushy it was! He had to stay with her, her husband, two sons two daughters and endless other horses, canines and felines at her home as he had done successfully and previously on occasion. So be it! We agreed with great relief and gratitude. We were on our way and all was set!

175

Now all that was left to be done in the planning department was to try and figure out what to do about all the sundry currencies which we'd meet en route and, of course, how much we'd need when we got there! The latter was impossible, so we decided we should take $30.00 in each of the five different currencies for expenses on arrival at each. Our longtime friend at Thos Cook and Sons, Ginny Greene, with whom I had dealt for five years while renting Cottages, Castles & Flats in the U K, provided us with this and with travelers' checks. It was interesting to us that, on advice from others, we took theirs and not those of American Express, as they are better known there, or were, due to the sometime British influence in that part of the world. Not being anything of a mathematician, I took a calculator with us that was worth more than its weight in gold from the start! As there were I believe 6764 Turkish Lira to the Dollar, and goodness knows how many Rupiahs per buck in Indonesia, it saved many a situation.

Finally, October 10th arrived and we were all off to Logan and an afternoon flight to San Francisco, thrilled at the thought of, for once, sitting in the front of the bus rather than the back, as usual! As the flight from San Francisco to Hong Kong was due to take 15 hours, or so, and we were not due to leave S F 'til 3.00 A M local time, we decided to stay overnight at an airport motel and meet friends of Moody's in Burlingame the next day which we did and most pleasurably. That evening, we went to bed early and asked for a 1.00 A M call due to the somewhat heathen take-off time. Why so early? Apparently, due to the ghastly approach to the one and only runway at Hong Kong's antiquated then-airport, that has to be made with the final turn onto it at 90 degrees and about 1,000 feet, if not a good deal lower over a densely populated area. Flights were not allowed to land before 7.00 A M each day because no one would get a wink of sleep! No wonder there was such great demand to build the new, modern, airport, which apparently is now one of the most amazing in the world (but a long way from the city).

Leaving for a 15-hour flight at 3.00A M is not my idea of fun, but we survived and in no time we were being pampered and spoiled by the most charming flight attendants on Singapore's Flight #1 to the Orient. I found that knowing what time it was anywhere en route was hopeless, so I just relaxed and enjoyed it all and the 15 hours really only felt like about six, thank goodness.

At one point, as we were approaching the coast of Taiwan, I was asked if I'd like a snack as breakfast was still hours away! Somewhat out of it due to my inability to sleep like my better half, who was corking it off beside me, I asked for a cup of hot chocolate. A few minutes later I was offered some caviar that I happily accepted! As I enjoyed both, though not together, I could not help but think of my nephew who runs a well-respected restaurant off Piccadilly in London, and how he would have had a stroke had he known of his uncle's strange and untimely selection!

As our luggage was just about the first off the plane on arrival, it was not long before we were through immigration and customs and were met by an Abercrombie & Kent agent with a Mercedes and whisked off to the Regent Hotel on Kowloon, the mainland. As always in the Orient, it seems, the entrance doors were opened for us by smartly attired young men with smiling faces, a warm welcome and, quite often, our names used for good measure! After a minute at Reception, we were whisked off to our room where the view for the next six days was utterly breath taking and constantly absorbing. Immediately opposite over the harbor were the skyscrapers on the island of Hong Kong and, between, the never-ending flow of ships of all sizes and nationalities including the constant procession, both ways, of the famous 'Star' ferries which take about seven minutes one way. Sadly, there were few junks passing in front of us while there, in fact only one that Anne was able to catch on film. Mark, who was on business in the Far East while we were in this city, joined us on our first afternoon there, and what a great place to have that re-union! His room was a few floors above ours and we had three days in which fully to savor his being with us!

The day following we left in the morning for a day in Macau, the sole Portuguese colony left in the world and about an hour's high speed ferry ride from H K. On arrival at the dock we were, like most tourists, set-upon by drivers who wished to take us on a scenic tour. As none seemed to speak a word of English and our Portuguese was 100% non-existent, sorting out this problem was real indeed. Add to this that none of us had a clue as to what an H K dollar was worth there, it seemed that we were doomed to taking a walk! No way! Number one and only son steps up and manages to persuade the MOST persistent of all the driver/guides to take us in his minibus for an hour's tour and that he'd be rewarded adequately, somehow or other, at its end! In no time did we see our conveyance and realize that it'd be with luck if three got into it, including chatty driver, let alone five! Remember the days when students by the dozen tried to get into one 'phone booth? This was a similar move!

For the first twenty minutes our driver gave us the grand tour of what appeared to us to be the recently bombed area of the town, stopping once where, with gestures and torrents of the local dialect, he

177

persuaded us to burst out of the bus. This was no mean feat out of this 'bug'! As we were in no man's land again, we could see no reason for our driver's excitement until we at last understood his shouts of what sounded like "Chila" to us. Only visible was rubble and a refuse-covered playing field and, in the background, an ageing high-rise building. What, it transpired, we were looking at was, for the first time ever for any of us, China and quite unnoticed nearby was the checkpoint between the two countries! As we were all so moved by this experience, and should have been according to our driver, it was decided we universally needed a pit stop! So! The driver we'd christened Kit by then, hustled us into his close friend's nearby gift shop, of course, to buy jade in gratitude for the use of its plumbing!

After two hours of a most interesting, colorful and amusing tour that gave us a real taste of the area, Kit bade us farewell after depositing us at his favorite restaurant where we enjoyed a great lunch at a most reasonable cost. Not one word of our language passed between Kit and us, but this good, cheery man did us proud and with considerable honesty. I was so glad to see Mark reward him generously as he left. He deserved every penny and we were lucky indeed to have found him.

That night, Mark took us, Annie, Moody and me, to the purlieus of Kowloon and to his favorite and authentic Chinese restaurant that he'd found on a previous trip. Suffice to say that this was an experience for which I picked up the tab and I'm still in doubt as to what, somehow, went down our throats! In my case that was, anyway, minimal because chopsticks and I had never had any mutual understanding at all and, in this instance, it would have been more than socially gauche to use either fork or fingers! At the adjoining table a birthday celebration was in full swing and, at candle blowing out time for the cake, it was an education to hear "Happy Birthday" for someone, whose name sounded like Ping Pong Pow, sung in Chinese!

Most sadly, Mark had to leave us to go into China on business the next day, but we so enjoyed a long and delicious lunch at the Hong Kong Club as guests of the parents of a dear friend of ours, Evelyn Treacy, from Boston. They were Judge and Mrs. Liu who came with their son and daughter-in-law. They entertained us royally and, also, were able to answer many of our questions about the future of their vibrant and exciting city. Between now and 1997 it would seem that life is not going to be dull there at all! I said the meal was superb. I didn't mention that the Judge forced me, you understand, into having the most memorable glass of vintage port with him after we'd eaten! When we bade farewell, I was most flattered by His Honor saying, "Michael, you are my kind of man!" You can be sure I'll never forget that totally unique moment!

During the six days spent at The Regent, the weather was warm and often hot and sticky, but luckily, we had no rain. All the way along, we were told that we were just ahead of the rainy season. This was the way we had planned it and hoped for, as it happened! To generalize, we were all fascinated and excited by Hong Kong, its people and its culture, not to mention the Chinese Arts and Crafts Center quite close to our hotel that we found to be an education in itself!

On the morning of October 18th our A & K guide was at the hotel door among all the Rolls-Royces and Bentley's that are usually there for taxi service, and took us to the airport to board our flight to Singapore but, sadly, in a Mercedes! I didn't complain too much, though! We made a brief stop at that superb airport and then flew on to Bali's Denpassar airport to arrive at dusk. We were met here and driven to the Oberoi Hotel via a back lane, it seemed, to avoid the very heavy and slow traffic along the famous Kuta Beach. As, again, our driver spoke little or no English and seemed to have a minimal idea as to where we were headed, we did have some nervous moments in his car. You know how one can be convinced one is being abducted on arrival at an unknown land, with an unknown driver, in the dark on an unpaved road?! All those hallucinations were most unnecessary...for us of little faith!...and soon we were being greeted in the wide open and most attractive surroundings of the Oberoi. It was steaming hot and humid so the outdoor and sunken bathtub belonging to our 'cottage', surrounded by exotic flowers and greenery, looked most beckoning before turning in after a fairly long day!

Early next morning we were on our way again to the airport where we began to meet others who were, like us, flying to Kupang on the western end of the island of Timor. Here we were to board the Island Explorer, our floating home for seven days. It was a passenger-carrying catamaran owned by the P & O Line and partially chartered on this voyage by A & K. The one we were taking was billed as "The Dance of Welcome" Cruise as we were to see this on each of the islands at which we would call on our way back to Bali. To instruct and guide us on these island visits were a most patient and charming couple. One was an Indonesian 'cruise director' for lack of a better term and his assistant was a young German lady from Jakarta, who knew her subject well and briefed us nightly with her colored slides on each morrow's venues.

As you might expect, we, the passengers, were a mixed bag! There were Yanks, Aussies, Dutch, Kiwis, Brits, Austrians, a total of 34 of all shapes, sizes and ages and, as usual, I guess I was the oldest!

179

The Explorer, built in 1985 and weighing 859 tons and 134 feet in length was both comfy and serviceable for the job she was built to do. Our cabin was not spacious by any means but who needed that when we spent so little time in it? It was the first time ever that I'd encountered a double bed in a ship's cabin rather than two single or a couple of bunks. The latter I had on R M S Aquitania in 1936 in 'Steerage', far below the waterline en route to my year as an Exchange Student in the USA.

The Captain and crew of our ship was Indonesian and couldn't do enough to help and make us feel we were most welcome constantly. Our meals both on, and off, the ship were very interesting and more than adequate...in fact darn' good for the most part. Happily, the crew detailed to cope with us when going ashore, or returning by Zodiac rubber boats, was always attentive and available. Due to heat and humidity this was a godsend, for hanging around waiting onshore after a longish visit somewhere would not have been our idea of fun!

The routine for each day was somewhat similar if one wanted to be involved in the events that were organized. You didn't have to go! Lazing around on deck and getting sunburned was fine if the spirit moved! In the morning we visited an event on shore and in the afternoon we'd go to a lovely beach for water sports, shelling or lolling about in the crystal-clear sea! We learnt much about local culture and saw the native islanders making their famous weavings such as Ikat and Batik. Additionally, usually a Dance of Welcome was performed by both sexes though once we were met on landing by fearsome looking men on miniature horses who came roaring, literally, down the beach at full gallop brandishing swords and assorted weapons to greet us! The effect was diminished a bit by the fact that the horses, minute as they were, had flowered straw hats pushed between and around their ears!

Each of the six islands we visited was quite different. On Sawu, the economy is based on the cultivation of the Lontar palm and the making of some of the finest Ikat. On Sumba we watched a ceremonial wedding preceded by the bargaining between two families regarding the dowry and, subsequently, the dancing and the killing of a pig. This, mercifully, was not carried out but there was no doubt that the pig that was brought in with legs tied to a bamboo pole, had not been appraised of the situation in which he found himself! He was convinced that he was for the unseen charcoal grill and screamed appropriately. Luckily, though he didn't know it, he was part of the act and was, for this time anyway, in no peril.

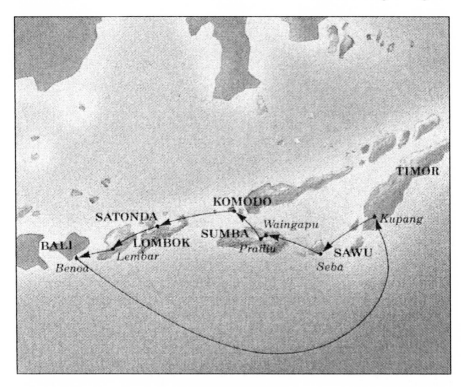

The Spice Islands
Map Courtesy of Abercrombie & Kent

It was on Komodo Island that Anne and I went our separate ways one morning. She went with others to see the famous 'Komodo Dragons' up close. I went fishing at 5.00 A M with as much success as I usually have...none! Thereafter, we both went in Zodiacs to look at thousands, literally, of Fruit bats that nested there. Much larger by far than our domestic bats, these critters had a wing-span of about a foot and a half and looked more like flying foxes, I was told. Never having seen such an animal, I can't attest to this but, happily, they stayed far from us and were in no way interested in our getting close to them. Anne reported on her return that 'the dragons', up to about nine or ten feet in length, were contained in their own enclosure and must have been fed recently before their arrival as deer were grazing nearby with neither paying attention to the other. Just as well, she felt!

It was most interesting to see, as we visited these comparatively close and small islands, the varying cultures from Islam to Hindu to Christianity and the different natures and habits of the islanders. For instance, those interested in selling their homemade products, after the Dance of Welcome, were infinitely more aggressive on Sumba than they

181

were on Suwa as we were warned they would be by our guides! Also, we became adept in the bargaining process that is everywhere there, and to me it made the process far more interesting and competitive!

On our final day on board, we docked at Lombok, an island that, until 15 years ago, or so, was totally isolated not only from Indonesia but from the rest of the world. As a result, it is often referred nowadays as 'Bali before tourists'! Instead of an open truck, this time we were taken in air-conditioned luxury to visit the Lingsar Hindu and Islamic temple. I only mention our transportation in this instance because it was a real delight in the heat and humidity to which we were becoming accustomed. On our return to the bus on each previous trip though, the crew had the foresight to supply us all with ice-cold face towels and the most delicious orange drink and that made all the difference!

After our visit to the temple and watching native dancers, we had the good fortune to visit a complete Sasak village, Karang-Bayan by name. Those who live there took the greatest trouble to give us insight into their way of life and the warmest of welcomes. It was apparent that they had less than few of this world's goods that we, sadly, take all too much for granted. It was equally apparent from their smiles and obviously contented looks upon their faces, that they were satisfied and happy with their lives in general, a unique experience these days for those of us living in the 'civilized' world. Confidently, I say that this situation seemed to us to be endemic, generally, to the Spice Islands we visited. Long may it last!

After a most cheerful and excellent farewell dinner on board, we docked at Benoa, Bali's port, and disembarked next morning to be driven to the Amandari Hotel. This is about an hour and a quarter's drive towards the middle of this lush, highly populated island where the people are, for the most part, Hindu. Temples, temples everywhere, but not a soul in one! That was our impression but we soon learnt that they come alive on special holidays and times of religious celebrations that are legion! Each village, all of which appear to adjoin, has three major temples and, scattered like salt and pepper everywhere, are little individual ones. Most have black and white or yellow linen 'skirts' surrounding the base and invariably have an 'offering' thereon for the appropriate spirit or God involved and, often, a tiny umbrella above to keep the sun off!

On Bali, we spent three nights in what Anne and I reckon is one of, if not the, most attractive, beautiful and unique hotels in the world. The Amandari is in a small vibrant town filled with artists and artisans. It is called Ubud, pronounced locally and phonetically, Oobould, (as in 'would') and, due to space limitations, suffice to say that this hotel is the very, very best. The fact that beautiful and colorful staff and management meet you with all our names on their lips as you get out of the car, with their hands together in front of their chests and bowing, sets the tone for everything else that happens from then on! The Asian service, both outstanding and conspicuous, is at its very best and the hotel and restaurant are delights. I so hope it will stay that way. The Amanresort Company has a really great reputation—well deserved!

Sitting next to us at lunch one day was a couple that heard us mention Boston.

"Forgive us for intruding", one said, "but we heard you mention Boston and we wonder where you live."

"Oh! We live in Westwood just outside," Anne answered.

You've guessed it for sure! They lived less than two miles from us and I doubt if either of us could have been further away from our homes anywhere! Who said that it was a small world, other than everyone under such a circumstance?

On October 28th we reluctantly left the Amandari with the view overlooking the rice paddies and river gorge from the huge full-length windows of our most luxurious rooms and were driven back to Denpasar airport with its temples and similar architecture. In short order we were back again on our favorite airline and en route to Singapore just 1½ hours away. They must have known I was coming on board because, in no time, I was offered a superb, 20 year old glass of port after, as usual, a delectable dinner!

On arrival we went straight to Raffles Hotel that, incidentally, had been closed for a couple of years for a total refurbishing. It was everything I had expected and heard about since I was a kid at my Dad's knee back in England in the 1930s! The ambience and quality had been maintained well with the introduction of modern and useful additions. On this occasion, our A & K guide was the most attractive and intelligent wife of a pilot in the Singapore Air Force. During our stay, she showed us the beautiful and rightly famous botanical garden with its dazzling orchids and then to the highest point in town to view the majestic harbor. Like Hong Kong, it must be one of the busiest in the world.

In no time we were in touch with Anne's friend, Becky Meigs Rives and her husband who taught at the American School in town, and who very kindly invited is to dine at their favorite restaurant for Chinese food. I was a bit depressed at that idea as you may remember the problems I had in Hong Kong! Not to worry! Everything, including the handling of chopsticks, went finely! It was here in Singapore, that our traveling companion, Moody Ayer, developed over a while a more than painful sore in her mouth. She said it seemed to be caused by a piece of bone which, suddenly, had appeared in her lower jaw. The pain really became no joke for her and we wondered what on earth to do as she started to talk about flying home. In the event, Becky came to our rescue and took her to her own dentist nearby who, promptly, had Anne take her to the local hospital and soon the pain was dissipated, thank heaven! We never did hear how the bone appeared or what caused it, however!

I should have mentioned just now the very first thing Anne and I did on arriving at Raffles. We voted! Before leaving home, I was a bit incensed to find that I was, then, unable to vote in advance on an absentee ballot due to their not having been printed in time! With great patience the Town Clerk of Westwood, Edie McCracken, listened to my carrying-on about becoming a U S citizen in 1952 and how I had never missed voting in an important election before. Immigrants are funny that way, I guess! Anyway, she asked where we were going to be on Election Day, so that there would be time to get the ballots back by airmail. We told her we'd be at Raffles in Singapore. Whereupon she guaranteed to get them to us before we left there. You can imagine how pleased we were on our arrival to hear that they had been there at the hotel for a week! We completed them immediately and sent them home where they arrived with time to spare we learnt later...not that it did the results any good, unfortunately!

Before leaving this spotless, modern and capitalistic city that owns the most beautiful airport, subway and transit systems, we were invited to have lunch at The Singapore Cricket Club, an adventure and experience in itself! I could almost hear the snap of the red-leather ball on the willow bat and imagine my ancestors sitting on the grass or in deck chairs watching, doubtless sipping a Singapore Sling between their moustaches and beards! I had no idea whether, or not, I had any ancestors there, but they should have been! We, too, enjoyed Singapore Slings in Raffles' Long Bar and dropped the husks of the peanuts left for us on the tables onto the floor with abandon! This, we gathered, was a tradition and all husks are left either on the tables, or dropped to the floor by clients or the staff, and then swept up at the day's end!

One evening, to indulge in some local and real Asian color, we dined in the hotel where there was a large Bali promotion going on. The

184

costumes and colors were outstanding but, to the somewhat unenlightened like us, Balinese dancing does go on, and on and on! This we found was not unlike the music that accompanies it. We wondered what on earth 'heavy metal' must sound like to a middle aged Balinese though, to look at both sides of the cymbal!

Anne and Mark in Ubud

Next stop, Istanbul! A long overnight flight of 12 hours, or so, with a stop in Saudi Arabia on the Persian (or Arabian) Gulf, goodness knows when, but sometime in the middle of the night! There were only three of us in our section of the 747-400 and about eight to look after us. Never had we had it so good! I was delighted when, sometime before our landing at Bahrain, to off-load passengers, one of the stewards asked me if I'd like to meet the captain. Naturally, I agreed and in no time was speaking to Capt: Evans who, believe it or not, had been in the RAF as a night-fighter pilot as had I, but *not* in WW2!

Thankfully, he was much younger than I...how did you guess? I was highly interested to learn that he had been the Captain of a 747 that, some years before, had had a four-engine flame-out over a volcano in Indonesia due to ash in the air. He, I learnt, is one of two who have suffered such a hideous predicament and, somehow or other, brilliantly got the four engines going again before hitting the ground. The second was a British Airways pilot flying over the sea. In RAF World War II parlance, that unpleasantness would have been known as a 'revolting development', for sure!

It was with great sadness that we had to say goodbye to the Singapore Airlines' crew and staff on arrival at Istanbul. All three of us decided that, whenever possible we would fly with them—provided we were lucky enough to be flying their routes again! They are a really great airline in every respect.

Going to Istanbul from the pristine cleanliness of Singapore was quite a shock, but easy to take! The Ciragan Palace Hotel (phonetically, 'Chireyen'), on the north side of the Bosporus and overlooking it, is part of a Sultan's palace and, like the Regent in Hong Kong, offers guests a magnificent view of ships of all nations as they pass.

Here in Istanbul we did what most visitors do and were guided to the Topkapi Palace, the Blue Mosque and, among other sights, The Bazaar! Now, I'm not the best and easiest person with whom to shop as Anne probably will attest, but The Bazaar boggles the eye and mind literally and I wouldn't have missed it. In fact, my better half somehow arranged it that we went there twice! The whole is such an immense rabbit warren that I feared we could get lost therein, but not to worry! I was almost certain that Anne could wind her way amongst the nearly overwhelming amounts and selections of GOLD as if she lived there! Our one and only misfortune in town was to catch a cab whose driver spoke not a word of English and was an antique as well! Shades of Macao! We asked to go to St. Sophia's mosque, but our driver had totally different ideas. He decided that we should attend services at the Suliman Mosque which we were convinced was in the opposite direction as we'd been told previously. You think traffic is bad in the States? Wait 'til you have a taste of it in Istanbul! It was so bad that stopping was almost out of the question so, when we saw the railroad station we decided we'd bail out and would know where we were. First though, we had to give our driver a handful of Lira that was, we were sure, much more than he expected because he produced a never seen before grin with appropriate farewell gestures as we leapt for the sidewalk and moderate safety. It was from here that Moody caught her original flight home. With her dental problems, that was a blessing, for sure.

As the Istanbul to Boston flight was such a long haul, we decided to stop at the Dolder Grand Hotel a few minutes from the center of Zurich. Anne, as expected, loved the main street...the Bahnhofstrasse...the Newbury Street of Boston, the Fifth Avenue of the Big Apple, the Rodeo Drive, the Champs-Elysées (etc), and I found real, honest-to-goodness, cheese Fondue! Swissair did us just as we'd been told they always would, excellently, on the flight home! All we needed was a 7, repeat 7, course repast en route home and a 'snack' as we flew over the St. Lawrence. The snack, amazingly and with considerable restraint, we passed! As we disembarked at Logan the Swissair agent handed us a note for complimentary service at the airport and on home. What a way to go! What a great way to fly around the world in 29 days for the first time! How lucky could we be?

It came as quite a shock to Anne and me when we awoke on June 8th of 1993 to realize that we'd been married for 25 years! How time flies when you're having fun! A good friend of Annie's and mine, Julie Schniewind, who had known Anne for ages and was partially responsible for the two of us getting together, decided that she'd be more than generous and give us a party the day before and invite some of our closest and dearest chums! This was to be held at a delightful rooftop apartment on Boston's waterfront with superb views of the harbor one way and the skyscrapers on the other! Enhancing it all was perfect weather.

I managed to mumble a toast to Annie that went like this:

"Starting tonight, tomorrow is unsurprisingly a very special day for Annie and me. Thank you all so much for joining us in the celebration of our first 25 years! Thank you, Julie, for making this affair such a delight in all ways but, also, for getting Annie to notice me in the first place, 25 years ago! We are lucky indeed having you all as our close friends for Lo! these many years. We are most grateful for your considerable part in our lives together.

I surely would be remiss if I didn't wax a bit sentimental at this happy milestone! With the exception of one or two passing glitches many years ago, which invariably are the lot of all marriages, Annie's and my 25 years together have been to me about the happiest and most exciting years that any couple could spend. We've been up and down, to and fro over our planet; we've been blessed with good health. We have super friends, dear and loving animals and beautiful belongings both generously given as well as inherited and collected. We have so much for which to be grateful.

Annie is responsible for all this, I well know. A kinder, more caring and most loving personage would be very, very hard to find and I feel sure you will all agree. If I have any reason *not* to have hair as gray as hers, she is the cause! She gets me, and keeps me, going for these and all the other reasons I know so well. I know that I am the luckiest of men.

Please join me as I drink with much gratitude and more love to my very best girl, Annie."

I know that some of the above is repetitious but remember, please, that I quote a toast!

I bet you have sat through quite a few seemingly endless, and sometimes ribald, poems read in honor of a relative or friend's anniversary or birthday. We sure have, but one this year we thought was excellent and right on the money; it was written by our good friends, Karen and John MacDuffie, and I think you might get a chuckle out of it as well! We did.

To Anne and Michael on their 25th Anniversary

Dear Michael and Anne
Yes, my friends, it is true -
We are all here to share
Your 25th with you.

Can you really believe
25 years have passed?
Seems to me I remember
People said you'd not last.

Was it 6 months or 6 days
Before you'd be through?
Well, you're still hanging in there,
And you're still happy, too.

What you've done in the meantime,
All the places you've been:
Europe, Bali and Hong Kong—
All the sights you've seen.

You've safaried, you've sailed,
And you've photographed all.
Then you share it with friends,
And we all have a ball!

And that's what I think of—
The friendship, the fun
The effort you make
For us each...every one.

It's friends they're your hobby,
And you're both *non pareil*
At loyalty and caring.
So now, friends, I say

Here's to you, Anne and Michael
May your next 25
Be as fun and fulfilling.
May you still be *alive!*

Carmen and Norman

I think that is one of the better ones, even though I am anything but humble by printing it! Karen has the knack of producing such odes as this we've learnt over the years. We love to try, too, but usually wind up being hysterical! Once, when Anne and I were driving to Connecticut for the wedding of Jane and Lanny Parker, we started to compose a rhyme on the way. We both became, as I said, so hysterical at our efforts that Anne managed to drive into the car in front of us! Added to that, Annie forgot to put into the car the dress she bought to wear at this special event so had to wear the dress she stood up in (Bad English!) for the whole week-end! The dress for the wedding actually fell off the bed at home before being packed, so Anne never saw it when checking her luggage prior to leaving! Of course, she was blamed for this oversight by her smug husband! The first shock we had this year occurred on January 20th. William Clinton was inaugurated. Enough of that though and all that followed for years. March 13th was the day one of our major blizzards and on the 29th Anne and I left for our annual and perfect stay for nine days at Coco Point.

On our annual holiday a couple there, among many over the years, made a considerable impression on Annie and me. They were Carmen Dell'Orefice with her friend, Norman Levy. You would, probably, recognize Carmen right away with her mane of silver-white hair, should you meet her on the street and say, "I know that striking lady, who on earth is she?" Well! She is, I think, the best looking lady of her age I've ever known and no wonder. She is still the top model for her age in this country. Luckily, we got to know her and Norman one evening and became quite good friends! Norman and she appeared to be totally dotty about each other and they were a very real joy to be with for walks on the beach and the occasional dinner! Norman, who must have been around 75 then, give or take a few years, was just like a head over heels teenager and it was a real tonic to see how mutual and solid their affection was one for another during their advancing years!. I really don't mean to make out they're *that* old, but you know what I mean! It made Annie and me wax quite sentimental, too, particularly as I am probably about the same age as Norman! Sad to say, we have seen neither of them since, but we have spoken to Carmen occasionally and she tells us that they are still behaving like teenagers! What a great pair they make! I have a photo that Annie took of both of them on the C P L beach that proves the point!

On September 5th, one of Annie's best and oldest friends, Beth Williams...'oldest in time' said he rapidly, married Rob Ladd in South Dartmouth, MA. This not only was an epoch-making day for them but, also, for us because we have had the fun and pleasure of knowing and enjoying Beth for years. Sadly, she lost her late husband Jeff and thereafter showed the greatest guts and ingenuity in raising her three children, Jeff, Holly and Sam, under really tough circumstances. Time has proven that she did the greatest job of this and I think all of her friends, who are legion, shared pride in her, as did we, of course. It was our delight to try and help whenever we could, just by being there for them, and, speaking personally for a minute, my life has been enhanced indeed, not only by Beth but by her family, particularly her eldest, charming and thoughtful son, Jeff. As Rob moved out west from this part of the world ages ago, it meant that Beth would be joining him there at Ft. Collins in Colorado. Selfishly, that was sad for us, but not to

191

worry! It all sorted itself out well, as you'll see, should you still be with me, for they both, happily, have remained close to us.

Right around this time, too, Anne and I drove up to Vinalhaven in Maine for Bodine's 80th birthday celebration. As they do so often, Jackie and C S Lee had us to stay, with umpteen others, in Jackie's Uncle Ham's and their special house, Cracroft, on the Thoroughfare. Additionally, Sandy, Bodine's son, had arranged to charter the 'Pauline', a charming old, but modernized, boat which could sleep several of us during the weekend thereby easing the numbers at Cracroft. What fun we had on board, and on land, too! By chance, for the view from Cracroft of yachts and ships passing by is always exciting, Anne happened to look out and there the 1930 rejuvenated J boat and Americas' Cup challenger, Endeavor, was going by under full sail and the Pauline happened to be, also, in the picture! Some contrast! Some picture!

Bob Groom who, with his dear and pretty wife, Monica, we'd gotten to know well since our original meeting in Trinity Church some years back, kindly invited me to a dinner at the British Officers' Club in Boston. I had quite a history with this long-lived club, having been invited to join it when I first came to live in America and Hamilton in 1948. At that time, the club was located on State street and I used to drive up from Hamilton on Wednesday nights for get-togethers of people from all branches of the British services, quite a few of whom were of WW1 vintage. Busy as my late wife and I had been with bringing up Wendy and Mark, and with me trying to make a few bucks on which to live, I began to feel I couldn't spare the time to go and find myself listening to good old Brits giving forth about their experiences in WW1 while quaffing warm beer. You can see how short sighted and intolerant I must have been, but that was why I resigned, and frankly have sometimes regretted it since. I was able, however, to help the club find some new digs on one of the wharfs down town before I left and that made me feel better!

Anyway, along comes Bob Groom, O B E. R N (Retired:), (Order of the British Empire. for those that are not sure and aware of that prestigious award given personally by the Monarch.) asking me to go with him to one of the club's special meetings. It was special because we had to be dressed in dinner jackets and wear miniature medals and, also, because Bob was going to be the Speaker. The latter he did with great effect and interest by giving us the story of his experiences, starting before and during WW2, in the Royal Navy. I wouldn't have missed it for anything. It was a very special event and I was proud to be asked as Bob's friend.

Monica Groom

Bob Groom

Christmas at Home in Westwood

The year ended with Mark coming home for Christmas to be with us as usual and my mother-in-law, who came for the day. We are always so appreciative that Mark makes the effort to fly back from Reno at that time of year. Sadly however, due to his work, he can stay no longer than five days and always seems to have to return by air from Logan on the day after Christmas, leaving at around 5.00 A M. Misery! As usual, it was a most cozy time, enhanced by the presence of Radley, who charmed the pants off everyone, as he always does! Maybe that's not quite the right description for his effect on my mother-in-law, but at least she was tolerant of him!

1994 started off with a major shiver. 18 inches of snow on January the 8th and the 15th produced the coldest temperature in 10 years. It was on the 17th. that L A had its violent earthquake. Some start! As soon as we returned from Coco Point in April, I was off alone to England to be with my sister Betty for her 80th birthday. Harry, her husband, had arranged a gala affair at his club, the Garrick in London, and that was a great success. Besides being an age-old meeting place for actors and actresses over the years, one never knows what famous face and person may be there. This time, I was able to meet again many friends and relatives I'd not seen for ages, not to mention my nephew and his wife and their sons, of all of whom I am most fond.

Eight days later, my sister called me after I'd flown home, to say that Harry had fallen down the stairs at the Glebe, their home in Wilmington, Sussex and had broken his neck and had died immediately. What a ghastly shock for them all there. Annie and I did fly over again for his memorial service at the end of June which was held at a big, crowded church in Eastbourne, close to Ascham, the prep: school at which Harry had been Headmaster. The music and the readings by my nephew and his sons were most memorable, as was the singing of 'Pie Jesu' by the school's choir of young boys. A big reception afterwards enabled both of us to refresh friendships with, again, many whom we had not seen for years and my sister stood up to the ordeal nobly, We were so glad that we could be there.

Betty and Harry, Her Husband at The Garrick
On Her 80th Birthday

On August 29th a dear and longtime friend of mine in our Hamilton days, Connie Taylor, had her funeral service in Wenham. Again, so many of my old friends from the years 1948 to the present were there which was heartening and to see many who were among the pages of my first book. Moody, Ruth, David & Lexa Ayer; Steve Palmer, Joe Robbins,

Johnny Lawrence, the Forrester Clark family, Natalie Brengle and many others were there, to mention but a few.

Now, I want to introduce you to Henry and Judy de Jesus! We met them this year, I think, due to my never-ending search for a decent English crumpet! One day I visited a fish shop near home and, much to my surprise and interest, I found a packet of crumpets above the fish and on the counter! The last place I'd expect to find such things! I bought the package promptly and returned to have one for breakfast. It was delicious, so wrote promptly to Sharrocks Bakery, the makers in Fairhaven, MA. (a) to congratulate them on making what I felt was the most authentically British crumpet I'd found over years of search here and (b) to ask where I could find them closer to home. Goodness knows how much later, Annie answered the 'phone one day and came to tell me that a 'Henry de Jesus' wanted to talk to me. "Henry who?" I replied stuffily! To cut a long and most satisfying story to the marrow, I spoke to Henry who was devastated at being so long in answering my call about his **Sharrocks** crumpets, but he and his wife never seemed to stop making the darn things, and that was why!

After hearing what Henry and Judy were doing, and as my memory was still more than aware of what, years ago in 1949, Jackie and I were trying to do with our small marmalade business, I couldn't help but offer, as many had done to us back then, any help that I could to this courageous and incredibly hard working young couple. Most happily, they agreed to this and the four of us have been good friends ever since. Over the years we have seen them grow remarkably and they now market their several 'deliciousnesses' through a fine chain of food stores. This is in addition to their private label thatI had used for my former Hamilton business. I offered this to them as a very small gift and was most proud that they accepted it for use on each packet. Henry, totally typically, insisted that the label bear a tiny replica of my initials in one corner! Look carefully! A more hardworking couple there just cannot be! Up at 3.45 A M to drive to their 'factory' in New Bedford and home often not until 6 or 7 P M. With Henry pouring batter all day long from a heavy metal container, it is amazing that they both can cope, but they do and in spades! 1/800/627-0385 will get you a super packet, or two, at a most reasonable price if you'd like to try!

On September 3rd. Jeff Williams, about whom I wrote previously with affection, got married in Chicago to Jen Rauch. Anne and I were invited and we had a great gathering at the University Club there of his family and friends from the east. The family in this case meant, Jeff's younger brother, Sam, and Holly. both great kids! It was the first visit ever to the Windy City for me, and Jen's family treated us all royally.

The Sharrocks Crumpet Label

During this year, too, we were informed that I had prostate cancer, which set the cat amongst the pigeons a bit. When being told this, I must say that I uttered an expletive that was a little ungentlemanly, but then Annie did too, simultaneously, so that made it all right! Suffice to say Dr. Bill Shipley at Mass General did his thing most successfully, and Annie hers by driving me there every day, bar Saturdays and Sundays, for eight weeks for radiation treatment. What a performance! Thank God, I've just about forgotten about it all since, but I'll never forget the kind, sympathetic, efficiency of the trio who coped with me day in, day out. Carrie Donahue, one of 'my' team, tiny and thoughtful as always, came in one morning brightly (at 7.00 A M yet) and said "O K Mr. W-W. Take your pants down, please" To which I found myself replying, "Carrie! You're the first lady who has said that to me in at least forty years!" Bless her heart, she invited us to her beautiful wedding on the Cape to which we went and had a super time, and we still try to stay in touch with her and Greg her husband, even though they've moved from Beantown, and Carrie from MGH. We planned all this prior to leaving on the trip that follows because, had the cancer spread at all, we couldn't have gone due to having to have the radiation treatments as quickly as possible.

You may well say, 'I wonder if Michael does a darn day's work ever, judging from all the junkets they seem to go on!' It does look a bit as if I gave all that up ages ago, I guess, but no way! I work away at The Registry daily during the week, but when we're away, I can invariably get Martha Richardson, a Painting Specialist of the Registry, to keep an eye on incoming orders and my office in general.

Having just explained how I manage to keep my nose to the grindstone with work, I'm now happy to tell you that we've managed to collect enough people so that we may lead them on our second round-the-world tour, first class all the way! Again, our friend, Greg Johnson, 'Mr. Indonesia', will be our guide and companion on this journey and Sandy Lindsay, Greg's agent on the west coast, will make all the arrangements and bookings that we and Greg have suggested. Again, this time, we were able to obtain an excellent round the world price for first class tickets that we were lucky enough to get on our first trip, mostly on Singapore Airlines and Swissair. This trip was billed by Greg as 'MICHAEL WYNNE-WILLSON'S 75th BIRTHDAY PARTY, and that it was, all the way around!

I mentioned Natalie Brengle just now. She was one of the first who, with her friend Fife Symington, said that they'd like to join us. Fife had the effrontery to be older than Nat and I who are the same age! Anyway, Fife had been Ambassador to Trinidad, knew everyone everywhere and we were delighted to have them come with us. Our friends Ken and Sally Burt suggested that we contact Ken's roommate at St. Paul's School, to see if he and his wife might like to join us. They did, indeed, and we were glad to welcome Jan (1) and Brad Middlebrook from Boca Raton. They, in turn, asked good friends of theirs, Jan (2!) and Charlie Waldner, also from Boca Raton, so we had a party of eight guests including us and, of course, our incredible mentor and guide, Greg, who flew in to check on us for a night or two at a time to see that we were having the trip of our lives and leaving us all delightful gifts along the way! He certainly did spoil us all, not only by his intimate knowledge of wherever we were but, also, by those who were on hand to manage and guide us at each stop that we made and by the special and surprise arrangements that he engineered for us.

For ease of management, we all flew by couples to San Francisco, where Greg had us booked into a hotel for the night. On the night following, October 20th, we all flew by Singapore Airlines naturally, to Hong Kong (Annie and I were in seats 1A and 1B around the world!) Here we stayed at the Regent again. From Hong Kong we flew to Bangkok and the Orient Hotel; then to Bali and the Amandari and Amankila Hotels. In Jogjakarta, Java at the Santika Hotel and, finally, the Duxton in Singapore. Raffles had really become a bit too pricey we felt, though doubtless it was as good as ever! It was here in Singapore that we parted, sadly, with our charges as time constraints were closing in on them so they all flew home from there.

Annie and I went to a small island about an hour's ferry ride out of Singapore's harbor for three nights on a most interesting little island called Batam, *not* Bataan, and a resort there named Turi Beach. At the time, it looked to us as if the Indonesians, who own the island, were thinking of making it into their 'Hong Kong'. Jack Nicklaus was even 'building' a couple of golf courses there among the huge buildings that were going up around what looked like a major port in the making. Greg, of course, arranged that visit for us, and that was complimentary, thanks to his friend the manager! Spoiled, weren't we? Sadly and at that time, there were fires raging over Kilimantan (Borneo), so the whole area there and in Singapore was shrouded in noticeable smoke, but that did little to spoil our enjoyment. Back to Singapore, the best ever airport we believe, where you could lunch off the floor amidst the orchids and aquaria! Then we flew off to Delhi in northern India on Oct. 28th, (same seats!) for a night, or two, and on to Agra by train, scary due to speed! As expected, we were mesmerized by the Taj Mahal, and then on by an equally scary Indian airlines flight of an hour, or so, to Khajuraho to look at another big temple, famous for its erotic statues! Why Greg arranged that stop for us was most surprising, I thought! Back to Delhi on another, somewhat scary and over-filled, flight and then after a couple of days in Zurich, directly home by Swissair. What a magnificent and memorable experience all the way!

Perhaps the best way that I can relate to the high spots of this trip is by asking myself questions:

What were the most memorable sights?

1. The Taj Mahal for certain;
2. The two temples at Borabador and Prambanam, the first Buddhist and the other Hindu; both not too far from each other at Jogjakarta in Java;
3. Indri, our adorable Indonesian guide! That's only my assessment, naturally;
4. The Reclining, Golden, Buddha in Bankok;
5. Annie trying to stop an elephant on a main street in New Delhi, then trying to talk her way out of paying for the ride that the 'mahoots' (?) thought she wanted!! All she wanted was a photo;

Courtesy of our Guide

6. My son, Mark, sitting next to me from Singapore to Bali on Singapore Airlines in seats 1C & 1D in first class, and being serenaded by several gorgeous hostesses bearing the first of my six Birthday cakes; then his remark to me, "I'm very impressed, Dad, do you always travel like this?" "Naturally", I replied, "of course";

7. The gold, real gold, that seemed to be everywhere we went in and outside many of the palaces and temples of Bangkok, plus the layers of gold paper which were attached to some of the Buddha statues by the faithful when offering prayers.

What were the most unnerving moments?

1. The main station in New Delhi at 5.30 A M, trying to find our train to Agra in a bedlam of people, carts, cows, smog, cyclists, tiny cars and more people;

2. The death-defying speed of that train once we were off and running!.

3. When our Ambassador guest found himself most unhappy with his room at the Amankila on the island of Bali. Suffice to say we are all good chums again now and he soon, thereafter, did a 180 degree turnaround;

4. When all our guests got a bit fed up with my being greeted with a 75th Birthday Cake at every stop along the way with singing and carryings-on with each one! The crew of our Singapore Airlines flight back to Singapore was more than sad that they had not been informed about 'the 75th Birthday Cake' routine, so the Captain and crew most kindly signed one of the expansive menus for me! I think that was close to the final straw for all even though, of course, I was most appreciative;

5. When Anne's and my luggage became lost on arrival at the old Hong King airport and all our guests' were first off the flight and put aboard the awaiting Daimlers from the Regent Hotel! It was the beginning of our trip, of course, and we were mortified that it should be 'our' luggage that held up the whole party;

6. Prior to take off at Delhi for Zurich. Annie and I were separated, in customs, and our luggage searched from top to bottom and Annie was next to strip-searched! Why she was, heaven knows, but we sure held each other's hands on take off and thanked the Lord that we were out of there;

7. When Annie treated me to the very first massage I'd ever had in my life for my birthday, and I was ushered into the 'massage parlor' of the Bangkok Oriental hotel and into the hands of a gorgeous, shy, Thai masseuse! I didn't have a clue what I was supposed to do!! As she spoke no English I gathered that quickly and, maybe, you can understand my confusion! Anyway, please, don't even think of getting any inaccurate ideas!

What was the worst experience?

I think it must have been one evening in Hong Kong, when Anne and I were talked into going, by Charlie Waldner, for dinner at the Floating Restaurant in Aberdeen, not on our schedule and at one of the towns on the other side of the island to Hong Kong. I'd heard of this vast Chinese restaurant only because, I seemed to remember, that it was built upon the side of the sunken liner 'Queen Elizabeth', and you've probably seen photos of it. The 'Lizzie' caught fire there, I think, many years before and prior to being broken up. It was bad luck that Charlie remembered his father telling him that the one thing he should do, if ever near Hong Kong, was to visit this monstrosity! Why? Because he won the discussion as to whether, or not, we should all go! It was by far the very worst meal we'd ever encountered on this or any other trip we had conducted! There were probably at least five tours, if not more, all clamoring to be fed at the same time...tours of at least a hundred bodies each, from every nation in that part of the world barring Australia. They were probably there, too, but we never saw them! May I suggest that, somehow or other, you avoid this floodlit steel palace? It is on all the lists of 'places to go and dine' out there and, what's more, many movies have been filmed there!

What was the greatest fun?

My actual birthday supper at the Amandari Hotel in Ubud, on the island of Bali, took the cake! Henry and Char Gray, the manager and his wife, outdid themselves, as did Greg, of course, with their arrangements and, above all, having my son Mark there with us to join in the festivities. Mark had flown back from China, where he'd been on business, to be with us all and I was so happy, excited and grateful that he did that for me! He really is a good and special young man!

TEN
1996 - 1999

This is the year of Annie's 55th Birthday and it was her great admirer and our friend, Harold Sedgwick, who announced that he wanted, again, to give a birthday party for her! I *am* into birthdays now, am I not? Anyway, it was a memorable affair and, again, I'm going to include his 'toast' to her with pride:

"To Anne Wynne-Willson on her 55th Birthday...

I rise to propose a toast to our guest of honor who today is having a birthday. We salute Anne with love and affection and with gratitude for her many gifts.

Wherever Anne goes she exudes electricity...when she comes into our midst we sparkle around her. She makes Christmas Christmas: she transforms a hot, humid, August day into solace and enchantment around the pool; she comforts the sick; she brings cheer to the lonely. Everywhere she spreads happiness.

Anne, your friends who are legion, thank you from the bottom of their hearts on this your birthday. We are so glad you were born.

H.B.S. February 6th 1996

Is it any wonder that I am more than proud to have had Annie as my wife, for 34 years no less?

On April 1st. we drove to Logan for our annual visit to that heavenly place Coco Point Lodge. We left home the night before we were due to fly, actually, as a blizzard was upon us and we decided we'd be really smart and spend the night in an airport hotel at Logan so that we'd have no trouble in getting there at the crack of dawn on the 1st. No way! When we awoke we could barely see out of the windows of our room because the great grandmother of all blizzards was howling across Boston, and continued for two days. Seldom had we been hotel bound before, but this time was almost fun but, also, darned expensive! Annie spied someone and her daughter eyeing us as we climbed the stairs in the hotel and recognized the mother. As there was nothing else to do after meeting said charming couple, we decided we'd all better meet for a drink, or two, or three...as there was nothing else to do, mark you! After a most amusing time for two days and an expenditure of heaven only knows how much, we saw that we could get to the American Airline's departure place and fly off to paradise! We've only seen our friend once since then...her daughter was off to the U K if I remember correctly...and that was in church!

Happily, our friends Susan and Steve O'Brien were at Coco Point at the same time as we were. That of course, brought back many delightful and hilarious memories of many years ago when we first met them there. Annie and I have dined out on that story and chain of events but, darn it, I really don't think I'd better relate it! It was all quite on the up and up, but it might be just a wee bit unfair to them both to tell it *in a book!* Suffice to say, it started a really great and mutual friendship for the four of us for many, many years...at least we think so! Hope they do!

It was in this year, too, that Hamilton Lockwood died. It was Ham who owned the super house on the Thoroughfare between North Haven and Vinalhaven islands off Rockland, ME. to which our friend, Jackie Lee, Ham's niece, seemed to invite us and her chums to stay each summer! Not only did those two do that delightful thing but, so did our dear friend Bodine Lamont, who, also, had a house with the most heavenly view out to sea on another side of the island nearer the village. Bo, too, would often invite us for a long weekend, and both Jackie and she would manage, most generously, to have us for drinks and dinner during our stays. What fun we had! Jackie and her husband, C S, together with their two delightful children, Christopher and Jennifer, seemed to love having weddings and anniversaries there, and no wonder as it was so beautiful and the house so large and stately. Annually, at some chosen summer moment, jumping onto the Vinalhaven ferry, would be: Lanny and Jane Parker from Providence, Barbara Welt and her late husband from Albany, Jane Sherrill and her friend Mike Magruder and, of course, Radley, who was always allowed to visit with us when staying at Bo's. As you've probably gathered, I was crazy about that lovable Yorkie, but Bo gave me a good run for my money in that department! He loved her, too, and always had as good a time as we did! Unlike me, he was incapable of doing anything wrong! Annie and I and Radley have so much, over so many years, for which to be grateful to all those kind and incredibly hospitable people!

Remember Eleanor Coolidge from Book I? I can't let this year pass by without mentioning her and the fact that she died during this, her102nd year. She was truly 'a very present help in trouble' to my late wife, Jackie, and me when we were struggling to start making marmalade in Hamilton, back in 1948 to '50. She, with her husband Bill, ran Kettle Cove Industries in Manchester on the North Shore and there was nothing that she couldn't, or wouldn't, do to be of help to us. I always tried to keep in touch with her as long as she felt like a visit, call or note and tried so hard to have Willard Scott announce her 100th birthday on the TODAY show, but failed sadly! She was *such* a great lady and true friend.

Three Stringer Girls from The U.K.
With one old exhibitionist on Barbuda; Kneeling are
Ann Damphouse and Julia Price (Kern)

Anne and I started off 1997 with a visit to Florida to stay with friends, among which were the Middlebrooks who came round the world with us the last time; Guppy and Camie Ford, he's our Senior Appraiser in my Registry and Betsy Philcrantz and her husband. She was a school chum of Annie's. After that good piece of 'sleeping around' for free, we went to Captiva for a few days! This was the first time we'd been there and we enjoyed it greatly.

My 60th Class reunion came as a bit of a shock to those of us still around! Quite a few of us old souls showed up, however and, as always, it was great not only to see my fellow classmates but, also, to see how great the school was looking in all ways under the leadership of its Headmaster, Chuck Hamblett and his wife Carol.

Edward and Louise Collis in Oz

July saw us on our way to Las Vegas to meet Mark and celebrate his 42nd birthday. The reason we went there, rather than Reno where Mark lives, was because we three went to meet Pat Reynolds, Annie's biological cousin! The two of them had gotten in touch, so they decided they should have their very first meeting over lunch where Mark and we were staying at the Luxor! That was a truly happy and exciting moment for them both, and not a little for the two of us 'boys', too, as you can guess. Pat then, very kindly, took us to her home for a couple of nights so we could all get to know each other and, all told, it was a tremendous success!

August 31st. was one of those days, one of very few, that all of us will remember exactly where we were, or what we were doing, when we learnt that Princess Diana had been killed in Paris. We, also, will hardly forget the day and those following her funeral in Westminster Abbey on September 6th.

Not long after that event, we both were off to the U K to be at one of my great-nephew's wedding! Edward Collis was being married to Louise Bahar, a most charming and decorative young lady who, we both felt, would be a sparkling and great addition to the family! We were 'right on' as it turned out! The occasion demanded that Annie buy a hat that, like Louise, was highly decorative but, unlike Louise, was more than broad! Humping it across the Atlantic in the back of the bus was *not* my idea of fun, let alone carting it around the south of England before the event! It was greatly admired though and, believe it or not, still gets a workout once in a while and looks no worse for mileage flown!

My nephew Robin and his wife Pooh did a superlative job of organization and planning, as Louise's parents live here in the U S, and in addition to the actual ceremony being held in an age-old church in Fulham on the outskirts of London, the reception was held at the Hurlingham Polo Club nearby. Suffice to say, it was a *most* memorable and enjoyable event and one that we would not have missed for anything. It was great for me, particularly, as I was able to catch up not only with my sister but, also, with many other relatives and mutual friends whom I'd not seen for ages.

After Nov. 15th the wedding day, we enjoyed a great reunion with Peter and Sue Ansdell, who got me going in the Castles, Cottages & Flats business some years ago and, also, the Stringer family, our chums whom we see at Coco Point Lodge quite often and happily and who live just outside Portsmouth on England's south coast. On December 1st., Dr.

Henry Mankin, MGH's Chief of Orthopedics, removed my right hip and 'popped in' a new one! He did this with singular success and professionalism. However, after a session of hiccups for 13 days and a stay at a rehab: near our home in Westwood, the dam' thing 'popped out'! This not only was, as far as I was concerned, 'exquisite pain' but, also, a bit terrifying as Henry's last words to me were, "Michael, if you pop this out, get yourself another doctor." Thank goodness he was kidding!

As it happened Mark arrived home for Christmas at precisely the time that the ambulance pulled in, lights flashing outside our home. It had gotten lost en route, and then got lost again, with me screaming my head off inside, trying to find the way into Boston and the MGH! Mark, following in our car, was *not* impressed with the ambulance company involved, nor was I! I decided, while still screaming and en route to MGH, that driving in a hearse would be, and certainly looks, far more comfortable and less painful than driving in what I was in! It seemed to be lacking any springs whatsoever! As for what happened when we got to the Emergency Room at MGH, I think it had better be left untold. It may not have been surprising, however, as it was the Sunday night before Christmas Day, so I'll leave all that to your imagination. I was anything but a happy camper and let all and sundry know, because I was determined not to let it happen again to any other unfortunate. Suffice to say, after several months, I did have the opportunity to meet the Doctor in charge of the E R there who, in the interim, had written me a most concerned and apologetic letter in reply to my broadside from the President on down., and found him to be a charming and, again, a most concerned Scotsman!

Anne, who has volunteered at MGH for years, and I, have the greatest admiration for so many of the medical staff there that we know and think most highly of the whole operation. Mine was a most unfortunate, unique, happening at a most unfortunate time of year and I felt that anything that I could do to negate its happening again would be helpful. I've been led to understand that it was.

It was early in 1998 that a more than kind and thoughtful gentleman wrote to me from New York. He owns a most successful business called 'SUNDAY Productions' which provides the music dubbed onto TV commercials. I'd met him only once before when I was trying, on a whim, to throw myself back into the radio and TV 'commercial' business in New York. That was a bust that neither my young and successful advertising friend, John Osborn of B B D & O, nor Hilary Lipsitz his friend, who gave me both great help and the use of his office, could overcome! However, it was Hilary who wrote later inviting both Annie and me to New York as his guests for a couple of nights!

Incredibly, this generous man had convinced himself that I must have won the war single-handedly as a night-fighter pilot in the RAF, and it was his wish to let me know that he admired my compatriots in that force greatly and that he wanted me to know it and show his gratitude!

Regardless, off we went to the Big Apple to meet Hilary and his wife Ethel where he put us up for two nights in The Millenium Hotel close to his office in Times Square and gave us a marvelous time. He gave us tickets, front row center, for 'Ragtime' the usually 'sold out' musical at that time; lunches with a notable guest who was also an RAF admirer and of its aircraft of WW2 and numerous other surprises. In all, this was a four-star time, none of which I deserved at all but one which we enjoyed to the very fullest. How lucky could we get?

Beth and Rob Ladd

It was in early June that we flew, for our 30th. anniversary toot to Denver, once again, to spend a day or two with Beth and Rob Ladd in nearby Fort Collins. After the usual happy time with them, we rented a car and started our drive through the Rockies. This was a trip I had been anxious to make for years and I so hoped our advanced planning would serve us well. It is a drive that I would highly recommend to anyone who has not had the chance to do it as yet. With this in mind, I'll list where we went en route to Colorado Springs. Our first stop for the night was at Grand Lake Lodge in Grand Lake, which straightaway gave us a feel for what was to come. The next night we spent in Vail at the charming Swiss-looking, Christiana Lodge. This attractive ski resort reminded me a bit of St. Cergue, the village my late wife and I visited after WW2 in the French Alps. On to Snowmass and the Silvertree Hotel, and the next night at the Redstone Inn in that colorful, peaceful and high up village.

We'd heard much about our hotel and its restaurant in Ouray, CO, our next overnight. Called the St. Elmo Hotel and situated on the broad and long Galena Street, it is as unique as can be! We really expected a stagecoach, or two, to drive up while we were there! The restaurant was excellent. Try to arrange a stopover in this most special of places should you be anywhere near. During our stay we visited and went into a nearby, disused, silver mine which was an educational adventure. As I write, it seems to me that it looks as if we did nothing but stop for overnights! That's not at all what happened as the scenery we saw in daytime was magnificent and ever changing. For instance, after leaving Ouray (pronounced phonetically I believe, 'ooray', as in hooray!) we were faced with driving down the hair-raising *Million Dollar Highway,* so named due to the cost of building it some time ago. I flatly refused to drive this as I'd have probably jumped out of our car and jumped off the edge! The road was built, somehow or other, on the edge of a mountain and there was nothing between us and a drop of heaven only knows how many feet from that edge! My brave wife decided that, if we were to finish this super journey she'd have to cope, so we started at the crack of dawn hoping that the smallest number of cars and trucks would be met as we descended. She performed this scary task magnificently apparently, since I only occasionally lifted my head from reading being too chicken to look out. One must continually drive on the 'wrong' side of the road furthest from the vertical drop and edge! Mercifully, nothing much was coming in the opposite, winding, direction so, in my antiquity these days, I'm more than surprised that I now am such a chicken about heights and getting near edges having dizzy heights!

Heck! I used to fly when young and behaved crazily thousands of feet above the ground, no doubt, but now I panic if my son even gets close to a big drop, let alone me! This, of course, he loves to do whenever possible! The worst he's done so far was to ask me to take his photo when standing on a shaky promontory over the Grand Canyon! Being a good father, I did as I was asked, but darn' nearly threw up afterwards!

After pulling myself together, I started to drive again, avoiding a few thunderstorms that were rattling and bouncing among the mountains around us, and eventually we got onto the San Juan Skyway, finally pulling into Durango and the New Rochester Hotel. Like them all, so far, this hotel had become steeped in history since being built in 1882. It was made more interesting by the many photo blowups of the legion of movie stars, of my era and before, who had made movies in this exciting part of our land!

After a good look around this vibrant city we drove off to the Mesa Verde National Park—also in Colorado. To this ex Limey of many a year, this was a true experience! Up, up and away we drove to reach this incredible plateau with its fascinating burial grounds, Indian homes dug into the face of the sandstone hills with many still recognizable as such, not to mention the awe-inspiring views in all directions. Go there if you have half a chance! More and more during this journey, I realized that we, as a couple, have been incredibly lucky in having been able to visit places around the globe, but have not really taken the time, nor the opportunity, to see our own, magnificent, country and its endless beauty and scenic treasures. Time will tell you that we have, just a bit anyway, taken care of that situation!

The Gray Family
In Wareham at Margot Gray's Wedding to Jeff Gaul

A long, long, drive through New Mexico to Albuquerque was next where we picked up Mark, at the airport there, and then on to Santa Fe and the Hotel St. Francis for a night at the Inn of the Anasazi. The Anasazi is a super hotel, by the way. In Santa Fe, Annie and I and Mark walked for miles being typical tourists and seeing as much as we possibly could in our allotted time. How we love that town! The adobe houses; the San Miguel Mission that they say is the oldest church in our country; the Cristo Rey church and a visit to the Bandolier National Monument site of the Anasazi Civilisation circa 1200 A D, were bound to be remembered. Additionally, you must see the inexplicable stairs within the Chapel of Our Lady of Light in town. These stairs were built without nails, nor any visible means of support, by a mysterious man who appeared out of the blue, completed the job of building the stairs that seem to defy gravity, and then disappeared without trace or payment! Now they have banisters that have been added, but back in 1852, when they were built, they had none. See them, for sure! This town offered us such a new and exciting experience, and when we were there, June 21st. to 23rd. It was hot, but not insufferable by any means though I gather it can be. Most sadly, Mark had to return to work in Reno from Albuquerque that day, but he, like us, was entranced by it.

A night in the 'arty' town of Taos and a memorable visit to, among several, the comparatively modern museum bearing the name of Millicent Rogers, the granddaughter of one of the original founders of Standard Oil. We were intrigued to learn more about her and seeing many of her spectacular collections of Navajo and Pueblo jewelry, to mention only two.

Our return toward home just had to include a visit to our young and great friends, Margot and Jeff Gaul. Margot is Judy Gray's younger daughter, Judy being one of Annie's oldest and dearest friends as I must have mentioned! Jeff most kindly took us on a special tour of the Cripple Creek Gold Mine where he works and, also, of some nearby mining towns not far from Colorado Springs, none of which we would have missed for anything. To my uneducated eye, very little seemed to have changed in the mining towns since horses and buggies prevailed on the main street!

As usual, returning to our home on the 27th to the warmest reunion with Radley, was delightful though tinged with regret due to our time away not having been longer! Isn't it always that way? Having Radles to greet us, however, made all the difference and off I went with him again on our regular, daily, walks 'around the block' with all HIS admirers greeting HIM again like mad and wanting to know where HE had been, not me! The story of my life!

My 79th birthday came and went quietly on 9:13 and was made noticeable only by the appearance of five beautiful but hungry deer on our back lawn and, later, 25 yes 25, wild turkeys! I'd never even seen one of those, wild, big and rather clueless birds before in my life! Don't tell that to Bob Gianuso, the best of all mail delivery persons (we used to call them Postmen!) however. He was surrounded by the darn' things in his van one day near us and they were so hostile that they didn't let him get out to deliver the mail! Bob and Radley and I got to know each other well on our walks, and I was delighted to learn that Bob's son got a super job for himself in the computer business, I believe, and is now doing well in New York. What a huge difference it makes if one is lucky enough to have a thoughtful, kind and helpful Postman! We were so lucky in having Bob as ours for many years and are so grateful to him.

I struggled for quite awhile to try and think of something different to do by way of celebrating Annie's 58th birthday on February 6th, 1999. She is, as you might guess, the only girl in the world to promote well in advance her HALF birthday. Sadly, this doesn't meet with any notice from her husband, so he feels that he'd better 'step up to the plate' for her legal one! What I did this time, however, was to go to a very small, Swiss owned and operated, hotel on Commonwealth Avenue called The Elliot, and book a bedroom and sitting room for that night and make a reservation for dinner in their good restaurant. That done, I asked a few of her dear friends, all gorgeous of course, to come for cocktails thereby insuring that I was the only male present! I know I had fun and certainly hope that everyone did. The two of us had a darn good dinner, too!

Around this time, too, we made our annual visit to Coco Point. Before that we enjoyed visits from Robin and Pooh Collis, my U K 'belongings'; 'Yum Yum' Schooler, our friend of many years; Chip and Julia Kern and their, son Ben, and celebrated Harold Sedgwick's 91st birthday at the Harvard Club with Bob and Monica Groom and Frank and Weezee Gardner.

Somewhat typically, Annie decided to invite her class at The Beaver Country Day School to our house for its 40th Reunion and 21 radiant 58-year-olds attended! From where I sat, it looked like a howling success and even the two boys, Radles and I, enjoyed it, too!

As you've gathered by now, Page and Lee (née Osborn) have played a large part in Annie's life, as have their children. May found us charging off to Connecticut for the wedding of Page's son, John, to, as you would expect, a charming and highly decorative girl called Leslie. It was John, perhaps you remember, who was rapidly climbing the ladder at B B D & O in New York and had been so helpful to me before. Like most weddings, this was a blast and drew an outpouring of both families. We were lucky to be included and it was such a significant event that 'Annie's Hat' was dusted off and brought forth.

As this event was such fun, so sad was the news that my dear friend of many, many years, Moody Ayer of 'Wenham les Bains!' as she was wont to say, had died. Her late husband Fred Jr. and I had become friends shortly after I arrived in this country to live in 1948. My late wife Jackie, Fred, Moody and I saw much of each other for many years. Happily, Annie and Moody became good chums a few years after we married and we always kept in close touch with her and her children, Ruth and David. 'Mood' and I had so many laughs and happy times over the years. I will, always, miss her and her acute sense of humor. It was a relief for me to know that I was one of the last people to be with her. By chance, I dropped in on her—as I did quite often at her home—the day before she died of emphysema. Her funeral service, and subsequent burial in the Wenham cemetery, was held on June 24th.

To cheer us up again, guess what! My 80th Birthday was upcoming...a most sobering thought! Beth Ladd and Martha Marshall, two dear and longtime chums of ours, quite definitely made the decision that I *was* to have a dinner and dance at our house on that day and they would organize and cope with it if I'd provide the necessary tent on our back lawn! Knowing a wee bit about the cost of renting a tent, I hedged a bit for a few days but, eventually and happily, agreed so we were off and running!

Beth and Martha did a really bang-up job of the whole evening, which happened to be beautiful. The tent went up, the invitations went out, and, of course, Eddie Madden's orchestra was engaged and, of course too, Mary Flinn from The Country Club without whom we could not have a party, was asked to come and deal with dinner and all that entailed! Radley even had the place of honor! He was getting on then, in fact his 14th birthday was upcoming, so he was placed in his basket between the garden door of our house and the entrance to the tent, so that he could check on all our guests, and vice versa, as they came and went. Special for individual table decorations was the addition of little US and UK flags!

You'd expect me to go on and on about this event, but I won't! I have to tell you that, without doubt, it was one of, if not *the*, finest events of my life! About 80 real and close friends came and several said things that were totally exaggerated and unnecessary, but highly appreciated anyway! To mention names in this case would be excessive, obviously. However, I must mention my dear friend, Joannie Baker, who managed with her husband Nick, to come, somehow, in spite of her acute illness then. Also, Mike Mallardi, my special chum from Radio Press International days. He drove for miles from Suffern, New York, to be with us. I felt spoilt rotten, and Radles, too, and I was so very grateful to all who did so much for us including Annie, naturally. What fun!

With Wally Savory in Cushing, Maine

This really does seem to have been becoming a somewhat hectic year! The life of The Appraisers' Registry continues interestingly. Of particular note is the fact that I now have a partner to share in its future, Wally Savory (Segundo) by name. Over the years as the chap who had managed our family insurance, not a big job I assure you, he and his wife Charlotte have become our good friends. Occasionally, on our walks with Radley in the Hale Reservation behind our home, Wally asked me about my Registry. Eventually, as I was wondering how long I could run the business on my own and at my advancing years, I asked him if he was thinking of buying it. Not that there was too much to buy, mark you, other than lists of fine families from over the years for whom we'd done appraisals, and a few bits and pieces of office equipment, and me! Anyway, much to my surprise and delight, Wally came back with a suggestion for partnership wherein I would keep on doing and enjoying what I had been for years, and he would pay me half of his offer down and the remainder when I wanted to quit, if ever, or else was in a pine box! I couldn't have asked for a better deal, so partners we became. The Registry became known thereafter as The Appraisers' Registry of New England LLC, which included 22 appraisers within its membership who could respond to almost any appraisal request, regardless of how unique it might be. We still do barely any advertising, but now have a website, appraisersregistry.com, for those who might want to learn more about us and view the credentials of our first-rate and professional group of appraisers. I started all this about 23 years ago, by the way...a rather shattering thought, for sure!

Walter and Penny (Ryan) Lennon
At My 80th

218

The Ryder Cup was at our club this year and that was just about the most exciting finish we'd ever heard of, or seen! As usual, all members of our and other clubs near and far, were asked to assist in any way that they could. My involvement was most minor, but enjoyable. I was attached to the driving pool of people who fetched and delivered the professional players from wherever they were staying. This involved for me quite a few trips in and out of town, but as we were asked not to communicate, when driving anyway, with our charges, I didn't get to know any of them too well! Between you and me, I always talked to them while driving, but don't tell a soul!

Latimer (Tim) Gray

219

This paragraph, or two, is most hard for me to relate. It involves our longtime and admired friend, Latimer (Tim) Gray, husband of Judy, Anne's close friend and father of Melinda and Margot, Annie's two goddaughters. I can't bring myself to go through all the shattering events, but enough to say that it was a freak accident that totally paralyzed him from the neck down. He died peacefully about two weeks later on October 5th from the injuries to his spinal cord.

The celebration service for Tim's life on October 8th in Tabor Academy's chapel in Marion was proof, should anyone have needed it, that this kind, thoughtful and caring man was loved and admired by hundreds who came from far and near to be with his immediate family and Sam, his beloved younger brother and wife Gerry. Some of us were honored and invited to be ushers at this event. For me it was a signal one and, as with Moody, I will always be proud to have been counted among their friends.

On October 6th Annie and I had to make up our minds that, as Radley's back legs seemed to be giving out, which we learnt meant kidney failure, and eyesight, too, we had to do something with the advice of our Vet. Because we would be out of the country, we made the very difficult decision that the most humane and the kindest thing to do would be to end his wonderful and caring life. What a ghastly decision to have to make! 14 1/2 years ago, when we had to put down Tinsel, you may remember that that was a disaster and a situation in which I felt I could never be involved again. It was all too much. Now, faced with the same situation for Radles, I totally chickened out and poor Annie had to cope. Martha Marshall most kindly came too, and drove her to the vet. She had called before they left to make sure that they would take Radley immediately and do what had to be done. There, Annie was asked by the nurse if she wanted to be with him. She declined politely, remembering the unpleasantness of all those many years before. She and Martha then went outside to wait. As they waited the nurse reappeared. Being surprised to see her so quickly, Anne asked if the job was done, and it had been. Whereupon Anne apologized for not wanting to be with him and much to her surprise, the nurse said that she wasn't surprised at all. It turned out that it was the very same nurse who had cared for Tinsel when we had to put him to sleep 14 ½ years before and had remembered the agony of Dr. Prescott having difficulty inserting the needle into our Yorkie's tiny vein. She told us that Doc Prescott had never forgotten that incident until the day he died. Annie was stunned that the nurse had remembered that incident so long ago, but it was so traumatic with both of us screaming and crying at the pain that poor Tinsel had, momentarily, to endure, that how would she ever forget? She asked

Anne if she wanted to see Radles for the last time and, after struggling with this decision, she finally agreed. He was brought out to her wrapped in a lovely, soft, white blanket, looking very much at peace, with his tiny pink tongue barely showing out of his mouth.

Radley, R.I.P
1985—1999

After returning home Annie told me that, after I'd hugged him for the last time before she and Martha had driven off, this dearest of dogs seemed utterly content and quiet and, on arrival at the Vet's, he still was which was never, ever, the case when we drove into that driveway before. It was if he knew where he was going and soon, in the office, he never made a move and lay quietly in Anne's arms all the time. She felt sure that he knew that this was his time; that he understood and by lying quietly it was to make her feel convinced that we were doing the right thing for him.

Everybody loved him...most of all me! That night, with considerable difficulty, I felt like writing what follows:

'A DOG'S BEST FRIEND'

Man's best friend has always been known as the dog, but I so hope that I have been the best friend that Radley has ever had. Anne always said that he was 'my dog' though I was unsure that that was always the case. He tolerated us both and, I'm sure, in his rather off-hand way, accepted us both lovingly as his 'belongings'.

Thank heaven I was never a *master* to Radley. Like any handsome, charming and un-yappy Yorkshire Terrier, he was his own master. He dispensed his affection as he saw fit, but always in the best of taste among his own two-legged types and, of course, his own four-legged ones. He was well aware that he was more than attractive and 'cute' with his button-nose and, in winter, his hair that fell to the ground on his either side like curtains! Everyone told him so but he could never be accused of conceit. Radley, or Radles as he was often called amongst other terms of endearment, seems to have been 14 ½ years young for ages and occupied the distinction of being his home's eldest in dog years...98 ½ to be exact.

Now, with little sight, hearing or smelling capability, I cannot bear to see him shy away from shadows, people and me when I want to hold or pat him. Consequently, my wife and a dear friend have taken him to meet the late Tinsel, Minus, Duchess, Mr. Smith, Sprocket, Melas, Consol and Puffin, not to mention Perky and Ugly our late cats. These are just a few who, like Radles, have showered love and licks upon me and mine for years and years. How lucky and honored we are to have been counted, perhaps, among their friends.

I shall miss you unbelievably, Radles. Thank you for your boundless love, loyalty and happiness.

Just so that life should not become humdrum, Annie and I left on Oct 10th, by prior arrangement of course, for Los Angeles and Australia! What a heck of a year this is turning out to be! Never a dull moment!

Why did we set off for Oz? Because my great nephew, Jamie Collis and his fiancée, Natasha, decided to get married in her home town of Brisbane where her parents lived, so we thought that, as his parents, Robin and Pooh and his elder brother, Edward and Louise his wife, were going, his great uncle and his wife should be there, too, to enlarge our family's representation! Actually, it was just another excellent excuse for us to fly off for our third 'round-the-world adventure and, by the way, we can now say that we have visited all seven continents! Also, because of my good friend and school chum, Jum Falkiner, at Radley and later in the Royal Australian Air Force in the U K. He was shot down, badly burnt, and became a P O W for the rest of the war (Book I). He returned to Oz thereafter and lived near Melbourne and most kindly invited us to stay. It was in 1984 that they came to stay with us and we had a great time with them.

First, however, when we flew into L A, Mark flew down from Reno and guess who came to dinner! Mark's birth mother! What an excitement! We knew that, after Annie made her search for her parents successfully, Mark decided that he'd like to as well, so off he went to Susan Darke at The Adoption Connection in Peabody, MA. as Annie had done previously. In time, they turned up trumps by finding his birth mum out in California and that started a great friendship for us all. Dinner was the greatest time and when it was time to leave I gave Ann a hug and we both said, simultaneously, into each other's ears, "You have a really great son!" It doesn't get much better than that!

With Mark's Birth Mother

223

The following day, before flying out on Qantas that evening, Mark, Annie and I visited one of my most favorite ladies, the Queen Mary, tied up in Long Beach! What a host of memories that brought on for me! If you remember, on one of my crossings on her, this one during the war en route to New York, I lucked out with my Radar Operator and, because I had an introduction to the Purser, we wound up in a special cabin for two below the Bridge. We had been served early-morning tea daily by our steward, which was unheard of and would have been vetoed for sure by the Big Brass, had they heard about it!! This was after I found myself in a cabin normally for two, but which had then 7 or 8 very Senior RAF Officers therein, when I was just a lowly Flight Lieutenant! I figured quickly that I'd have a pretty sticky time with that lot, so bounded up to see the Purser to introduce myself. Thank heaven, through his son who had been so badly hurt in a night flying accident close to me, he knew that I was coming and did he ever do us proudly! (Book I, just for a change!) It was Mark who found this very cabin, as I'd explained it to him, and we now have it photographed for posterity!

On October 13th we boarded our Qantas 747 and landed for gas and a stretch in New Zealand for two hours, or so. Sitting just in front of us on the way to Aukland was Bill Paxton, the well-known actor. Being moderately archaic, I didn't know too much about him, but Annie sure did and we had a brief and interesting chat with him. He was on his way to do some film work on the South Island, so he off-loaded on landing. We then flew on for three hours and arrived in Melbourne, having crossed the International Date Line so we 'lost' the 12th, on the 13th where Anita, Jum's wife, greeted us. Even though we'd not seen her for years, she looked just the same! She whisked us off to their farm a bit more than an hour away in Moriac, Victoria. There they have their 600-acre farm where they work the land, sheep, ducks etc: and, of course, Anita's lovely garden in which, it seemed, rabbits abound. Before breakfast, Jum can be seen sitting in his dressing gown indoors while trying to shoot them through the open window! Most likely, they were sitting up on their hind legs looking at him! Anyway and surprisingly, he quite often succeeds which, for an old prune of about my age, isn't bad! Wild cockatoos, with their beautiful, yellow, plumes and under-wing colors, are in abundance and most noticeable to us, who have only seen a few in zoos at home.

The first drive Anita took us on after the one from the airport was to Barwon Head on the Bass Strait where, on a clear day, one can see the island of Tasmania. Then off to Geelong (pronounced 'Jillong') Grammer School, (the Brits would call it a Public School and we here a Private one!) which looked very similar to Radley where Jum and I went to school in the U K centuries ago! It was here that Prince Charles was sent when that age for a year, or so, you may remember. Here too, Jum's family the Falkiners, had much to do with its building and, particularly, the Chapel.

New South Wales was our next day's destination to visit what was once Jum's family's Merino Stud Sheep Spread (farm). This is in the village of Conargo where there is only a General store and pub, where his Dad and family owned the world's largest Spread of a million acres. Boonoke, (pronounced Boonik), was the station we visited and was one of four on this mammoth plain where Jum had lived as Manager after returning from Radley school in 1937, or thereabouts. The grazing lands go on as far as the eye can see and it is known, also, to be the flattest place in the world.

After a tour of the family's beautiful homestead, now owned by Richard Murdoch, the newspaper tycoon, Jum decided that we should, at last, try to find some kangaroos. This idea was brought about by the total lack of them on our travels so far. Six of us in two jeeps sped off in opposite directions hoping to find some to corner. We did, about 40 of them all hopping about so fast that we could barely keep up with them. It was a great experience that we'll never forget, racing around miles of the flattest territory trying to get close enough to take photos!

We had, also, been starved for the sight of a Koala, as was Annie for the want of holding one! Jum, in fact, put up a dollar prize for the first one seen. After much scrutiny in the back seat, I spied one at last, high up and munching away, on the leaves of a tall eucalyptus tree by the roadside. At least, we did now know that they existed, and I was a buck richer! Just to prove a point, Jum had Anita take us to a Koala Wildlife Sanctuary the following day. Here she hoped she could get the owners to let us in so that Annie could have her great wish granted. Much to our surprise and delight, the powers that be invited us into the enclosure where there were several of these most cuddly characters recuperating from mild injuries in the wild and where they were about to be returned. They really do have tremendous charm!

A couple of hour's flight to Sydney for three nights was next on our agenda. Our first visit there was, unsurprisingly, to the most famous Opera House right on the Circular Quay. There are sure to be no seats available, but let's just take a chance and try at the box office for a couple for La Boheme tonight, I suggested. Incredibly, there was a single in Row A and one just behind it in Row C that had just been turned in! Did we ever luck out?! We found it interesting that many of the cast were Asian, as was the lead Tenor. The evening was made even more memorable by our dinner at the Bennelong Restaurant, part of this well-known complex.

**The Collis Family
At Jamie's Wedding**

Our next 1 ½ hr: flight had us in Brisbane to meet my nephew, Robin, and his wife, Pooh who had booked us into a modern and delightful place overlooking the river. They arrived from the U K the next day, somewhat exhausted after 36 hours without sleep. After being joined by Pooh's brother and wife from New Zealand, Robin drove us all for five hours north to Hervey's Bay, pronounced Harvey's! Here in the small, but attractive airport, we boarded a 16-seat plane for a ½ hour flight to Lady Elliot Island, one of the southern, and smallest, of The Great Barrier Reef. It is an Eco/Educational paradise for hundreds of birds, fish and turtles which were beginning their mating season. After more and still necessary sleep to catch up, Robin wanted me to walk around the island with him...at least, ¾ of the way...which we did in about ¾ of an hour!

As the island is not too far from the Equator, it got mighty hot there, but rained a bit, also, so we were never too uncomfortable and though there was electricity for our 'bedroom and bathroom' huts in which we slept, other amenities with which we are spoilt at home and probably take for granted, were not available.

Natasha and Jamie in Brisbane

On our return flight and drive from 'our' island, we stopped for a night at The Eyrie Escape, a Host Accomodation (a k a 'B & B' in the USA). Peter and June Rogers had just opened this idyllic property with the most magnificent views in all directions. It could house all six of us and they deserve tremendous success as their food and ambience is extra special. There were eagles flying around us as we enjoyed the outdoor hot tub! Everything that was arranged by Robin for us in Brisbane and on the island he did on the Internet! A really great job!

October 30th was the wedding day! Jamie and Natasha, the bride and groom arrived at 2:30 this morning from the U K! Edward, Jamie's elder brother and his wife, Louise, flew in yesterday, taking 22 hours to get here and will leave for the U K again tomorrow evening taking the same time to return, so they were in Brisbane for 52 hours total then an additional 22 hours to return home all in the 'back of the bus!! If that is not brotherly love and family togetherness in extremis, heaven only knows what is! The wedding in Brisbane Park, conducted by a lady Justice of the Peace, was super. The bride was gorgeous and it was a tremendous three-family gathering that, for all of us, was unique and exciting!

The next event planned for Jamie and Natasha was to be a 'Blessing Ceremony' to be held near Robin & Pooh's home in Surrey. We had these wonderful 'around the world' first-class tickets that cost only slightly more than first-class from New York to Lisbon both ways, so what to do?! With this in mind and as Anne and I were half way around the world anyway, I persuaded myself that it'd be cheaper to keep going all the way around it! So! The Collis family flew off back home, and A and I continued to Hong Kong with Qantas, who were beginning to know and spoil us well! 8 ½ hours got us there and to the brand new and vast airport. No more RH turns at less than 1,000 ft on the 'final'! Sadly, it lost A's luggage for a while but it was delivered safely, a few hours later, to the Regent Hotel on Kowloon Island, one of our most favorites and where we had the same room overlooking Victoria Harbor as we did the last time we were here.

As we'd been 'on the trot' for quite a while, we were comparatively national-news-less! As it happened, we were met and greatly saddened by the amazing story and loss of that great golf champion, Payne Stewart. Then we read about the awful crash of Egypt Air's flight that occurred on the wedding day.

Our three-night layover was just as wonderful as it had been for the last visits there a few years ago. Since then the Chinese had taken over so we were interested to see what changes had been made, if any. The only noticeable one, we thought, was security. Police with guns were very much in view whether on the streets or in the 'malls'. They were in no way bothersome. They just seemed to be keeping an eye on things generally.

Our favorite thing to do was to go back off the beaten track to what Annie refers to as 'the Old China' where the tiny shops were to be seen with their owners crouching by the entrance. Many did speak English so it wasn't 'just looking'! If something was seen that was of interest to purchase, Annie had learnt well the art of bargaining in Africa and had become quite adept at that art!

The walk through the 'Farmers' Market' is an extraordinary experience with all the fruits and vegetables lined up so neatly and all appearing so fresh. The live chickens with their heads being cut off was anything but pretty, but it was all part of the daily life led there, so we just took it in our stride! "When in Rome...!" After walking several blocks, we found ourselves back on Nathan Street where the more modern shops are and where you can shop 'til you drop! There's no doubt that among the best parts of travel and the best education is to see the culture, or cultures, of other countries, if possible.

The one big, important shopping toot we just had to do during our time there was to find some sort of fake flower to put on Annie's straw hat that she had bought really as a beach hat for the Barrier Reef island, but intended to use as her wedding hat in England and at the Blessing Ceremony. She was darned if she was going to carry one from Boston around the world...and without any conceivable doubt, **I was not about to,** and have it arrive in mint condition! She'd need a black hat to go with her black suit, but some color to spice it up and not look as if she was off to a funeral rather than a wedding! **Well!** In a nutshell, this minor errand caused the following: A Star ferry ride to H K island, at least an hour's worth of wandering around crammed streets asking where she could find such a thing, a highly expensive lunch at the Mandarin (Oriental now) Hotel and further shoving through worse crowds after asking for more directions to find the perfect flower! Now we knew, indeed, what it meant and what we'd seen of, the Chinese way of living in H K and the ever-present fight for life on its sidewalks! Add to these few, unimportant, things the fact that it was, without doubt, the hottest day that H K had had in a thousand years and you can understand the state of mind and condition of this particular, antique husband!

Finally, **Eureka**!!

Annie found a vendor on a side street that, actually, sold real and fake flowers, boas, you name it! Although not perfect, she knew it was going to be the best she could find before I threw my second ticker attack so, for **ONE DOLLAR, U S,** she bought a big, orange, fake flower that would go with her black and orange scarf. Phew! Now, of course, we had to find our way back through all those 'bare' streets to the Star Ferry! To say that it was a king-sized struggle in an understatement, but she constantly wants to hold high the looks of the Wynne-Willson side of the family at the wedding, and you must know how the English love to wear hats at weddings, surely?! To be fair, which of course I am under such stressful situations, the hat was a crowning success!

Our flight to London via B A took 13 hours and 40 minutes, but after that hat business, it was a breeze, believe me! A great few days followed with the Blessing Ceremony where we caught up, yet again, with the family, including Betty my sister, and many, many friends of old. Tishy Nugee was there! She was the daughter of John Nugee, my housemaster at Radley, near Oxford, when I was there from '33 to '36. She wasn't born then, of course, but it was so great catching up with her again after so many years.

With the Blessing Ceremony completed, and such fun, the next problem was how to bring the hat home! Annie had already made a decision about that, I found, with relish and relief. Guess what! She had 'most generously' left it with Pooh, it now being probably, worth all of $8.00! I'm willing to bet it finished its life in the trash there, but it really did serve its purpose well.

What a super trip that was, as I hope you gathered!

After we'd got home and a bit settled, we called up our close neighbor for 21 years, Karl Stuntzner, just to see how he and his wife were and if all was well. Anything but, we learnt most sadly. While we were away, Mary, Karl's wife, had died suddenly. What a shock and we felt so for him and his daughter, Marion, whom we'd watched grow up so well and beautifully over the years.

By and large, though exciting often, '99 was a grim one due to the loss of many close and dear friends.

ELEVEN
2000 - 2002

I wonder if some of you have been to Captiva Island on Florida's west coast, as opposed to Captiva nearby on the mainland or, maybe, joined by a bridge. Anyway, Annie and I took a beachside cottage there for a few days in February and invited Beth and Rob Ladd as our guests. All of us loved it because it was quiet as could be; no cars, just golf carts to get us to the small ferry landing and shop and two small restaurants, one pretty good for dinner.

It takes about half an hour to get to the island from the mainland and it is well worth visiting the nearby supermarket that is close by the dock to take supplies with you. Should you run out while in your cottage, there is a pleasant young woman who has built quite a business by taking your order, going back to the mainland to fill it and returning it to you on the dock that evening for a reasonable charge.

Our cottage, #10, had the very best view of the lot across the channel looking east, north and west and of the abundance of fish and dolphins and shore birds—moving constantly and with certain magic. The plethora of shells on the unspoiled and moderately people-free beach was unique, superb and highly collectable. We even had a quiet, tame, blue heron that came daily for snacks on our deck.

The cottage we rented was adequately furnished, clean and fairly comfy. This was more than complemented by its view and position. We've been tempted to return since then but, sadly, the owners don't seem inclined to make what we all felt were quite necessary and inexpensive improvements for the price charged. It is a pity because Safety Harbor is a peaceful and attractive spot for these days, we think.

While in Florida this time we stayed for three nights with my senior appraiser and his wife, Guppy and Camie Ford, at their comfortable home overlooking the beach near Sarasota. We flew back home on February 21st. On March 9th it was 70F degrees for two or three days and on the next it was 33F and snowing! "Oh! To be in *New* England now that Spring approaches", to misquote someone famous! Who? I've not a clue!

August 27th was a really ghastly day. As we often do at this time of year on Sundays, we drove down to Padanarum and the little church

231

there called St. Aidan's for the service and to hear our friend Spencer Rice preach the sermon. That, we think, is always masterly and invariably draws a SRO congregation!

**Harold Sedgewick
With the Harvard Football Flag**

As was our habit, Harold Sedgewick joined us so we could drive him to church at 8.00 A M sharp to get us to the church on time! Anne went out to greet him. She took his bag with a bathing suit in it because we were going to have lunch with Molly and Joe Dow plus a swim, and put it in the trunk of his car. She returned to the house and, as she closed the kitchen door, turned and could only see Harold's feet behind his car.

Obviously, he had gotten out of it, locked it and collapsed. Anne ran to call 911 and, in no time, the Westwood ambulance was there and, after his condition was checked, she followed it to the Norwood Hospital where he died about 20 minutes after leaving our house. What an awful shock that was. What a loss to his hundreds of friends near and far, to one of the loves of his life, Harvard University and, most of all, his family.

On September 7th, his family arranged for a memorial service at Trinity church in Boston that was not only a fitting celebration of his life, but was just what he would have loved! He was such a kind, thoughtful and caring person and *such* fun! His niece, Lee Bagwill and John, her husband, who live hard by St. George's school, made most of the arrangements for his service and, happily, through that considerable sadness for so many of us, they have become good friends of ours.

John and Karen MacSnuffles' daughter, (that's what I've always called my special friend John, whose proper name is, of course, MacDuffie) named Carolyn, got married to Dan Chapman this September and that cheered us up greatly. She acknowledges that I am *the* oldest person she's ever, ever, known and paid me the singular compliment by writing her thesis about my life! What a risk she took! Anyway, most luckily and amazingly due to its subject, it was accepted. Carolyn is a talented Social Worker and Dan a College Administrator and they're such an attractive young couple.

While on the subject of beautiful and young maidens about whom Annie and most of our friends say, quite rightly, that I am enamored, Dana Osborn, whose brother John I mentioned herein, is right up there! She married Brett Harpster in May and what a great event that was at Trinity and, thereafter, at the Chilton Club. Dana is a nurse at Mass General where she seems to work day and night and Brett is an upcoming lawyer. Like her brother John and his wife Leslie they are, together with Julia and Chip Kern and Christopher and Jennifer Lee, our most special young people on this side of the Pond! I'd probably be in deep trouble if I didn't mention here that Dana is the daughter of Page Osborn who is Annie's age and a dear and special friend of us both. As I told you earlier, it was her father who was the first to interview me for a job when my late wife, Jackie, and I moved to Hamilton, MA from New York City in 1948! He was President of Forbes Lithograph Co. and had the smarts to by-pass me! Finally, one other dear couple that I want to include is Sam and Jen Williams who got married recently. Sam and Jeff and Holly, who lives on Oregon, are the progeny of my friend Beth and her late husband, Jeff.

September saw both Carolyn MacDuffie's wedding and, of course, Harold's Memorial Service. A few days after this we left for Las Vegas where we met Mark who flew down from his home in Reno and spent two amusing nights there with us and Camie and Guppy Ford. Many carry on critically and at great length about this 'sinful city' but really, if one goes there determined *not* to be critical and *not* with a 'nose-in-the-air' attitude, it can be great fun and not as exorbitantly expensive as many other cities. Mark managed to do wonders and got us five tickets, at the last minute, to see "O" (Eau), the Water Show produced by Cirque du Soleil, a French Canadian company and a truly memorable and fascinating spectacle at one of the casinos and among the very best I've ever seen.

Having rented a car, Mark and the two of us set out to see Zion and Bryce National Parks and the Arches. I'd always hoped we might be able to get to these unique and beautiful places and found each to exceed expectations. Luckily the weather was perfect and it was great having Mark to do the driving for us in a leisurely fashion...*some* of the time!

Later in the year we flew to Edinburgh, via Heathrow, and there were met at the airport by Jill Brewster who lives near by at Lilliesleaf, such a delightful name, and her close chum, Sheila Morrison from Harrogate. She, also, had a small Yorkie with her who traveled with the four of us in a big, comfy, van all over the western coast of Scotland and the island of Skye. This was a wee bit tough for Annie and me at first having Wesley with us, as you can guess after Radley, but we soon became quite fond of him. Jill had arranged the trip for us as she knows it backwards due to being in the Cottage rental business, and that is how we met some years ago as I wrote. We had such fun together and it was such a treat for me to go through so many places where my Dad and Mum took Betty and me in our 'caravan' before WW2!

The places to stay Jill chose were great and one, Skeabost, was of particular interest to me. It is on The Isle of Skye and now it is in one of the houses that the McLeod family owned when Dad went there to teach one or two of the boys back in 1927, or so. It is now called The Skeabost Hotel and it was a delight for me to be able to leave photos that my Dad took of it all, and Dunvegan Castle nearby, that included one or two of a young boy of about 4 or 5 years of age who was one of that clan, Ruaraidh (ph: Rory) Hilleary! Some time after arriving back home, I received a most charming letter from him recounting his memories of that time and thanking me so much for the photos.

Towards the end of October we fulfilled another long-term mission. Every few years, it seems, there is the Welsh Festival of choirs and, this year, other choirs from this country and this time Australia, at the Royal Albert Hall. Friends had attended one year and to hear them speak about it made me determined to go. However, this time there was an added incentive, though a most sad one. Gordon Heald, husband of Betsy, had died not so long ago of Lou Gehrig's disease and he had been a great part and promoter of 'Saengerfest'—the men's choir in this part of the country who, not only hosted the United Kingdom's choir here recently, but also, we heard, was going to have a brief memorial service during the Albert Hall concert. In the event, this never came about, which saddened us. The grapevine told us that many friends and former singing colleagues of Gordy were heading to this event from the Greater Boston area. So we called Betsy and asked if there was any chance of our getting tickets and tagging along! Being there was just like going to a popular event in Boston! People we knew, or recognized, all around the row where we sat! The concert was every bit as exciting and stirring as we hoped it would be! Such a magnificent sound! Combined choirs of hundreds of men's voices singing stirring songs many of which we knew by heart! As I wanted to be sure to remember how to spell Saengerfest, I called my chum, John Drake Ross, who sings with this group, most of whom are from Massachusetts, that was formed in 1904. He told me as well that it was formed by 4 Harvard Medical School students and, ever since, all correspondence to the many individuals now members, all are addressed as 'Doctor', regardless! John now lives on the Cape and tried, with me, to republish 'AWAY GAMES" you may remember. His family, related to Sir Francis Drake of U K naval history fame, is buried in the little village church of Musbury, near Axminster in Devon we found, when we were staying with Robin and Pooh. They took us a few yards to it from where their house is, to the village church and we read all about it. I, too, found John's name in the Visitors' Book there that he'd signed a few days before, so Annie and I sent him and Martha, his wife, a P C back home from there just to let him know that 'Big Brother' is always watching! It was fun catching up with them at the Albert Hall a few days later and to let them know about their visit to Devon and our knowledge of it! My great-nephew, Jamie, and Natasha his wife, most kindly let us stay in their flat near The Oval which was fun, and then a brief visit to Robin and Pooh at their lovely house for our first time.

In November we made an epoch-making decision to make an offer to buy a house in Dedham, only about five minutes away from Orchard Circle in Westwood where we'd lived so happily for 34 years. Why did we do this, you may ask? Because Annie felt, most strongly, that due to my hip we should be in a house that has its master bedroom and bathroom on the ground floor and, besides, I wasn't getting any younger! Our new home is so configured and is free standing in a condominium where the outside is managed. I, if the truth was known, was getting tired of coping with mowing, gardening and looking after the little pool and garden we had in Westwood and, also, having my office in the dark basement where, believe it or not, I spent much time!

Our Pondside Home In Dedham

On December 7th we signed the P & S agreement for our lovely new house with the continuing and excellent guidance of our friend Lee Higgins, who had been our first-rate real estate agent and, also, George Killgoar, our most competent and caring lawyer. Mark came home on the 23rd for Christmas. This is always a brief, but great, excitement for Annie and me, and that day we took him to meet Tucker and Terry Aufranc, the charming couple from whom we bought our new house, and as we were certain he would, he loved the place. With that important piece of business completed and a Merry Christmas under our belts, Mark flew off home to Reno on 'Boxing Day', the 26th at the crack of dawn, never a happy moment for us!

During January of 2001, Peggy, who had not been doing well in Clark House, the medical section of Fox Hill Village near our home, gave us all concern due to her possibly having had a stroke. Her age then was 94. As can be imagined, this was a frantic time because, a long time before this, we had made plans to go to Egypt on February 8th with

Abercrombie and Kent as our guides. We had always wanted to go there to take an extensive tour of the Egyptian artifacts and ruins but, also, to take a voyage up the Nile on their boat. We were more than concerned about Peggy and what we should do, unsurprisingly, even though she didn't recognize us and was becoming weaker by the minute. All involved made it more than clear that we should go, however, as it was felt that she might linger on for days or weeks. In the event, after really struggling with every aspect of the situation and taking everyone's advice we decided we should go as planned, but not without concern, on the 8th and confirmed this hurriedly with A & K.

As things turned out, it was not a dull week. On January 28th we were told, finally, that Peggy had had a stroke. On the 29th we signed the agreement for the sale of our house in Westwood. On February 5th Peggy died. The 6th was Annie's 60th birthday. On the next day Anne made all necessary arrangements to have the Memorial Service for her mother after our return home, and on the 8th we caught a Swissair flight to Zurich and on to Cairo. We had quite a wait in Zurich airport, but this wasn't tough to take, and that evening we flew on to Cairo where we were met by a most charming, Egyptian, A & K representative, who welcomed Annie with a huge bunch of beautiful flowers! That's the way to go!

Of the several exciting trips we have made under the guidance of Abercrombie and Kent, I believe the Egypt one was the best from a research and guide point of view. To be blunt, I was a bit scared of being overwhelmed by information from high-powered Egyptian, English-speaking, guides. Not so, in the event! Our principal guide, Hesham, was by far the most helpful, understanding, patient and, above all, knowledgeable Egyptian gentleman you could imagine and everyone both admired and learnt greatly from him. He became a good friend to me and, at the end of his time with us, I wrote him a letter trying to express my appreciation for all he'd done for Annie and me. This he received just before our farewell dinner and he amazed me by saying that he had never once before received such a letter, and he just didn't know how to thank *me!* I think of him often because of the Middle Eastern problems that surround us and of the many discussions I had with him about them. I was particularly interested to catch his somewhat scathing, but veiled, remarks when speaking to a group of us, regarding the crash of the Egypt Air flight off JFK in which all aboard perished. He didn't say so, but made it abundantly clear to me later that the reason for it was that there were, in his words, many Egyptian pilots on board who'd just finished their training in the U S and that the cause must be put at the door of sabotage and the Israelis. Far be it from me in my ignorance to argue this one, but it surely brought home the age-old problems that fester and threaten to explode in that entire area of the world.

After visiting the incredible National Museum in Cairo the next day, our guide took us to the airport and we flew a short distance to Herghada on the western side of the Red Sea to board our 'home' for next few days, the M/Y Callisto. She is a delightful, 20-plus-passenger ship of Greek registration and Greek crew. As it happened, there were only eight of us passengers on board due, we believed, to the international situation in those parts. After quick overnight sail northeast, we disembarked at Aqaba, the most southerly, and only, port of Jordan that abuts Israel and Saudi Arabia at that point. We then jumped into a bus and drove off to Petra, the Pink City of the Desert—one of, if not *the*, most extraordinary sights to my way of thinking in the ancient world (dating from 20 centuries ago, in fact!). Frankly, it blew our minds and Anne and I will remember it vividly always. In spite of the heat, we all walked, with Hesham at my side due to my hip, for about 40 minutes down the Siq gorge, a winding chasm. The origin of this truly unique site is not known for sure, but it might be from torrents of water over the centuries, or by a fracture of the earth. This is the main entrance to this incredible 'hidden' city of ages ago.

Just as we approached the end of the Siq, we were asked to get in a line and place one hand on the shoulder of the person in front. We walked like that, having closed our eyes for several feet and then were asked collectively to open our eyes wide! There before us was the front of the incredible Treasury, carved completely out of the pinkish sandstone. Additionally there, lying on the ground right in front of the front door, was the omni-present camel illuminated by a shaft of sunlight from above. What made it even more dramatic was the fact that the 'inside' of the 'building' was in ruins and only was about ten feet in depth, so the pink front of it, fully illuminated by the bright sun, was stark and seemed to be all that there was.

Due to the considerable heat, going down and up the Siq, it was decided that I would a take a horse and buggy ride back up that I didn't mind at all! When, and if, the situation ever improves in that area, I so hope that all who have not been able to visit this appealing place will. It is, I believe, an experience of a lifetime with which Annie agrees most heartily.

On another day when the Callisto was docked in Aquaba, we were taken, by car again, to the Wadi Rum desert to visit a Bedouin camp through which, most interestingly, we were taken and given a tasty and unique meal and then on into the desert to watch and ride camels! The ride was rolling, but absolutely nothing like that given us on the way in our large jeep by a crazed Bedouin! I was convinced he was out of his gourd as he drove at around 70 to 80 mph up, over and down the innumerable mounds of earth and sand that we had to cross making occasional right-angled turns, just to keep us in awe of his prowess, I could only presume! What really ticked me off, however, was that whosoever was our guide in our Jeep was highly amused at our predicament and did less than nothing to rein in Jehu, the spaced out driver, in answer to my pleas!

**Petra—Our Very First View of The Treasury
As We Left the Siq**

First-Time Camel Jockey

Last-Time Camel Jockey!
Wadi Rum, Jordan

Not long after that visit and after boarding A & K's 'Sunboat 4', a larger boat for cruising up the Nile to Luxor, I distinguished myself by coming down with the most miserable strep throat. It says something for A & K that they called up one of their doctors from vacation to board the boat to look after me as I had a high fever. Due to this I missed quite a few of the side trips to such famous relics as the fabled Colossi of Memnon and The Valley of Kings to mention only two. Thank heaven I did not miss the drive for five hours across the Sinai Desert from the Red Sea to St. Catherine's Monastery of 'Burning Bush' Biblical fame. We drove in a convoy of about 20 cars well covered, at departure and arrival and at points along the way, by gun-toting guards and armed cars. It seems that there'd been a 'spot of bother' with marauding bandits quite a long time before we got there! As you might guess, it was as hot as Hades along the way, but we were in an air conditioned bus, as always, with supplies of ice-cold water in bottles for drinking and, also and as always, an armed guard on it to calm any nerves anyone might have! Between you and me, I thought that that was overdoing a bit having him with us but, in hindsight, it was just as well, perhaps!

Luckily, my 'personal doc' did a great job and by the time we got to the Aswan High Dam, and the lake created to control the waters of the Nile, I was in fine fettle again. At Abu Simbel where we flew on a brief hop, we saw the colossal temples of Ramses II and his queen, Nefertari. They're 'only' 65 feet high and a unique sight if ever there was one! On our final day we drove to the Sphinx and the Pyramids in Giza, which really seems like a suburb of Cairo. To me, like all I'm sure, it is amazing that one never sees the palatial hotel and town which appear to be just a few hundred yards from the Sphinx. There it is, however, and never does a photograph show them, unsurprisingly! How very lucky Anne and I were to go on that adventure at the time that we did because it is doubtful that we'd take it now, things being the way they are in the Middle East, for sure.

After we got home on March 1st. the most exciting news about Annie's Vincent Club award was awaiting her. Linda Stikeleather, President of the club this year, called to give her this news and about which I've already mentioned. Mark, also, flew in from Reno to be with us for Peggy's Memorial Service at the Church of the Redeemer in Chestnut Hill the next day. This was a most fitting affair, I felt, and one of which she would have approved heartily, especially the Homily that was given by the Rector, Dick Downes.

Wally Savory, my partner in The Registry, had coped well in my absence, so well in fact that we popped off to Coco Point for our 24th consecutive annual visit of nine days on April 3rd. On April 19th. Toby Worsley Fox Collis was born in England to Louise and Edward. He is my first great, great nephew! Good show!

On May 31st the movers came to start getting us out and, on the 1st into our present home in Dedham. Who were our movers? Over the years, The Registry had been called by Gentle Giant Movers to appraise one, or two, things that had been damaged by them in transit. Their catchy name stuck in my mind! So! When the time came for us to shift, I gave them a call and said, "I'm not sure if I should be doing this, but I'd like you to move us!" In the event, they did a super job for us, but I occasionally call them hoping that they may have, perhaps, dented something, somewhere, so that we can do our appraisal work for them again!

On June 1st, Tucker and Terry Aufranc, moved out of their lovely house and we moved in after signing papers right and left! One great joy about our new abode is that my office, which used to be in the cellar at #29, is now over the garage at our new digs, and how light and airy and expansive it is! Wally has christened it The Appraisers' Registry's World HQ! I feel very spoiled to have it and Annie has made it so comfortable and workable. Tucker used to use it as his art studio. He is a first rate artist, by the way, as well as being a prominent and respected orthopedic surgeon! Happily, they didn't move too far away!

I'd be remiss here if I did not mention the most kind book-signing Barbie and Ernie Greppin gave me for Book I, on September 9, 2001. It was a lovely evening in their garden and quite a few brave souls showed up to hear Barbie introduce me and Before I Forget (Book I), more or less this way: "I did enjoy your book, Michael, and was most intrigued by the fact that you seemed to do little else during WWII, other than drink too much and leap into the sack!"

To this I replied, "I know, Barbie, but you must remember that I was 21 back then, unmarried, and by no means alone in these antics, for sure!"

The Second Day of Infamy occurred on September 11th. that the world now knows only too well. We were both at home when Monica Groom called to tell us and that the networks were reporting the shocking, mind-boggling events in New York. What a living nightmare.

Barbie Greppin

I can't remember whether, or not, I've told you this, but about two or three days a week, I fall out of the sack at 5.30 in the morning to go with Annie to jump up and down at Healthfit, a modern and efficient health club in nearby Needham. Why? Because I want to be around as long as I can and because I'd feel more than guilty lying in bed while Annie goes alone! Add to this the fact that the place abounds with gorgeous, young, healthy and cheerful (even at that heinous hour) trainers who, for a modest price, will beat the bejabbers out of you on request! Of course, I exaggerate yet again! We happen to have a very special trainer. Her name is Lisa and she and her husband, Bob, are becoming good chums of ours. Lisa twists and turns us both once in awhile and generally gives me the word about how my head will be parallel to the floor unless I straighten out and up! They once most kindly invited us to go and watch Bob play Wheelchair Rugby. I tell you that game, and those who can play it, simply by their existence, deny me the right, ever again, to complain about anything. Inspiring.

Christmas in our new home was something else! Robin and Pooh came over from England, Mark came home and Annie gave a lovely party for them and some of our friends on the 21st. Mary Flinn from the club, as always, presided over the affair so, with Annie's arrangements and decorations, it was a howling success (or so 'they' said)! Having Number One and Only Son and 'my Belongings' with us from the U K made it perfect!

One sadness occurred. Our longtime helper and once-a-week visitor, Ellen Kelly, decided to retire. We have missed her.

Robin and Pooh with the W-W's
Christmas, 2001

SOME RECOLLECTIONS AND
THOUGHTS, NOW WE'RE UP TO DATE!

Today, June 8th 2002, is a perfect one and it just happens to be Annie's and my 34th anniversary! I've said it before and will again, I bet, as it is so true, "How time flies when you're having fun" and, at the risk of being slightly sloppy I'll add, "when you're in love!" We have just received an email from my one and only son, Mark, from Reno, wishing us well, too, and that means so much to both of us. Like all fathers, I guess, I cannot believe that he'll be 47 in a month, nor I 83 in three for that matter!

As 34 years of marriage is not perceived to be a major milestone, even though I think all anniversaries are nowadays, we are not having any great celebration. Our good chums, the Greppins, who have their 39th anniversary this very day as well, are coming to share lobsters with us this evening and that'll be fun!

I've found that, in recent years, I seem to have become more intolerant than I was! Maybe that is the norm with increasing years, but I don't necessarily mean over major things and happenings. These are little, perhaps inconsequential, things that drive me nuts! I know I am sticking my neck out with some of you by listing them, for sure, but I'll risk it!

Split infinitives: You'd think by now I'd be used to them, particularly because I doubt if they are ever mentioned by a modern teacher of the English language. And, they crop up in the New York Times and in published "highbrow" fiction and even nonfiction.

'So fun' in place of 'Such fun':
Now *really* Elizabeth!

"You know" and "I mean":
This hiccup, that has now taken the place of 'hang on while I think of what to say next' or what takes the place of inhaling, or exhaling or both. One person on TV said 'you know' at least once if not more, in each *sentence* he spoke through the interview! We counted!

'Like I said'
There really should be a law against this statement, and 'Like in' can be added!

Gold:
That is displayed anywhere on a person, **other** than on fingers, wrists, earlobes or circling the neck.

S U Vs:
These steeds eat gas; I can't see around them when driving behind them and they promote excessive 'driver-power'. This'll get me into a peck of trouble!

CAPS...with their visors on backwards:
Why? Is it to keep the sun off the back of the neck?

Belly Buttons on view.
Who needs them and why expose them twixt shirt and whatevers?
Surely this exhibit is humdrum, or is my age showing?

Bill and Hillary:
I cannot help but blame a high percentage of our country's recent
social and moral problems on these two, due to their behavior when in
office. One more than t'other, I admit. They both make me nervous and
apprehensive now.

The Boston Globe:
Even though I still take it and always had to tell, Dave Taylor, its
long-term publisher and my late treasured friend, I couldn't cope with it!
Being a true gentleman, he never responded! It does seem to get more,
and more, liberal though.

Drivers:
Who refuse to move out of the fast lane. Why do they never look in
the rear-view mirror?

Drivers:
That park illegally in 'Handicapped' spaces and leap out of their cars
like spring lambs.

Limp handshakes:
They send chills through me.

Excess junk mail:
The number of catalogs that clog our mailbox day in and day out
that, when added to millions of others over the years, will destroy forests
throughout the world. We, due to our name, usually get at least two or
three; one for Wynne and the other for Willson and some with only one
'L', of course. Such unforgivable waste.

Telemarketers
Who call me 'Mike': It is about 30 years since I was known as Mike!
Not that I really mind from chums but, to be called that at my age by
someone who has never met me, gets my goat! How stuffy can I get?
They often ask about the state of my health at that time. Frankly, I don't
believe they give a hoot, and I usually say so. That's how stuffy!

Pretty young sales-girls who say: "Have a nice night!"
I know they mean well, but I think that that is my business and not
theirs! They'd think I was a dirty old man if I replied, "I hope we both
do!"

"I'm good"
When asking the young, and not so young nowadays, "how are you?" and the reply is, "I'm good!" I often find myself replying that I'm not too concerned about their morals. About their health, however, I am!

State Police
That are assigned to park for hours/days next to a few guys, or more, who are digging up the road, watching or having lunch. (I fear this is a Massachusetts anomaly). My spies hint that they are being paid overtime for carrying out this dire necessity. Such waste of time and money must drive *them* crazy?

Finally, I've recently had a most interesting series of emails with an Englishman whom I have never met! He found me via my cousin, Bill W-W, my hero ever since he was at Oxford when I was at Radley. I'd very much like to include one of Sam Eedle's letters regarding my Dad, if I may, as it was news to me, more or less, and I'd enjoy sharing it with you!

July 2. 2002

"Dear Michael,

I have now finished reading your book (one, i e.). I read it while on holiday for a few days in Devon during early June. You have certainly had a busy life - the book was most enjoyable. As a dog-owner myself, I particularly enjoyed the piece on 'Minus', and I was interested to follow the marmalade-making venture as I run a graphic design business from home and encounter similar challenges. I get round the time/employee problem by employing outworkers.

I leant on a friend to dig out your father's obituary last week, and here it is. Hyphenations are exactly as seen, and the squared brackets in the test occur where the type ran into the gutter of the bound paper, thus making it difficult to read.

Did you get the scan from Robin Collis's picture that I sent earlier? All the best. Yours, Sam"

Obituary. Bristol Evening Post. 15th July. 1937, page 11

Batsman Dies
County Cricket Ground Tragedy
Brother Of Bishop Of Bath And Wells
Innings Of 19 Playing For The Men O' Mendip

"The third tragedy this season at the County Ground, Bristol, occurred last evening during the match between the Gloucestershire Regiment and the Men O' Mendip, when Major Linton Frederick Wynne-Willson suddenly collapsed while walking back to the pavilion.

"Major Wynne-Willson had made 19 (runs) and it was at the close of his innings that he had a sudden heart attack.

"A doctor was summoned, but it was discovered that Major Wynne-Willson was dead. The body was taken to the Bristol Infirmary.

"Major Wynne-Willson who was 58 years of age, was a brother of the Bishop of Bath and Wells, and Preb. A.B. Wynne-Willson of Long Ashton and an uncle of J.P. Wynne-Willson, of Bucklands (Hatch?) Nailsea.

"He was the son of the late Rev. William Wynne-Willson., rector of Codford St. Mary, Wilts, from 1873 until 1891. He was educated at Winchester and Trinity College, Oxford. During the South African War he served with the Oxford University Volunteers and later received a commission in the West India Regiment.

KEEN SPORTSMAN

"On the outbreak of the Great War he was gazetted to the 5th Norfolk Regiment and was sent to help train the 13th Gloucestershire Power Battalion with whom he served in France.

"In 1917 his health broke down and later he was transferred to the Royal Flying Corp School in Norfolk.

"Since the war he has run coaching establishments for boys preparing for the Universities and the Army at Hayes, near Shaftesbury; Alderley, near Wotton-under-Edge and High Littleton House, Timsbury. A keen, all-round athlete and sportsman, he at one time played cricket and hockey for Norfolk County. In 1907 he married Miss Elizabeth Beaumont, of Weymouth, and has one son and a daughter. The funeral will take place at Chewton Mendip Church on Saturday, at 2,30."

250

Now, you all know more about my Dad than I ever did up to a few days ago, thanks to my friend in England whom I've not met...yet! I knew, of course, that Dad died in a cricket match four days after I returned from my year at St. George's in Newport and I was able to attend his funeral at Chewton Mendip's church with my family. Some of the preceding was mostly news to me, however!

**Dad, Betty and Mum,
Circa 1916/17**

Some may remember my writing about my 'surrogate' son, Peter Tunley. His next job, after being Manager of The Country Club about 16 years ago, was as Manager of The Stanwich Club in Greenwich, CT. This year Annie and I were incredibly pleased and proud that he had the honor of being elected President of The Club Managers' Association of America. His wife Connie and his two sons, not to mention his dear mum, Jeannie, must be equally proud of him, if not more so!

Speaking of Peter and of his association with TCC, I'd be more than remiss if I did not remember and mention as friends the following members of TCC's staff, some of whom have been there since 1976, or longer, when I gratefully became a member. They are, roughly in order of entering the front door, Ethel MacFarlane, David Chag the General Manager, Sean McSwiney; Bob Corenki; Vincent LaFleur; Steve LaCount and Mary Flinn who you have met already! Two who have retired from the club, but who we miss greatly, are Tim Ryan and Mary Lou LaPlace. Annie and I will always be grateful to them all for the ways they assisted in so many of our happy times.

Camie and Guppy Ford

252

Annie and I are incredibly happy, thankful and content in our comparatively new home. Number one and only son is still working away successfully in Nevada and enjoying his skiing and climbing as usual. We haven't heard from Wendy for a long time. For the first time in memory there are no animals at home. After Radley left us, we really felt that it'd be wrong and unkind to have another dog due to traveling and leaving him, even with Elsie to look after him, should she continue running her kennel!

The Appraisers' Registry of New England LLC and its 22 members are well and seems to grow in stature annually. I'd be lost without it because I'd be bored rigid with nothing to do. My partner, Wally, and I seem greatly to enjoy our work together and have fun doing so. When, and if, I ever retire and he takes over fully, I so hope that he will get as much enjoyment out of the work that we do now and the association we have with our members. They are a great group.

Many ask me, due to my age and WW2 experiences, I guess, what I think about all that surrounds us in our country today. Like most people, I find that hard to answer. Bluntly, I wish for security reasons that there was no television as there was during WW2. It seems to me that we tell the world just about everything we're going to do, when and how, before we do it and that scares me stiff for our armed forces and all who have the country's security at heart. That the print medium seems to follow suit is as discouraging. With everyone's 'rights' being tantamount these days and that of 'making money' seeming to be the only things that matter, no wonder that every scoop and rumble comes at us all day every day as a 'News Alert'. It may sound heretical these days, but what we did *not* know, mostly in WW2, was usually good for us and enabled us to get on with what we were doing which, quite frankly, was enough to worry about. It is often that I remember well, and how we greatly enjoyed the days when, all day long, hour by hours, radio and TV did not shout at us how somebody, somewhere, has died, been murdered, raped or ruined in some ghastly way or another. What in heaven's name are we supposed to do about it, other than feel shocked, sad, helpless and useless and, in my case, infuriated? It is awful that it happens, but this has been broadcast for so long now that it is obvious that it does no one any good, in fact it appears to make matters that much worse by it's continual exposure. Enough already!

Getting Saddam out of there is, I truly believe, essential. Not too original a thought! However, if that happens and war is the result with all its attendant horrors, I pray that we, and whoever is with us, can figure out how to cope with and manage what follows. I do not believe that anyone on earth can read those tealeaves. Additionally, I wonder, as do many, what would happen should Saddam have shoved all of his stock-piled horrors, if he does have them which seems the case, across the border into Pakistan, say, and the inspectors come up empty handed? That, it seems to me, would set the cat among the pigeons and be a lasting problem.

I have told you that, in our family, I am the only one out of step! Annie, Mark and Wendy are all adopted. I was not! I've mentioned herein how I so hoped that I would be able to include, in this memoir, Annie's personally written story of HER SEARCH. I am delighted to say that now I can!

The Appraisers

(Back Row): Dan LaCroix, Bob Landry, Guy Dillaway, Bruce Bower,
Norman Hurst, Albert "Guppy" Ford, Robert Mussey, Peter Combs,
Steve O'Brien, Jr., Martha Richardson, Ken Van Blarcom,
Wally Savory, Susan Forster, Bob McMillan.
(Front Row): Martin Booker, Michael Wynne-Willson, Brigitte Fletcher,
Johanna McBrien, Grace Yeomans, Millicent Mali.
(Unavailable For Photograph): Chris Reuning, Bob Harkey,
Keith Gagnon, Rick Walsh.

I was always told by my Dad and Mum to leave the icing part of the cake to last and have always found that, in the main, to be a darned good idea, providing it wasn't whipped away when I wasn't looking! Now, I use Annie's words, bar a very few thereafter, as the icing on this effort. To me, it is the best place of honor I can give it and I know, and am quite sure, that you will enjoy and, marvel at it, as I do every time I hear her relate it. You all, by now, know that I'm a bit of a promoter, and have been for years. I think the following story, her story, should get much wider publicity than I can give it, don't you? I hope you agree.

At my sister's funeral in Guilford Cathedral on March 23, 2002, I was thrilled to see relatves and friends of many years ago. I was so particularly pleased that my cousin and hero of old, Bill W-W, was able to be there!

My Hero of Old, Bill Wynne-Willson, Age 91
At My Sister Betty's Funeral

Part Three

ANNE'S STORY
BEFORE I FORGET
My Search

By

Anne P. Wynne-Willson

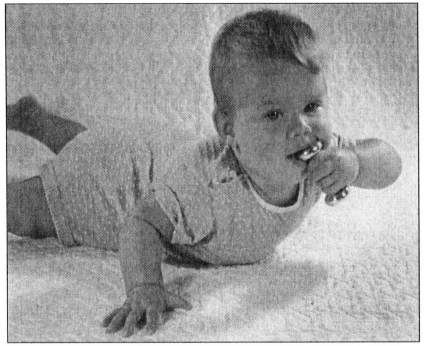

Aged 7 Months

Although this book is the sequel to Michael's 'Before I Forget', he has asked me to write a little section of it, or maybe it will only be a chapter. We will see when I get there.

My tendency was to begin..."Once upon a time there was a little girl," but then thought the better of it. This is a real story about adoption, how I grew up and a search that didn't begin until I was 54 years of age.

I was born on February 6, 1941 ten months before Pearl Harbor and was adopted by Peggy and Cam Patterson from Weston, Mass, six months later. I was brought home to their summer home in Marion, on Buzzards Bay. The first picture taken of me was when I was seven months old by Mother, who was doing a lot of wonderful photography herself at the time. I looked like every other baby that age. Adorable, of course, but chubby and smiling, with a typical silver rattle of that time in my hand!

I won't bore you with every scenario of my life because this is Michael's book, but I had a happy childhood doing what every child does as they grow older year after year. I had a roof over my head, ate good food although Mother was a meat and potatoes cook, saying that she "cooked because we have to eat." I guess I gathered at the time that she actually hated to do it. However, after Pearl Harbor and the United States entered the war, things began to change in our household, like so many did during that time.

My mother was 35 years old when I was adopted and my father was 48. They had been married 10 years. He had fought in the Border Skirmishes, and World War I. He wasn't able to graduate from Harvard with his Class of 1916, because he had already entered the war. So you can imagine how tense things were when he decided to volunteer his services for World War II at the age of 50 or 51. It would prove that he really was too old to go to war, but as he was an expert in transportation he felt it was his duty to serve his country. When I was 3 they sold the dream house they had built in Weston, said goodbye to the help, Helena and Fred Sturk, and off we went to Norfolk, Virginia where the Army sent him. I don't really remember much that happened there except that a little boy that I played with came down with polio. Consequently, I spent a good deal of the time in the house because Mother, naturally, was afraid I might catch it. I also remembered seeing a yellow fire engine from my bedroom window. For years I talked about seeing this yellow fire engine and I don't think anyone ever believed me. About 14 or 15 years later on my way up to Williams College to see my beau at the time, traveling on Rt. 2, I saw a yellow one backing into the firehouse in Gardner, MA. *Phew!* My remembrances had finally been validated.

When Daddy was sent to Okinawa, we came north and went into the house in Marion for the summer. Because we had no place to live due to that house having had no heat, Mother had to rent a house in the village for the next two winters. Unfortunately Daddy came back from the war a handicapped person. Although it was never diagnosed, Mother felt that he had acquired some sort of a fungus on his hands and feet that was very painful and made walking very difficult. For the rest of his life he used a cane. When he finally came home to the new house they bought in Chestnut Hill, MA, he sat in his chair for a year and did not say a word. I have no recollection of that. To Mother's credit she got him going again and back to work at Patterson and Wylde with his partner of many years, Jack Wylde. He never played golf again. I think it was because he was President of the Massachusetts Golf Association from 1937-1939 that he was offered a golf cart that would be made for him, long before the days of ever having what we use today, so that he could get back on the golf course. He refused partly because he didn't want to be singled out. He did manage, though, to get back onto the curling rink at The Country Club in Brookline, and curled for many years.

I realize that when you get older sometimes things become bleary in your mind, but I do *think* I remember when I was told I was adopted. I think I was about 5 years old and remember walking with Mother down a street in Boston, jumping over the lines on the sidewalk making sure I didn't step on the crack. I remember her telling me then that I was adopted. Of course I know that I didn't understand what that meant, but I seem to remember the incident. I don't ever remember that I was told I was chosen and therefore special, but I bet that is exactly what happened. I just don't remember that part of it.

I was sent to The Park School in Brookline, and Alford Lake Camp in Union, Maine for three summers. When I was in the 4th grade at Park I remember having a teacher, Mrs. Wilder by name, who always picked on me and scared me to death. I would try to hide behind the person in front of me so she wouldn't call on me, but invariably she would. I was so petrified that it was then that I am sure I began not to listen in class, especially in math. To this day I can't add and subtract...well I can, but you know what I mean! I am not a numbers' scholar. It was much later that I would learn that this behavior was what was called Verbal Abuse. When I got to the seventh grade I was sent to The Beaver Country Day School in Chestnut Hill where I stayed until graduation. I loved Beaver and made many great friends there, many to whom I am still close today. I wasn't a great student but I did well in sports, playing everything that I could. I was tall, but somehow someone else was always taller, so I never made the Basketball Varsity although I always seemed to be the manager! I did play a mean game of field hockey, however! I owe that to one of my favorite teachers, Pippy Rooney, now Pippy O'Connor, who pushed me to the fullest, screaming at me running down the field, always trying to make me do better. I wasn't happy about the screaming at the time, but realized later that she was doing it for my benefit. She awarded me the MVP in hockey in the 8th grade and I received a gold hockey stick for my charm bracelet. Pretty heady stuff in those days! Pippy remains a good friend today and for years I would follow her around a golf course. She was an excellent player, had a gorgeous swing and won the 1955 Massachusetts Woman's Golf Championship. She continues to teach golf today and is a big supporter of junior golf. I worked so hard at my lessons, and before I knew it, it was Graduation

Day. Yea! I made it! I was really and truly sad to leave the hallowed halls of the school and I knew I would miss all my friends, but another chapter was beginning so off to Mt. Vernon College in Washington, D C, I went.

After graduating from College I moved to Boston at age 21 into an apartment on Charles Street with two of my Beaver Classmates, Jane Conant, and Paula Crampton before they moved out to San Francisco. I lived on Beacon Hill for 6 years working at the Harvard Graduate School of Education and The Harvard Divinity School. The latter was only for about 6 months. I must not have been the divine type! I hated it and didn't like working for a woman who decided not to give me much, if any responsibility, so I took a job at The New England Aquarium in 1966 as it was just being built. It was here that I met Michael who was working as Public Relations Director for The Boston Zoological Society in the same building on Long Wharf, but down the hall. Jackie, his wife, was still alive then but died about a year later.

The Vinalhaven Party
Back Row Lanny & Jane Parker, MF W-W, Jim and Sally Gilliatt,
Dixon & Barbara Welt; 2nd Row Jane Sherrill, Ham Lockwood
Front Row Christopher & Jennifer Lee, A P W-W, Jackie and C.S. Lee

Having met Michael, I thought he was good looking, charming and, most important to me, funny. Having a sense of humor I find is what gets you through life with all its twists and turns. My roommate, Julie Wight, thought he was good looking and thought I ought to go after him. My comment? "Oh yea, he is just about to look at me being 20 years younger" Her reaction? "Well, if you want to remain an old maid for the rest of your life, fine!" I didn't go after him, but shortly after that I began to date him, but didn't dare tell my parents that I was dating a man twenty years older than I was and a widower who had two children. Help! What would they say? I was 26 at the time and I think Mother was beginning to wonder if I was EVER going to get married. I had a savior who unknowingly stepped in. He was our dear Minister, The Very Reverend Lawrence H. Whittemore, Jr. He had left The Church of The Redeemer in Chestnut Hill for a higher position in Bethelem, PA, but came back the next year to marry the daughter of a friend of ours. When he asked Mother if there was anything on the horizon, meaning men for me, Mother wistfully said, "No". He cheerfully told her that at age 26 the next step would probably be marriage to a divorced man or widower! Bingo! So, when it came time to break the news the barrier had, thank goodness, already been broken by Mr. Whittemore. We were married on June 8, 1968. I was 27 years old. Michael lived in Hamilton on the North Shore, and the word went around that it wouldn't last 6 months. Well! We are about to celebrate our 35th anniversary. Not bad going, I'd say!

Life went along as most marriages do, although at 27 I took on one husband, two children, two dogs, two cats and one horse, not to mention the gerbils and any other pets inhabiting the house. We all survived, but it was tough sledding for a while. I chose to move into Michael's house in Hamilton because the children had lost their mother; their father had re-married, and the house was the one thing still stable for them. Although Wendy was the one who was always pushing the marriage, in the end she wasn't so happy. Mark on the other hand just sat back to see what this strange woman was all about. To this day I give him great credit for giving me a chance. Pretty big stuff for a 12 year old! The person that was the nicest to me when I moved into the new house, was a lady who lived down the street named Rommie Vaughan. I knew of her a little through The Vincent Club because she wrote so much wonderful music for many shows. Her daughter Jackie, who I slightly knew growing up, came back into my life because of our first invitation to Vinalhaven, Maine, their summer home. For the first two years of my married life I was grateful to Rommie for her warm friendship. Although sadly she died in 1971, it was the beginning of over 30 wonderful years of trips to Vinalhaven. We always knew that when the children went off to school we would move into a house of our own. What we didn't know in planning this was that, in the end, we would move off the North Shore to Westwood. That was two years later in August of 1970.

Karen Thornquist MacDuffie

John MacDuffie
Photo by Carolyn Chapman

Judy White Gray (Now Mrs. Harvey White)—
My Oldest Friend
Photo by Tim Gray

On January 31st, 1978 my father died after spending two years in a nursing home. He had an automobile accident in Marion brought on by what I now think was the beginning of Alzheimers. That name was just becoming known at that time because of Rita Hayworth's behavior in airports and airplanes. In the end she was diagnosed with this disease, and it was at that time that Daddy's mind began to get very confused. He was a very kind and gentle man, but in the nursing home he began to beat up his roommate with his cane. He would never hit a fly with a flyswatter, so this action was clearly out of character. Mother, two years earlier, had moved from the Middlesex Road house in Chestnut Hill to a single two-floor condominium, still in Chestnut Hill. Her eyesight was becoming worse due to glaucoma, and her disposition wasn't making Michael's and my life any easier. It was like the 4th grade all over again. She eventually had to move to the Assisted Living section at Foxhill in Westwood, one of the new Life Care Community Centers, where she could have supervision. She went in hating it and hated every minute while she was there. The last two years of her life she lived in Clark House, the nursing part of Foxhill, where she died from a stroke at 94, two months short of her 95th birthday on February 5, 2001. It was the day before my 60th birthday. What an incredible last eight years I had with her and I still pray that she is finally at peace. I hung in there with her through thick and thin and I am proud of that.

I was very lucky to have been adopted by these two wonderful people, who took me in and gave me a home. Heaven knows where I might have ended up. However, I think that no matter how lucky one is to be chosen, I have come to feel that every adopted child needs, and should know, their roots if only to get medical information. If you were adopted in my era of the 1940's, all the records at that time were sealed. That was just the way it was. I had thought about doing this many years earlier. Michael and I went down to City Hall, and when I found out I had to go before a judge to get my records, I froze and we walked out of the door. Through most of my life it never occurred to me to want to go on a search to find my biological belongings. Why would I, living this life that was handed to me? Of course, I always wondered, and when General Eisenhower was elected President, I thought...well, could he and Mamie be *my* parents? This happened on several occasions, some with famous people and some who were friends. There was a girl who lived in the neighborhood whose name was Karen Thornquist. She remembers very vividly my asking her if she was adopted. She didn't understand what that meant so went home and asked her mother if she was adopted like her friend Anne. I was thinking that maybe she could be my sister because we looked so much alike. Oh! What comes out of the mouths of children! Both of us went to Alford Lake camp and we ended up at Beaver. She was two years younger and as you know, at that age, two years made a huge difference. Eventually she married

John MacDuffie, and we re-connected and have been friends for years. During the 1964 Goldwater Republican Convention, there was a picture in Time magazine the week after the Convention of a girl holding a bunch of balloons. It was me! It was my twin, I was sure of it. That of course, got me thinking again.

Basically, I was a happy child, had wonderful friends, learned to cope with any difficulties at home and just lived one day at a time as I grew up. Although I grew up with absolutely no confidence, today I look back and realize I had my friends and teachers that I loved at Beaver who, in a way, became my extended family. My closest friend in life was Judy White who I met in a tree at The Park School. I can't remember who was in the tree, but I think I was. She too grew up in Chestnut Hill and Marion. Because we were only children I think we just gravitated to one another. Her parents, Mr. & Mrs. Henry K. White were absolutely wonderful to me and I loved them dearly for their kindnesses to me, and their support. I always have thought of them as my second parents. When Mr. White died in 1976, I was left his wonderful Chelsea clock with his initials on the front that now sits proudly on our living room mantel. I was also left a beautiful gold and diamond bracelet when Mrs. White died, and the best part about that is I remember her always wearing it. How lucky could I be? It never occurred to me that people would ever leave something to me in their estate. When Judy married W. Latimer Gray known as Tim, in 1962, she was 21 years old and I was her Maid of Honor. Six years later she was my Matron of Honor and only attendant. I am the Godmother of her eldest daughter Melinda, and took over the responsibility for her youngest daughter Margot who was about four.

Pat and Wally Meigs
(Known Pat Since Age 15)

What would I have done without Page Osborn and her parents always having me to their home. Years later her younger sister, Lee Higgins would help us with the sale of our house in Westwood. Things do come full circle if you live long enough. I met Pat Hobbs, now Mrs. Wallace Meigs, when I was 14. There was a 15 years age difference between us, but for some reason we just clicked and she has been a part of my life since then. She and Wally were married just 6 months after we were and as couples we have continued a great friendship. I give great credit to Jane Conant Batchelder, Kathy Whitelaw Stanton, Marny Stevens Gannett, Penny Fuller Graham-Yooll who have stuck with me since grade seven. I think, also, that being an only child, and having older parents, I spent my life wanting to be with my friends and taking every opportunity there was because I didn't want to miss a thing. There was a great big woolly world out there and I wasn't going to skip a beat!

Mother always said that she really knew nothing about my biological parents. The only thing she *did* know was that I was the product of a young woman and an older married man. She didn't even know in which hospital I was born. Anything to do with adoption then was tight, tight, tight! I can't remember how old I was when I noticed that on my birth certificate it stated the residence of my parents was listed as New York. I was curious because as far as I knew they never lived in New York, but I never went further with my thoughts and put it out of my mind. Years later I would understand why they did that.

I have learned that when you write a book, or in this case contribute to a book, one has to be honest or else there is no reason to tell the story. My story here is the tale of an adoption search, not really about my growing up, although I felt there needed to be some biography of my early life. Although Mother had this abusive personality due in part to her own up-bringing that included the loss of her mother at age 7, an abusive nanny for 8 years before she and her brother finally told their father, (she was fired the next day), the death of her brother at 25 climbing the highest mountain in Chile, her anger lasted a lifetime. Somehow I got rolled up in all the frustration, but it was the lack of communication and emotional support that was the most difficult. She was a very accomplished woman; a great horticulturist, a great sport's woman in riding and her love of horses as a young girl, and golf and curling as an adult. It wasn't until after her death that The Winsor School sent me their latest bulletin with an article about her and her memories of her time there that stated she "excelled as a Winsor athlete, playing field hockey and basketball." I never knew that. So much for communication! After her death I found out, through relatives, so much that I never knew about my mother and her life; for some reason she just didn't want to let me in. We hardly ever met up with my Baltimore cousins, and only later in life "found" we had cousins just across Route 9 in Chestnut Hill. Martha and Arthur Tucker and their two daughters lived just a biscuit toss away, and I never knew it until I went to Beaver. I am not sure Mother ever knew it and it was just happenstance that she and cousin Martha met. They were first cousins. After Mum's memorial service, I needed to call my cousin Kathy Worthington in Baltimore to tell her the news. I had met her only a few times in 60 years, but now we e-mail each other all the time. It was this lack of communication that was very confusing to me. There was so much I never understood, and Kathy filled me in on some things that surprised me so much.

Beaver Classmates
Top Row Penny Fuller Graham-Yool, Kathy Whitelaw Stanton
2nd Row Jane Conant Batchelder, Me And Page Osborn

It was now time for me to get on with my search and to try and find my biological parents. I did not do this out of anger myself. I want you all to know this. The older I got the more curious I got and after all, at 54, time was running out, maybe, to find my biological mother alive. After spending 52 years of not really wanting or thinking much about doing a search, maybe this was now the time to try. Could I do this? Would I be strong enough emotionally to go through the process? Remember, the only thing Mother said she knew was that my biological mother was a young woman and my father was an older married man. Well, how young was young, and how old was old? I pretty much decided that probably my father was not alive, but my mother could be. If she was 20 when she had me, then she could be 74. Finally, two years later at age 54, I decided to go for it.

My incredible journey was about to begin. The first thing I did was to write a letter to Helen Moore who was an Associate Minister at Trinity Church in Boston. I realized that, as many friends as I had, I really couldn't burden them all with their having to keep a promise of not speaking a word about this. I knew I could trust these few really close friends but if it ever got out, whether it be after a drink or two or even a slip of the tongue, I would be in duck soup. You see Mother could never know this. She, like many mothers, just wouldn't understand and I understood that. I was not about to hurt her in any way so I went on the premise that what she didn't know wouldn't hurt her. This whole process was for *me* to know, and to get medical information. If I were lucky enough to find my biological mother alive that would be a bonus. I asked in my letter to Helen if she would be of help to me if, for any reason, I should fold under the search process. I had been told that it was a very emotional thing to do. I knew that being a Minister, and also a Clinical Psychologist, Helen would keep it "under the stole," meaning she was dedicated to keeping it quiet. I have now taken the first step and so now I must continue. It was a scary moment because heaven knows where this would, or could, lead. I could be traveling down a dark road, or it could be something wonderful. I just had to have the guts and decided that this was an opportunity not to miss. I would accept the consequences and deal with any rejections later. I was a big girl now and felt quite sure I could handle it. Although not a really religious person, I had to believe that God had a big hand in this. You will understand this later, I think.

**The Girls From Beaver Country Day:
Jane, Me, Paula Crampton Bungen And Penny**

Years earlier our friend, and now Michael's partner in his business The Appraisers' Registry, named Wally Savory knew I was adopted. He asked if I had ever tried to find my biological parents. I never lied to him and got around that by telling him that the files in Massachusetts were closed, which was true, and which was always my standard answer to that question. As they were sealed in this state it would probably be impossible. He told me that his neighbor, a lawyer in Boston, adopted two children and if I was ever interested I should call him to find out the agency they used. Later I remembered this and so I called him. I told him that I had this friend whose 5th child was adopted and that maybe one day she would want to find *her* biological parents. That friend was Helen Moore, although I never revealed her name to him. He gave me the lawyer's name and I called him. He suggested that I give his wife a call since she now helped out at the Adoption Connection, the agency they used. Luck was with me because, by the time I called her, she was just about to leave the house for two weeks' vacation. I sat on this information for a few days, then screwed up my courage and called that agency in Peabody. Again I was fortunate because Susan Darke, the lady who began this operation 20 years ago at that time, answered the phone. Well! I nearly froze wondering what the heck I was doing, but I moved forward and explained to her what I wanted. I also told her that this was the top-most secret, and that no one must know about this, and could I have her trust? She was very soft spoken and sounded very sweet on the phone and I thought I could probably work with her. She said that she would send me some information about the agency and herself. A few days later a big brown envelope arrived in the mail. The return address was stamped in black letters "The Adoption Connection." Help! I phoned her immediately and said, "What are you doing to me?!" I told her that when I meant secret, I meant secret. She apologized and from there on all was well. How paranoid could I get?

I only had one piece of information to give Susan, and that was my birth date, February 6, 1941. It was the first time that I wondered if that was true, remembering my parents' residency in New York on my birth certificate. I knew that wasn't true. Susan told me that the birth date had to be accurate to make it legal. I did find out later that my parents used Mother's Aunt Emily Stevenson's address for protection so no one could find me, or maybe it was visa-versa, I didn't know. I guess I am not the only one paranoid! I thought at first that maybe I was adopted though a New York lawyer. I asked Susan how was she ever going to find any information with just a birth date. She obviously wasn't at liberty to tell me because that is one of the reasons she has a 90% success rate in finding parents for children and children for parents.

The reason why Susan began The Adoption Connection was because she herself was given up for adoption and when it came time for her to find her biological parents, there was no avenue for her to go. She also had a double reason. She also gave up a child for adoption. The only thing that I know is that she has worked very hard to put together this organization to help herself, but ultimately became successful in helping so many others looking for their biological belongings. I do know that she has an Assistant and many volunteer researchers in Peabody and clear across the country. She told me that there might be a wait of several months, but not to worry. At 54 I didn't have years, I replied!

I waited about 5 or 6 months, talking to her only occasionally. That August, Michael and I were planning to drive down to Hamilton to have lunch with his oldest female friend in this country, Moody Ayer. The Wynne-Willsons and Ayers had been friends since Michael and Jackie moved to Hamilton in 1948. Now that we lived in Westwood it was only occasionally that we got together. Michael thought it might be a good idea if we left a little early and stopped by to see and meet Susan Darke. After all, Peabody was on the way to Hamilton. He called her and she said she'd be delighted. She gave Michael directions, but said that she would like us to drop by the Cambridge Court House first. Why, I wondered, as it was a bit out the way? She told Michael that we should ask for Sheila and that she would have some sort of packet for us. I was very confused, to say the least, but we did as she asked. Remember it was only 6 months earlier that I began my association with Susan and she couldn't have found something already?

With The Rev. Helen Moore At My
Birth Mother's Grave,
Holy Cross Cemetery, Malden

We had no idea how to get to The Court House, but eventually we made it and found Sheila in The Family Court Department of the Middlesex County Division. She pulled out an 8X10 brown manila envelope, but first made me sign a release. I had to promise that I would not go on this search by myself. I told her that I was working with Susan Darke at The Adoption Connection, and she seemed very pleased about that. I signed the paper and she handed me the envelope. What could be could be, as I used to say as a young child waiting to open a Christmas present. I pulled out this very formal, legal, document that was folded three times. On the front was number 244955 and below that the name of Diana Marie Brackett. "Who is this?" I asked. "It is *you*", she replied!

I said, "Oh! God, my name was Diana Marie Brackett"? Then she told me that that was the name my biological Mother gave me. *Wow*! I unfolded this document and the next page read:

"To the Honorable the Judges of the Probate Court in and for the County of Middlesex:

RESPECTFULLY represents Charles C. Patterson of Cornwall-on-Hudson, N.Y. in said County, Orange and Margaret, his wife that they are of the age of twenty-one years or upwards, and are desirous of adopting Diana Marie Brackett of Cambridge, Massachusetts, a child of Nora Brackett of Somerville, Mass. which said child was born in Boston, Massachusetts in the sixth day of February 1941; that above-named child has been in the home of the petitioners since the seventh day of July, 1941 and that the petitioners are of sufficient ability to bring up said child and furnish her with suitable nurture and education. Wherefore they pray for leave to adopt said child, and that her name may be changed to that of Anne Warfield Patterson."

Well! Mother and Daddy never lived in Cornwall-on-Hudson so now you understand why I was a little confused when that was stated on my birth certificate. Also, I never lived in Cambridge, and I never lived in Boston either, but Boston is on my birth certificate.

It was dated the 3rd day of June 1942. Underneath there was both Mummy and Daddy's signatures. That was when I got goose bumps and felt the hair on the back of my neck standing on end, but it was nothing to what I was about to read which made me put both hands to my cheeks and say to Michael, "Oh! God, are you ready for this? The next name I read was that of Esther J. Stuart from The Avon Home. *That was the very same woman and agency from which Michael and Jackie adopted their two children*! First they adopted Wendy in 1953 and then Mark in 1955. Now what are the odds of that happening? I knew Esther Stuart only as a name on the Christmas List for years. I never met her, but heard much about her when discussing the adoption of the kids. Michael and I were both stunned. To think that Nurse Stuart was involved in my adoption in 1942 and 11 years later she was in Michael's house delivering Wendy to them in 1953, and again in 1955 with Mark! Am I beginning to see the hand of God in here somewhere or is this just pure coincidence?

In this packet, also, were many other documents such as the Agreement of Adoption executed by my mother, Nora Brackett, on May 20, 1941 where she gave me up to the Avon Home and authorized that agency to give me in adoption, without notice to her or the father. What an incredible wrench that must have been for her! Also included were my medical records and the results of the examinations that I had to have before being adopted.

Now we were on our way down to Peabody to meet Susan. Michael's thought behind this meeting was if she saw us, she might work harder instead of just working on the project not knowing those involved. She was thrilled with all the information we gave her because it meant she had much more to go on than just a birth date. She warned me that this still might take a few months, but not to be too discouraged. It turned out that there were two counties in this state that had opened their files. One happened to be mine, Middlesex County, and strangely enough the other happened to be Mark's which is Essex County. The reason that they were opened was because the two judges in those two counties were women! Now do you think God is with me?

My next assignment was to call the Cambridge Children's Services who had taken over the records of the Avon Home (Michael had always spoken of it as The Avon Nursing Home) when they closed, a date I do not know. I was to ask for Sandra (I can't remember her last name) and ask her for any unidentifiable information. This means that all the names would be blacked out. These records may be opened, but there was still some secrecy to this procedure. I explained to her my story but added that at my age it was probable that both parents had died. I felt I needed to say that in case she hesitated and I ended up with nothing. A few days later it arrived, and Susan was correct. Any and every name was totally blacked out. I tried to put it up to the light thinking I could figure out something, but no! Obviously I now knew my mother's name, but I was anxious to learn my father's. As I progressed I began to realize that there was no way I was going to find my father's name. I learned that in those days if you got a woman pregnant out of wedlock, somehow the man's name just evaporated into thin air. However, I now had 8 pages of information to sift through, and what I was about to find out was absolutely incredible.

My Birth Mother, Nora Brackett
Approximately Aged 38

What I was about to read was the record of interviews from The Florence Crittenton Home for Unwed Mothers in Brighton where I as born. Now remember, it said Boston on my birth certificate, and Cambridge on the legal form from the Court House. The first page was the medical summary from the hospital where I was born. It seemed I was a normal baby. My mother, (the name was scratched out but I already knew it) Honora Brackett, the Irish spelling for Nora, was admitted to the Florence Crittenton Home (FCH) in December of 1940. I had remembered reading a book several years before this search began about a woman in the same condition, and it was the norm to be admitted to this particular place at least three months before giving birth. Nora was born in County Cork, Ireland and came to the United States in 1925 at the age of 14, after completing what corresponds to our 9th grade, with her Mother and older sister. She had occasional jobs until she was 17 and then worked steadily since then. She did clerking in the A&P, 4 years at The National Biscuit Company and 5 years at J.P. Squires, a meat-packing factory. They lived in Somerville. She was Roman Catholic and had been at Squires in Cambridge, earning $24.00 a week when she arrived at FCH. She was described as friendly, talkative, vivacious and a bit superficial. She was 5'6" tall with brown hair with reddish tints and graying. She had a ready smile, dark brown eyes and clear skin. Her father had died several years earlier and she and her mother lived together in the second-floor apartment of a house in which her sister and brother-in-law (I am not sure whether they were married in this country or in Ireland before they came here) occupied the first-floor apartment. Her sister was said to be very bitter about this experience and quite concerned about money now that Nora wasn't working.

My father was born in Indianapolis, Indiana and also employed at Squires, earning $37.50 a week. He was married to his second wife and had one child. The first marriage ended in divorce. In regard to this marriage he said he "preferred not to discuss it…it was something of a mistake, but my wife is Roman Catholic, and I'll stick by her. That is my job." He was described as tall, about 6 feet and weighed 192 pounds. He was well built, with dark hair and eyes. He had a round face, wore glasses and was "nice in appearance". His features were regular except for a rather full lower lip. When interviewed for the first time on 4-1-41, he said, without hesitation, "I'm the guy…Nora, scratched out, is a swell kid…I have a swell wife and child". (From now on when I write in names you must realize that in this summary all the names were scratched out. The only name I knew was my mother's.)

In July of 1940 when obviously Nora was a month into her pregnancy, my father went through the firm's credit union and borrowed $200 to give her to "see her thru." He was paying $5.00 a week on this loan. For many years he worked as a truck driver for Squires, but in the summer of 1940 he was transferred to the sausage factory where he had less pay. Now he was back as a truck driver, but "felt like a heel" because he never told his wife. He was letting her think that he was still on the sausage factory's payroll. He told the interviewer that he was a World War I veteran and that he had been a roamer and had worked in 33 states.

This summary goes on to say that when I was born, Nora had decided that she could not keep me. She was anxious for an adoption placement. As she talked of this, "her eyes filled with tears." The social worker suggested several ways in which she might be able to keep the baby, but she answered, "No! No! I must give her up". My father called frequently, but Nora refused to see him.

The next few paragraphs suggest that there was much financial discussion about what to do. My father's son was seriously ill with a strep throat and that he was in debt to the hospital and doctor. The FCH worker said that my father must help to bear the expense of caring for me.

My mother's sister and husband were asking that Nora be allowed to return home as soon as possible. They were disturbed because her 3 months leave of absence was based on a "nervous breakdown," and they were fearful that, if she didn't return to Squire's soon, she would lose her job. The Social worker pointed out the fact that she, too, must bear some of the financial burden.

On April 2, 1941 there was a conference on what to do with me. This summary stated that Nora emphasized the fact that she could not look forward to keeping her baby "not only because I don't think it is fair to the baby, but because I can't stand my family's attitude. My sister would make it miserable for the child and I don't think it is fair to let a girl grow up without a name and without a father". She agreed to be responsible for one-half the board rate that would be approximately $2.50 a week. The arrangements were made for me to be admitted to The Avon Home's care on April 9, 1941. On the day of the parting my mother was "emotional, weeping and could not speak."

My Birth Father Harry Stingley

The rest of this summary primarily gives some of the background history that I found fascinating. My father was a Quaker of Dutch dissent. He made no effort to evade his responsibilities, financial or moral. He was sympathetic with Nora and her problems. He felt that the adoption plan was the best for the child because the mother's 'folks' would make it very hard for any youngster. He decided to stay away from the maternal relatives "because every time I went to see them they made a fuss and seemed more interested in getting every cent out of me than in anything else". My father spoke nicely about Nora saying to the interviewer, "Don't be hard on her and don't think ill of her. She is a decent girl. It was just unfortunate circumstances."

It goes on to say that he referred to his own wife and child. The latter was 4 years of age, born at Baker Memorial and he was said to be healthy and alert, "he knows some of his letters, can count fairly well and is very eager to get to school." In a letter to the FCH dated 2-14-42 he reported "my wife had a nine-pound boy on 1-18-42". He was apologizing for not showing up for an appointment and being "terribly slow" in paying and would do it gradually. He signed a financial agreement in the amount of $2.50 a week, and will pay at the rate of $1.00 a week until the bill is met in full.

At My Birth Father's Grave

The second half of this summary talked about Nora, my birth Mom. She made a smart appearance and was well dressed, a tweed suit, when she showed up for her appointment. She opened the interview by saying that she thinks the father "should be made to pay the full amount of the baby's board until I get back to work." She was reminded that he had already signed his financial agreement, and remarked that the responsibility should rest on both parents, and not on one alone. She agreed, but seemed to take the attitude that she was the one who suffered the inconvenience and physical pain; therefore she should not be expected to do any more.

The FCH felt that this attitude might have been due, in part, to pressure from her family. "They are pretty mad about it all". It seemed that she was worried about her job and annoyed that the father had gone on as though nothing had happened. She didn't see why it was always the woman who has all the trouble. "I was pretty decent to him. I could have told the boss or I could have told his wife. That would have made trouble enough for him...that is what most girls would have done, but I kept quiet for the sake of my job." She began to show some hostility, not necessarily against him as an individual, but against the community reaction toward an unmarried mother. "The least he can do is pay me for it". All this went on and on. She spoke appreciatively of the care she had been given at the FCH, but expressed resentment that they made her stay there for so long after the baby's birth and was afraid she would lose her job. Her family doctor had given her a statement for the factory doctor in which he stated that her illness was a form of nervous breakdown. She continued on, "I need that job and no one can say I am not a good worker...If I am going to lose my job I don't see why he should not lose his". By the end of this interview, it seemed to the interviewer that she was a self-centered person. Oh dear, oh dear!

This all goes on talking about my aunt and that she had two children, and my two sets of grandparents. My aunt was two years older than Nora. At the time of this interview on 2/21/41, my aunt was 30 years old. That meant that my mother had me when she was 28. Well, I guess I was off about 8 years. My original thinking was that she could have been about 20 years old or younger when I was born.

It wasn't very long after I read all this material that I got a call from Susan on September 6th, 1995. She had "found" my Mother Nora, but as I had expected, she had died. I think it was all hopeful thinking that she could be alive. She died at age 66 on February 11th, 1975 of ovarian cancer in a Braintree Nursing Home. I had turned 25 years old just 5 days earlier. Susan had found her obituary that was under the name of Williams, but it listed no husband and she could never find a marriage certificate. On her actual certificate of death under #12 it stated if 'married, widowed or divorced', but all it had was Frederick J. Williams and it didn't give the status. She was buried in the Holy Cross Cemetery in Malden. Michael and I drove out there and found her grave. She was buried with my grandmother who died in May of 1961. On December 6th Michael and I with Rev. Helen Moore, went back to the cemetery to have a small service of closure. Helen had put together a nice service where Michael did a reading and so did I. It was freezing cold and there was Helen in all her vestments having changed into them by the car. We were standing at the top of a hill and the wind was swirling around us. I laid a Christmas spray, with a red ribbon that I had made, by the stone and took some pictures. When we arrived at the cemetery we spoke to the man inside the gate and I asked him if it was all right to leave a wreath by the gravestone. He said it would be fine, but that it might not be there long. It didn't really matter because I had my pictures and if someone wanted to make their Christmas a little brighter, that was just fine by me.

People have asked me whether I was angry, or hurt, or felt rejected because my birth mother gave me up and the answer was always and still is "no." At some level, even when I was young, I somehow knew that there must have been a good reason and the most likely one was money. Emotionally, why would someone want to give up her child? The stigma in those days of an unwed mother was not the societal thing to be, and my father was a married man so there was no hope of her getting married to him. So it was both these reasons and her wanting me to have a better life. That was what I thought! Now after reading all this information from the FCH, I think my Aunt, Nora's sister, played a big part in all this. With me gone they could get on with their lives and society would be none the wiser. It was a very courageous act on her part. But what about the guilt feelings she must have had going through life wondering if she had made the right decision? No, I never blamed her for what she felt was the right thing for her and for me. Since September 6th when Susan told me she was dead, I often wondered if this decision, which must have caused incredible stress, could have been the cause for her cancer and death at age 66. Obviously we will never know, but it has crossed my mind more than once in the last few years.

In the meantime Susan was on a hunt to find my first Cousin. Again, it wasn't too long before she found him in Urichsville, Ohio. On September 16th 1995, I sat down and wrote him a letter that was a very tricky one to write. After introducing myself, and very briefly filling in some of my history and adoption, I stated that if my information was correct then I thought he was my first cousin. To make a long story short I was totally rejected. I could never even get past his wife. I explained to her that I wanted no money, only a picture of my mother and maybe they knew the name of my biological father. She wouldn't budge! Remember I went into all this with a clear head and expected this could happen. So now it was on to find his sister that would probably be difficult because we didn't know her married name, if in fact she did marry. Again, before long Susan had found her. This woman was amazing! My cousin's name was Muriel Reynolds, known as Pat. She lived in Las Vegas and was a cocktail waitress at the famous Golden Nugget Casino. This time I decided to forget letter writing, and after three stabs at screwing up my courage, I called her. She answered, so here I was repeating more or less the same thing I had written in the letter to her brother. She wasn't surprised that I had been rejected. She had been estranged from him since their father had died several years earlier. When I asked her if she knew anything about me she said that she did. Two years earlier when she came east to close up and sell the family house in Wilmington, MA, and move her father out with her (her mother, my aunt, had died a year earlier of Alzheimers), a lot of past history came out on the 3000 mile drive west. I became part of that history. She was very nice and hoped that we would keep up.

In July of 1997 we flew out to Las Vegas and met Mark for his 42nd birthday. He had flown down from Reno where he now lived and we spent 3 wonderful days together. I hadn't told Mark about my search until he came home for Christmas last December. I didn't want to do it over the phone. He was amazed! When we three met for dinner the night before we were all going to meet Pat for the first time, we discussed again the possibilities of him doing his search too. He also felt that adopted children should have the opportunity of knowing their background. Although he never talked about it, it turned out that he, like I had, thought about doing this over the years. After all it is a very normal thing to feel. At some level we needed to know our roots. The problem lies with the adopted parents because they have to be secure enough to go through the process too. I told him that now that I had done most of the work in setting this all up, that maybe he would like to go and find his parents. It turned out he was worried he would hurt Michael's feelings. Of course Michael, who is so progressive for his age, had been pushing it. Michael always wanted to know my background and was also interested in knowing about Mark's parents. Michael was never threatened about meeting and knowing them the way so many adoptive parents are. However, it was totally up to Mark. As it turned out I put his search into motion when I got home. Then Susan and Mark were in touch so the process was in the works.

The next day the three of us met Pat Reynolds at The Luxor, the hotel where Mark had put us up. We had a lovely lunch together. It was incredible to find myself sitting in front of my biological first cousin. I kept looking for any resemblance, but I couldn't see it. How far I had come! After lunch Mark went home to Reno and Michael and I went and spent two nights with Pat at her home. It was quite a gamble to do this, but we had a very nice time. She made her favorite pina colatas and the conversation seemed to flow and we three became very relaxed. We went out to sit by the pool, but not for long. The temperature was 112 degrees! She took me through all the albums that included Nora so I had a feeling about her and her life. As she watched me she told me that she thought I looked like my mother from the nose up. She could see some likenesses in my movements and reactions. Pat's mother evidently was quite difficult, but she loved her Aunt Nora who was sweet, kind and gentle. Pat gave me two pictures of Nora that she had copied for me and they are now in my study in the bookcase for all to see. Pat was a dancer but in the end was too tall to be a ballerina. Her Mother, my aunt, was not pleased that she went to New York to try to make it on the Great White Way. Pat thinks her Mother thought she would be teaching ballet in the basement of their house, but she wanted something bigger and better. Sadly that was not a success so she and some friends headed out west and ended up in Las Vegas. They became the opening act for Jerry Vale and Milton Berle. Not bad going! After persistent back problems, she became a cocktail waitress and has been at the Golden Nugget for years. The only real bit of news that I had hoped she might have was the name of my father, but she didn't. By this time I was beginning to realize that he really DID just evaporated into space.

At Cousin Pat's Home In Las Vegas

In September of 2000 we again flew out to Las Vegas to meet Mark and begin our trip down to Zion, Bryce and The Arches National Parks in Southern Utah. We met Pat again and had lunch with her. Sadly she lives too far away for getting together, but we do chat on the phone once in a while.

We finally came to a crashing halt regarding my father and it turned out that the only thing I could do was to go before a Judge to get his name. Here we are back again dealing with the Judge! I had been brazen up to this point so why quit? Now I was back calling Sheila at the Court House. I told her how far I had come with this search, but I guess I now had to go before a judge and plead my case. I told her I was pretty positive my father had died, but I would really like to get his name because I knew I had two half brothers out there someplace. In trying to set up a date she said not to worry, she would take care of it. The long and short of it was that I think she probably just walked down the hall to the Judge's chambers, pleaded my case and then sent Susan his name. It was Harry J. Stingley. Now, again, Susan had something to work with.

Well! Like everything else in this process, it didn't take Susan long before she called me. She had about 8 pages of Stingleys, many in Indianapolis IN, but there was one Harry J. Stingley, Jr. in Florida. She said this Florida one wasn't making any sense to her, but suggested that because it was the same name I should send the first letter to him. She would in the meantime send me all the other names. She told me she wanted this letter to be about genealogy and nothing about adoption. This way they wouldn't open the letter and get a blast of 50 years of past history about my adoption and life especially when they probably would know nothing about it. This way, I was breaking them in gently. I immediately wrote a letter telling Mr. Stingley that I was doing the family genealogy and that when I got to his name I couldn't seem to get any further. Would he be, by any chance, the son of Harry J. Stingley from Indiana, and if so would he mind getting in touch with me? I wrote to please call collect, if he wished. About three weeks later I said to Michael that it was obvious I was *not* going to hear from Mr. Stingley. It was a Saturday morning around the second week in October of 1997, and I was still in my bathrobe when the doorbell rang. I was on the phone with my friend Page, so Michael went to answer it. I could hear the man say, "is Mrs. Wilson there?" (I figured they were looking for Wilson with one L). Well, if anyone refers to us as either Mr. or Mrs. Wilson, we pretty much know that they don't know us, and that probably they wanted to sell us something. I know Michael well enough to know that he was about to say, "I am sorry, but we gave at the office," so I hung up the phone with Page and raced to the door. Normally I would not do that, but something told me I must see who this was. To this day I don't know why I did, because I don't usually greet strangers at the door in my bathrobe. Is God still playing a hand in all this?

I saw a man and a woman standing there, but when I looked at her I noticed she had an envelope in her left hand with another smaller envelope on top with a return sticker in the middle of that envelope. For some reason I had used that sticker instead of writing out my address. I threw my hands on both cheeks and said, "Oh my God, are you Harry J. Stingley?" He said he was. Michael and I became quite flustered, but quickly invited them in. They introduced themselves as Bud and Diane.

When we all settled down Michael said that he would go and buy some lunch, and disappeared. For some reason we had nothing to eat in the house. So here I was in the sitting room, still in my bathrobe, with two strangers I had never seen before. Evidently, when he received the letter he tried to call me but couldn't find anything with our address listed under "Wilson". They decided that they had better get in the car and drive up because if they didn't do it then, they might never do it. They went to the Westwood Police Station where they got directions to the house. I looked at him and asked him what he was doing up from Florida. He told me that they moved from Naples two years earlier and were now living in Woonsockett, R.I. Oh my God!

Something was really fishy here, because we all know that after six months to a year first class mail is not forwarded. Now, are you ready for this? Evidently, the man who bought their condo was putting out the trash at the same time as the neighbor. He just happened to comment that wasn't it funny that he should still be getting mail for Harry J. Stingley. The neighbor said to give the letter to him and he would forward it on because he still had the Stingley's address. Now really! What are the chances of that ever happening? Yes! I am here to tell you that there is a God and that all this was really supposed to happen.

Now for the heavy stuff! I asked Bud what he thought of the letter and he told me that he knew it was no genealogy letter, but that I was looking for someone. When I asked who that might be, he told me Rita. "Who is Rita?" I replied. "Rita is my sister from my father's first marriage". Oh! Lord, I said to myself, I now have a sister out there, too! I apologized that I didn't know anything about Rita, but he didn't seem disturbed. He and Diane hadn't seen her in years, but were just curious. She would probably be in her 70's now and could possibly even have died. Well! Now it was the time I had to tell my story but how would he and she react?

I told Bud that I might as well get to the heart of why they were here. I told him that if the records I had acquired were correct, he was my half brother. "Oh!" he said, "That doesn't surprise me". He went on to say that when he was around 12 years old he remembers his father leaving the house, crossing the street and getting on a trolley. Now when was the last time you heard the word trolley used? It is a great way to date this piece. Shortly after that, his Mother left and got on the next trolley and he remembers thinking that she must be following his Dad for some reason. Of course he never knew, but about two months later they moved from Watertown to Medway. He never thought of it again until this day. We talked for a while and I was trying to make things as easy as possible.

When Michael came back with the lunch, I then thought it was a good idea if I got dressed! We had a delightful time sorting all this out and trying to get to know one another. It turned out that "our" father, died at age 50 in 1949 of a heart attack. I was eight years old. Diane asked how I had gone about finding all this information and when I mentioned The Adoption Connection she had a big smile on her face and sort of giggled. It turned out that she had put up a daughter for adoption and the daughter found her through the Adoption Connection. I mean really, can you believe all this? All this was beginning to sound like it was right out of a soap opera! That connection has turned out very well for her and her daughter, as it was beginning to shape up for me.

Now I still had one more hurdle to get over. Who was going to tell my younger half brother, Kerwin who lived in Hopkinton, the BIG news? When Bud and Diane left, Bud told me not to worry, but that he would get in touch with Kerwin and explain the story. That eventually happened, and in January 1998, the 24th to be exact, I had them all for lunch. This would be the first meeting with Kerwin and his wife Judi. Kerwin was eleven months younger than me, born on January 18, 1942. I think I was a little nervous, especially as I had just gotten over the worst case of flu', so was on the weak side to begin with. However, Michael and I did our best to make everyone feel comfortable. I, at least, had had the advantage of meeting Bud and Diane earlier, but what did Kerwin and Judi think? In our many discussions it turned out that had I sent the original "genealogy" letter to Kerwin, he would have read it and tossed it in the circular file. I now give him a hard time saying, "just think what you would have missed!!" Judi says that she would never have let him do that, just because she was curious to find out what was going on.

With My Two Half Brothers, Kerwin And Bud, 1/24/98
(The First Time I Met Kerwin, My Younger Brother)

With Diane And Bud Stingley, Left,
and Kerwin and Judi Stingley

As this search began to unfold, it was hard for me to keep it to myself, but I had to tell someone. This was an incredible journey I was going on and there were only three people that knew about it. Michael, Helen and Susan. Was it about time that I let this secret out to a few good friends? Did I have the nerve? Well, after coming this far I guess it was time. I was, more or less, back to the beginning with making my friends hold promises, the one thing I was nervous doing in the first place. I was having lunch with my two Beacon Hill roommates, Julie Wight Schniewind and Jane Gray Parker, and for some reason I instantly felt compelled to tell them this big secret. Normally Judy Gray, my oldest friend, and who had been part of my life the longest would have been the first, but she and her husband Tim were on their boat in Florida. The phone method was not the way I was going to do this. I chose to do it personally so I could be a part of their reaction and get their promise. The promise was on a stack of Bibles not to breathe a word and then I would launch into it. I barely came up for air, and they certainly couldn't get a word in edgewise. That broke the ice for me in maybe feeling comfortable telling a few of my closest friends. I didn't tell everyone at once. It was over the next four or five years that it dribbled out, and then it was only about 10 people, if that! There always seemed to have to be the perfect time. Other than both Julie and Jane knowing at the same time, no one else ever knew who else knew. That was the only way I felt the lid could be kept on. I can't unfortunately list everyone now, because remember this *is* Michael's book! They all had to swear to secrecy and they all know who they are. I have to say that each and every one of them kept the secret and to this day I am proud of them and very grateful to them all. Above all it shows that it came be done. They came along on this journey with me, and I hope they had a good and interesting time. Thank you! Thank you all very much!

Now, just when you think this should be the end, I do have one more incident that needs to be told. It was something I never thought of nor ever dreamed would happen. The year was 2001 and by this time my new family was getting to know each other and I think getting to enjoy one another. Mother had had her stroke and her death was three days before we left for Egypt, my 60th birthday gift from my Michael. Her memorial service was planned for March 2nd, eight days after our return. My brothers indicated that they would like to come to the service. Although they had never met her, it was dear of them to be concerned and they wanted to be there for support. How wonderful is that! I certainly couldn't tell them they couldn't come. The night before the service I woke up to the fact that they would know no one. I knew that most of the people that would be attending would pretty much be my friends or know each other at least by association, but then there would be Diane and Bud, and Judi and Kerwin.

With Jane Gray Parker and Julie Wight Schniewind
(The first people I told of my search.)

I decided to give Michael a short list of some of the people I knew would be in attendance and who obviously knew the story of my search. Before the reception he said that he would make sure that my new biological family would be introduced to some of these people so they wouldn't just be standing off in a corner by themselves. In case Michael got caught up in the moment and didn't have time to do this little task, I also had asked some of my friends like Judy, Julie, Jane, Susan O'Brien and Gerry Gray, to keep an eye on them and make sure that they were comfortable. It seemed like a good plan to me! Well! My dear friend Julie was doing her job when she, being the first one into the reception, went right up to Judi and Kerwin and asked them where they "fit into this picture." Poor Kerwin absolutely froze as though he was a deer in front of headlights going err, err, err! He knew that very few people knew of this search, and he certainly didn't know who they were. Finally Judi said, "he's Anne's brother." Julie seemed satisfied and announced that she knew that story and promptly went over to get Sally Gilliatt. Now, Sally was a class above me at Beaver, but I only got to know years later when Michael and I became a part of a group with my close friend Jackie Vaughan Lee and Jane. For years we have all headed to Vinalhaven for summer weekends at C.S. and Jackie's house. Sally, bless her heart, came to the service to represent Jackie and C.S. who live in Texas. It was a lovely surprise. She was the one to get the surprise

289

though when Julie approached her and said, "Sally, you must come over and meet Anne's brother". Sally looked at her in the strangest way knowing that I didn't have any brothers. "Anne doesn't have any brothers," she claimed. Jane Parker in turn went over to Sam Gray and introduced him to the two boys. Because of my dating him years ago, he knew I had no brothers. Well, you can see where this was all going! I know I told all my friends that this was top secret, but I fully expected that his wife, Gerry, would have told him. I guess when she told him that it was TOP secret he tossed it all right out of his mind, so when he was confronted about it several years later, he had totally forgotten and was stunned.

I have to say that it was a lovely service for Mum and she would have been proud. I did everything that she asked me to do. She told me I could choose the music, and the only thing I added to her list was the Processional, "For All The Saints". I never meant for her funeral reception to be a family expose regarding my new brothers, but as someone said to me. "Don't worry Anne, you didn't do it, everyone else did it, so it was meant to happen." I wish, at some level, she could have understood adoptive children's desire to find their roots, and that, had she had a different personality, she might have gotten a big kick out of it. Sadly, I could never take that chance.

Jane called me the next day to say how nice the service was, and in the conversation was concerned that it all might have been a bit overwhelming for Bud and Kerwin and their wives. I immediately called Kerwin to check it out. They had a great time, thought everyone was wonderful and kind to them and enjoyed all our friends immensely. They said they felt like celebrities, not quite the thing to feel at a funeral, but everyone did their job. Thank you again my friends for being so kind and thoughtful. It is not easy coming into someone's house for a party where you know no one, but into a funeral reception with 50 people you had never seen before, must have been scary. Obviously they were up to the task, and I was proud to have them there.

Mark eventually found his biological mother. His chances of finding her alive were obviously much greater. She called him three days after he had written and sent his letter to her. She's married and lives in California. She had no other children. By the time Mark was adopted, Michael and Jackie had a little more information about his background. Things were beginning to loosen up. Michael knew that she had lived in Montpelier, VT, and had decided not to marry Mark's father. In 1999, when we were flying to Australia for the wedding of Michael's youngest great-nephew Jamie, Mark flew down to LA for two nights to be with us.

The second night his biological Mother drove to LA to meet us and join us for dinner. She was and is charming. Ann is nine years older than I. Guess what she told us she named Mark at birth? You guessed it, Mark! Sadly, Susan Darke at The Adoption Connection to whom we introduced Mark, was never able to find his father, although she did recently tell me she had some new resources and hadn't given up.

With Lee Osborn Higgins and Page Osborn
On My 60th Birthday

Both my sets of parents have now gone, but I have a new family and, as they say, life goes on. Obviously this is a different kind of family because it took 54 years to meet them and we have had other lives, but we have great giggles together and keep up regularly. Most searches don't always pan out for the best. This was a gamble and I beat the odds. It was sad that my birth mother had died so young. It would have been fun to know her, but things happen for a reason, and I think this ended the way it was supposed to end. God was with me the whole time.

This has obviously turned out to be more than a chapter. I guess that when I started I didn't realize how long it would take! Everything you have read is true. It has been handled gently in some areas, but that was done purposely. Life is not always a bowl of cherries, but my bowl is almost filled to the top. Basically, I have had a wonderful upbringing thanks to Cam and Peggy Patterson, and the most perfect life with Michael Wynne-Willson. My friends have been extraordinary, many of them who I couldn't mention in this story. Remember, this is still Michael's book. I thank each and every one of them, and they know who they are, for being there for me when things got tough. I owe a great deal to Susan because, without her this search could never have been done or completed successfully. I have kept up with her and have referred a few girls to her for help in finding their biological belongings. Truly, she is a great lady who began something to help herself, but in the end has helped thousands of us.

I am a very blessed lady, and I thank you for coming along for the ride.

EPILOGUE

Last night, July 3rd., we had our friends, Muffy and Billy Oates, for dinner. It was about 90 degrees F outside, so it was well that we were blessed with air conditioning in our new digs! Before dinner we had a chat about July 4^{th,} our Independence Day celebration. This had me saying something that surprised me. It was to the effect that today, the July 4th celebration, didn't get me too excited, even though I was granted American citizenship back in 1952. Having been brought up in, and fought for, the U K during the first 19 years of my life this, perhaps, is not too surprising. However, after my late wife, Jackie and I adopted our two children, we always had things we did plus the enjoyment of salmon and peas (a particular New England tradition on the Fourth), on that notable day. Of course, we were sure to take in Hamilton/Wenham's parade, but I always seemed to feel that my enthusiasm was a wee bit lacking in comparison to Jackie's and most of the others around me.

After I'd had my say, Billy asked me if I was more excited about the Queen's Birthday celebration, even today. "No", I said, without hesitation. That got me to thinking why? I believe because, at heart, I've become a really 'mid-Atlantic' person. I have great pride in, and am more than grateful for, my American citizenship. I am equally proud of my British heritage and that I was a member of the RAFVR. I do, however, get all excited and aggravated if someone makes what I believe to be unpleasant and inaccurate remarks about *either* country, and now at my age am quite inclined to say so! I believe this to be one of the perquisites of old age and, certainly, experience. Let's face it, if I don't have those perks now and make use of them, I never will. I've been waiting for them all my life!

I think it is quite a dicey business being an ex-something in a country not of one's origin! A very fine line has to be trodden when one is invited to make comparisons. They are usually odious, anyway! Whether, or not, one becomes a citizen of one's adopted country is a tricky and personal question to answer. I became one because I wanted to vote and felt that I should not voice opinions were I not a citizen. There were those in the U K who were somewhat put out by the fact that I so much as considered becoming 'A Yank', and this was hard for me to understand because, after all, people have been leaving the U K for centuries to settle elsewhere, become involved and raise families. I became a U.S. citizen because, with an American wife who had a heart-rending time in wartime Britain by trying to have children, I had every intention of staying here so that we could, perhaps, succeed. Sadly, that was not to be, but we were allowed and were considered fit to adopt two kids, and that was a great joy in itself.

Game Creek Restaurant Above Vail, Colorado
Our 2002 Christmas Card!

I have, all my years from age 16 on, tried to promote Anglo-American understanding and friendship which is obvious, I guess, due to my being awarded an English Union Scholarship to St. George's in 1936/1937. I see now in the strange times in which we live, things are so utterly different in many ways from the straightforward, somewhat blinkered, life that we led sixty years ago, or so. It is so on both sides of the Atlantic and the world for that matter, that this understanding, friendship and competition seems to be eroding a bit and that is saddening and worrisome to me, but I guess it is to be expected. The world seems to be becoming one unit, as did our great USA years ago. So! In the event, I am intensely proud of my country by adoption. But in a somewhat Anglican fashion, I so wish that, particularly now 'when there's a war on', we would stop shouting that 'we are the greatest, the best, the richest and strongest'. That must be totally infuriating, regardless if true, to those countries less fortunate than ourselves, and who have not had the countless advantages that we have taken for granted for years and about which we, occasionally, complain. Only the other day I heard from a friend who had been speaking at a conference to an African dignitary. This man, the dignitary, said that he just could not understand why we complained about anything because we have so much, much more compared to most countries. My friend replied that that was the problem. We do have everything but don't know how to cope with it.

Phew! It's 100 degrees F on July 4th '02, what a tub-thumper I've become, all of a sudden! Sorry if you don't agree, but 'them's my feelings'!

For those of you who might, perhaps, have read the first of these two efforts of mine, you may remember that it was dedicated to my first bride, Jackie, who died in 1967. You won't have had to guess too hard to discover that it is my delight to dedicate this to Annie who, as you may have gathered, is just one kind, loving, caring, patient and super special girl. Should you know her, you will know that that is next to an understatement! I am deeply, deeply, grateful to her for providing me, and Mark, with all of the attributes above and great fun as well for 34 years.

I, also, want to thank so many of our friends who have fussed away about my getting this, the second edition, finished. You know who you are. First, there was my good chum, Franklin Wyman, Jr., who struggled with Part I. Then there is Thomas Pickering Jones who, not only, has been trying to get me to see eye to eye with this new-fangled box of tricks to me, my computer, but also for making a stab at trying to edit all this. Both are jobs I wouldn't take, or have, for a fortune but he seems to be hanging in there and I am truly grateful. Ever since Book I saw the light of day, which was really a shock and surprise to me because it was never planned, I have been embarrassed by the shocking number of typos etc: that were within it and am truly sorry. I even had to insert a little 'disclaimer' apologizing for them in the books that I sold from home! Self-publishing is not something that I recommend unless one knows what one is doing, and I did not! Let us hope for the best in the near future! Another person who I should have thanked in my last book, but shamefully forgot, is Carol Weineck, who plugged along typing and struggling with the muddle I gave her for weeks on end. She is a charming and patient lady!

Then there is Harold Kosasky who came to dinner with his dear wife, Shirley, and said he'd love to do the final edit. I bet he wished he'd stayed at home! Finally, as usual, there is Annie. She not only wrote what I so hoped she would, 'Her Story' within for me but, also, read all this at least three times to be sure my memory was still accurate in print! It'll be no surprise to you that it was not! Thank each of you so very much.

At the start of Book I I, also, said that I so hoped that you and I would have fun should you be still with me when I couldn't think of much more to say! I've had a ball and do hope you have, too! I'm 83 now and, with luck, will be around to love life with Annie and be able to care for her, travel with her and not, repeat not, drive her 'round the bend' with all the bad habits and problems that I have now and which, most likely, will get worse by the time I'm 95! So far I've been married for 58 years with a 'time out' between and, without doubt, am the luckiest of men and the greatest promoter of the state of matrimony. I've had two great, great, friends and companions who have coped valiantly with me and I am incredibly grateful.

It is Armistice Day, or Veterans' Day, today and I've just about finished Tom Brokaw's story about his formative years. I admire him greatly, somewhat unsurprisingly, for his talent and his interest in 'old prunes' of my vintage that were around in World War II and thereafter. Strangely, he and I (when I got to this country) both started in similar fashion, though living in South Dakota was a far, far, cry from Hamilton, MA! His story of having to make his way as a small town radio announcer and being broke certainly rang a bell with me. That was, for sure, as far as any similarity went thereafter, however! Maybe you noticed!

"If only"...I was about to start the next paragraph with the two preceding words, but won't. I believe them to be, in that sequence, the two most depressing words in our language. Invariably they introduce something regretted which should have been done and was not, or something equally depressing. I must desist!

God only knows what will be happening in the future. It is, without doubt, a more than troubling and scary time indeed for our planet. Sadly, due to information overload, I think that, generally, our memories are far too short now and I do wish that the rest of the world would remember that it was a band of a Few who saved the day 61 years ago. Additionally, a banding of those in a great empire at that time, together with hundreds of those whose countries had been overrun, spearheaded that effort shortly thereafter and then, in 1942, there was the incredible effort and vast generosity of the United States of America that insured that huge sacrifice by the entire Allied Force.

Let us pray and be eternally grateful for all that we have, and have had, in this exciting, unique and wonderful country that welcomed me here to live some 54 years ago. Let us pray, even more fervently, that our country will stand in the world for as much, and more, than it has done in my lifetime for our children and future generations.

Peace, God bless, keep in touch and thanks be for a really great life...so far!

Michael

P S. You should know, and I've said ad nauseam, that I am more than lucky for endless reasons. The latest piece of luck, good fortune and good news is that my 'new' family, Kerwin and Judi, Bud and Diane, and Pat 'way out in Las Vegas, are a delight and we meet frequently with them together here and have fun, though, sadly, not as often in Vegas with Pat as we would like!

Addendum

Written on a scrap of paper in the trenches in France, circa 1915, this work of my Dad's, about which I had never seen nor heard, came to light after my sister died in 2002 and was given to me in May 2003 by my nephew, Robin, on a visit to us with his wife, Veronica.

Christ in Flanders

We had forgotten you, or very nearly-
You did not seem to touch us very nearly-
Of course we thought about you now and then,
Especially in any time of trouble
We knew that you were good in time of trouble-
But we are very ordinary men.

And there were always other things to think of-
There's lots of things a man has got to think of-
His work, his home, his pleasure and his wife;
And so we only thought of you on Sunday-
Sometime, perhaps, not even on Sunday-
Because there's always lots to fill one's life.

And all the while, in street or lane or byway-
In country lane, in city, street or byway-
You walked among us, and we did not see.
Your feet were bleeding as you walked our pavements-
How *did* we miss your footprints on our pavements-
Can there be other folk as blind as we?

Now we remember, over here in Flanders-
(It isn't strange to think of You in Flanders)
This hideous warfare seems to make things clear-
We never thought about you much in England-
We have no doubts, we know that You are here.

You helped us pass along the jest along the trenches-
Where, in cold blood, we waited in the trenches-
You stood beside us in our pain and weakness
Somehow it seems to help us not to whine.

We think about you kneeling in the Garden-
Ah! God! The agony of that dread Garden-
We know you prayed for us upon the Cross.
If anything could make us glad to bear it-
T'would be the knowledge that you willed to bear it-
Pain, death, the uttermost of human loss.

Though we forget You, You will not forget us-
We feel so sure you will not forget us-
But stay with us until this dream is past.

And so we ask for courage, strength and pardon-
Especially, I think, we ask for pardon-
And that you will stand beside us to the last.

Linton Frederick Wynne-Willson. Major.
'Mentioned in Dispatches' 1915

The End

POSITIVELY THE LAST ADDENDUM!

Since making a stab at finishing this effort back in 2002, Annie and I have recently returned from a really great sea adventure on Lindblad Expeditions' small (70 passenger) boat, The Sea Bird. From Seattle we flew to Juneau where we boarded the boat and then sailed, stopping at intriguing places and glaciers, up the Inland Waterway, to Glacier Bay. Great instructors and crew and well worth it, we found.

Before we left, I was told that I had Diabetes #2 by our good Internist, Doctor Katharine Treadway, of MGH. This was a bit of a shock, particularly as I gathered I was stuck with it and couldn't beat it. Never had anything like that before!

In the event, I decided I'd better do something quickly, so on the advice of good friends and Annie, I enrolled in a 4-day course at The Joslin Center's 'DO IT' Program in Boston. We, Annie came with me daily for support and education, too, learnt a great amount, principally that with CONTROL and EXERCISE, there is not too much to be worried about, for the time being anyway. I was interviewed daily for about 15 minutes by the program's Director, Richard Jackson, M D. and the ladies in charge of the several therapies which were deemed necessary including, diet, exercise and eye-sight to mention a few. One discussion with Dr. Jackson stopped me in my tracks! Mentioning to him that I was lucky indeed that I was able to catch the disease early, he replied at once that I was *not* lucky because I *had* diabetes. I could, however, control it for years if I did what the program suggested. This I, undoubtedly, intend to do!

I only mention this visit because, due to friendly influence, I did something quickly about having the disease and that delighted the staff on the program. Suffice to say, never, ever, had we received such first-rate individual attention, help, thoughtful caring and kindness under such circumstances before. From 7.30 A M to 4.00 P M for the four days, it was outstanding and, should you or friends ever contract this disease, either #1 or #2, do yourself, or a friend, a singular favor by recommending this program. This is an entirely unsolicited testimonial born of a very, very, special experience.

ABOUT THE AUTHOR

The Earlier Years

Michael Wynne-Willson was born in London, England, on September 13, 1919. His arrival must have been a severe shock to his mother, as she was 45 at the time. Educated in England until 1936, he was granted an English Speaking Union scholarship to St. George's School, Newport, Rhode Island, for one year. On arrival, rumor has it that on meeting Mr. Merrick, his future Headmaster, Michael allowed that he was there to broaden his *mind* and not his *education*. Merrick, who became a lifelong friend, confirms that Michael never once let him down!

Back in England in 1937 with war clouds forming, Michael was paid a visit by Jackie Chambers, a girl he had met in America. While in Paris the couple discussed marriage (as newly-acquainted couples were wont to do at the time), but with war imminent and money scarce, Jackie was to catch the *Manhattan*, the last boat back to the USA, from Le Havre. Michael joined the RAF on his 20th birthday, with hopes of becoming a pilot. But the RAF, lacking a sufficient number of training planes, sent Michael to an aerodrome far north in Scotland to peel potatoes in the Officers' Mess.

From 1939 to 1946 there were few dull moments: Night-fighter squadrons and experimental work in single and twin-engine aircraft; working with the earliest airborne radar; Michael's only war wound, shot in the head, etc., by a kid who thought Michael was a fox in the grass!

He trained as Gunnery Officer on Spitfires and then was off to RAF Station Greenwood, in Nova Scotia, to teach training instructors returning to the UK in the operational use of rocket-firing from Mosquito aircraft. Since no Mosquito aircraft capable of carrying rockets were available, frustration ensued.

In the midst of all this but away from the "D Day" landings (something Michael still regrets), the young flier found the time to marry Jackie in Middleburg, VA, on May 6, 1944, with substantial attendance of brother officers from Greenwood. The couple returned separately to England, Michael by air, Jackie by sea where during the voyage her ship developed engine trouble and was adrift for two days with enemy submarines all about.

Michael wound up his service with the RAF's Night-Fighter Interception Unit and Central Fighter Establishment. Once "demobbed" he found work with British European Airways (precursor, with BOAC, to the present British Airways) as an Airport Manager trainee, where he "ran" the fledgling Newcastle Aerodrome in the North. In the postwar climate in England, Jackie's medical problems (and good sense) in 1948 cautioned a move to the USA. The prohibition against removing Pounds Sterling meant it was "bare bones" transition, with little or no cash to spare.

Once in New York, installed in a $25-per-month cold-water flat, Michael pounded the pavements for Kent of London brushes. Next move was to Boston where Michael's "Englishness" qualified him to sell British cars for awhile. With the financial picture improving, the couple moved to Hamilton, Mass, where they bought a house and eight acres for $12,500. Over the next 15 years Michael would: make and peddle marmalade and assorted products, work as a radio and TV reporter in both the US and UK; operate a mobile broadcasting studio to cover major events on the East coast. Encouraged by the love and support of friends, Michael and Jackie adopted two children, Mark and Wendy.

All changed in 1967 when Jackie lost her brief battle with cancer. Michael, Mark and Wendy; the dogs Minus and Duchess, the cat Perky and Piglet the pony, continued to live in Hamilton for a while.

The Later Years

ollowing Jackie's death Michael devoted himself to raising his
en and turning himself into a PR man for the New England
m, and a Boston bank. It was not too long before he met Anne
, a striking woman a certain number of years his junior, and
f June they married.

rget...Again! is the story of Anne and Michael, a
ve couple who were never afraid to test the waters on
ways to earn a living. In the course of the past 35
d many delighted travelers on tours of the deserts
f India, the Far East and Antarctica. The tours
and a great way for the Wynne-Willsons to see
ss perspective they enjoyed but, well, maybe
hey not been the organizers.

A connoisseur of the finer things, in 1980 Michael had the idea to provide a clearinghouse for people seeking valuations on art, antiques and just about anything else. The Appraisers' Registry, Michael's brainchild, has since become a trusted resource for all types of appraisals, including even wines, antique cars and specialties such as *Quimper*, with a complement of 21 expert appraisers.

Before I Forget...Again! traces the peripatetic Wynne-Willsons through their many far-flung journeys. As organizers of numerous exotic tours, the couple managed to travel champagne-class "On a beer income," and Michael's keen wit and powers of observation never fail him, even writing as he is from his octogenarian perch.

The bonus in this book, however, is Anne's own story of the search for her birth parents, from a time when unwanted pregnancies were hushed and smothered in "homes for wayward girls." Anne's own voice is strong and courageous, and her tale should serve as inspiration to many other happily adopted people who, nonetheless, feel the pull to understand where they came from.